LEADBELLY

THE TRUE INSIDE STORY OF AN UNDERWORLD WAR

JOHN SILVESTER AND ANDREW RULE

JB

JOHN BLAKE

Published by John Blake Publishing Ltd,
3, Bramber Court, 2 Bramber Road,
London W14 9PB, England

www.blake.co.uk

First published in paperback in 2005

ISBN 1 84454 147 9

British Library Cataloguing-in-Publication Data:

A catalogue record for this book is available from the British Library.

Design by www.envydesign.co.uk

Printed in Great Britain by Bookmarque

1 3 5 7 9 10 8 6 4 2

Papers used by John Blake Publishing are natural, recyclable products
made from wood grown in sustainable forests. The manufacturing
processes conform to the environmental regulations of the country of
origin.

Every attempt has been made to contact the relevant copyright-holders,
but some were unobtainable. We would be grateful if the appropriate
people could contact us.

CONTENTS

ONE

BLOODSTAINS AND BULLETS

The gangsters became more confident that
they could literally get away with murder.

AUSTRALIA is the only country in the world that brags about its criminal history.

What other nation would adopt as its unofficial anthem a song like *Waltzing Matilda* – the story of a sheep thief who prefers suicide to arrest?

Ned Kelly, armed robber and horse thief, is a national hero. Disgraced policeman Roger Rogerson is Australia's best-known ex-detective – a celebrity crooked cop. Queensland's Terry Lewis is the only commissioner in the world to manage the unique double of being awarded a knighthood and a jail term for his services to policing.

From First Fleet convicts to the Sydney razor gangs, from painter and docker wars to bloody battles in the markets and 'hot shots' in the drug scene, Australian criminals see violence as the first tool of negotiation. But what has happened in Melbourne in recent years is unprecedented: a gangland war played out in public, whose participants have not hidden from scrutiny but actively chased headlines.

After each shooting it was the criminals and their connections who held press conferences and the police who were reluctant to comment. Some of the gangsters gained the public recognition of pop stars, only to die violently in public. Others tried to live in the shadows only to die in the dark.

The murders have inspired hundreds of sentimental death notices, which paint the victims as saints rather than the violent drug dealers and standover men they really were. The funerals attracted Melbourne's gangster community and its camp followers, mostly wearing the all black colours of the club and the mandatory designer sunglasses, often perched on top of slicked back hair or shaved heads. These extras in every funeral scene were the goons from Central Casting.

The size of the death toll varies from source to source because opinions vary about when the 'war' began and who are casualties and who are not. Who can accurately state when an underworld war starts? It's not as if the United Nations formally opens hostilities. Most in the media have decided the first murder that mattered was the exit of the charismatic Alphonse Gangitano on January 1998 but it is probably more accurate to trace the bloodshed back to February 1995 when Gangitano killed a gunman called Greg Workman in a St Kilda street.

There have been 33 underworld murders in Melbourne since Workman's death, most committed by professional hitmen on the orders of gangsters.

Not all these casualties belong to one 'war'. The fact is, these murders are not all related; some are one-off hits to settle old grudges or new 'business' disputes. But police have established that many of the string of killings are part of a bloody feud being played out in Melbourne streets. Two sides have emerged. A group of 'new boys' based in Melbourne's west seem to have declared war on the criminal establishment, tagged the Carlton Crew.

What is the motive for the war? Like most feuds, it begins as a dripping tap rather than a big flood – there is no single dramatic cause but a string of events. Incidents in this one include a dispute over drugs, a non-fatal shooting, a beating, a confrontation outside a private school, and an argument over a phone number. In mainstream society, arguments can end friendships. In the underworld, they can end lives.

So how did the war start? Just as a 100-year gale needs freak conditions to begin and then takes on a life of its own, in Melbourne the conditions that brewed for years finally combined to produce an underworld storm of bloodstains and bullet shells.

First there was police inactivity. In the late 1970s the then Chief Commissioner Mick Miller tackled organised crime. He backed intelligence-gathering to identify the activities of heavy gangsters and set up task forces to target and arrest them. He was prepared to invest more than 100 police to investigate organised crime.

But proactive policing seems expensive and, at times, hard to justify. In an age when police must account for every dollar spent there is no way to quantify the benefit of taking a young criminal from the streets before he becomes an experienced gangster. There is no column in police annual reports for prevented crime – thwarted murders, abandoned robberies, aborted drug importations. For all their talk of law and order, governments count the cost of crimes committed but do not always grasp the value of crimes prevented. This is as short sighted – and, ultimately, as expensive – as an insurance company that 'saves' by not subsidising smoke and burglar alarms for its clients.

3

Andrew Veniamin was a hitman suspected of being involved in at least four murders before he was shot dead in a Carlton restaurant on 23 March 2004. If police had targeted him when he was just a wannabe gangster he might not have grown up to be a killer – and ultimately a victim – in an escalating vendetta likely to cost tens of millions of dollars in police and court time.

The Miller model of preventing organised crime was eventually allowed to rust through neglect. Specialists such as the stolen car squad were disbanded and the drug squad was starved of resources and allowed to run without adequate supervision. Despite conventional wisdom that police should not be allowed stay in corruption-prone areas for long, Melbourne detectives were able to make careers in the drug squad. It was a costly mistake.

While the squad was losing massive amounts of amphetamine ingredients in controlled-delivery sting operations that 'went wrong', some senior police were more worried about checking office telephones to see if any of their detectives were organising to have a mixed grill with a crime reporter.

The outside agency given the charter to investigate organised crime, the National Crime Authority, also hesitated to target local gangsters. In 1989 the NCA, drawn like a moth to a red light, moved towards targeting white-collar crime and failed to police standover groups such as the Carlton Crew.

Some police had become too close to their informers. Drug-squad jobs were sold out and seized drugs stolen to be resold back to the underworld. Put simply, some police changed sides.

Over the 1996–97 summer break confidential police files on a major investigation were stolen from the drug squad. An internal investigation failed to find the offenders but recommended a major security upgrade. The recommendation was ignored.

In the late 1990s the drug squad finally had success with a controversial controlled-delivery programme, arresting many of the big players. But this belated success was overshadowed by the taint of corruption – a scandal was breaking. A police task force was set up to investigate the drug squad, and many serving and former police were charged with drug trafficking.

This created another key ingredient for the underworld war. The trials of about 12 people charged by the drug squad were delayed because some detectives due to give evidence for the prosecution had themselves been arrested.

At first, the drug trials were delayed to allow corruption investigations to continue. This broke the underworld food chain. The usual process is that as major criminals go to jail, new gangsters take their places until they are themselves arrested. But with a freeze on trials many men who would normally have been in jail were bailed and back on the streets, reclaiming their sales territory from newcomers.

The result was that there were simply too many drug dealers in Melbourne. It became a game of musical chairs in which the loser usually was shot.

The next element was the police response to the murders. Each case was treated as an isolated event. Whichever homicide squad investigative team happened to be on duty was assigned the latest killing. Senior police did not want to admit that many of the cases were connected and traditional police methods were simply not working.

Potential witnesses would not talk. For example, Lewis Moran lost his son and stepson to hired killers but refused to co-operate with police. If he thought his silence would impress his enemies he was wrong. He was later shot dead.

Andrew Veniamin knew he was likely to be killed but told his parents that after he was gone they should not talk to detectives.

Another player who was shot and survived refused to tell police the name of the gunman. Homicide detectives would eventually be assigned new jobs. Meanwhile the underworld-killing backlog grew and the gangsters became more confident that they could literally get away with murder.

By mid-2003 senior police set up a gangland task force, codenamed Purana. It was the right move, but way too late. The task force was assigned a series of killings that appeared to be connected. While the murders continued Purana began to target the main suspects. It was, and is, a process that takes time because of the painstaking surveillance that has to be carried out using highly technical methods. But it pays off eventually.

One year later the Purana team had made 22 arrests, charged suspects in relation to three murders, uncovered alleged conspiracies to murder four men and made inroads in seven further cases.

Purana investigators also jailed some of the main players from the New Boys and the Carlton Crew. Which poses the question: why was the police response so slow? And how many of those victims would have been alive if the task force had been set up in 2002?

In 2003 there were 11 organised crime-related murders. Many of the victims had been active members of the underworld for years. They had the lifestyles of the rich and infamous but they did not work. They managed to live lives of five-star luxury on unemployment benefits.

One suspect was involved in multi-million dollar property developments and even after police seized his Ferrari and other luxury items he was able to get a sponsor's hat signed by Formula One champion Michael Schumacher when he was invited (while on bail) to enjoy VIP corporate hospitality at Melbourne's Grand Prix. Appropriately, he gave the hat to his barrister.

Another well-known gangster decided to use some of his money for self-improvement and commissioned a full set of dental crowns to give him a film-star smile to go with his Hollywood income. When the dentist presented him with a bill for $55,000 he went to his Mercedes and returned with the cash.

But perfect teeth didn't bring him any luck. In fact, his expensive dental work was ruined when he was later shot in the head. This shows the wisdom of dentists and other professionals not extending credit to gangsters and dealing on a cash-only basis.

Police were to be embarrassed that some men who had been gangsters in Melbourne for years had survived without apparently becoming the target of consistent investigation. Assistant Commissioner (Crime) Simon Overland was to admit police had 'dropped the ball' on organised-crime investigation.

'We just haven't had the right systems in place … You lose focus on the less immediate but perhaps more serious.'

Police say the underworld war has shown that they must go back to aggressively targeting organised crime, even if it is an expensive ongoing commitment.

While the anti-corruption Ceja investigation has unearthed disturbing connections between serving and former police and sinister gangland figures, the Purana task force has found worrying relationships between a group of criminal lawyers and their clients.

The detectives believe the lawyers have crossed the line and become 'players', not objective officers of the court.

One prominent lawyer was eventually charged with conspiracy to murder – a charge he strenuously denies. He chose to give up his practising certificate while facing criminal charges. Another disbarred lawyer was charged with the same offence. One man with heavy legal connections and who had worked in law firms was murdered. Two others who worked in the law were charged over another gangland killing.

In one case police monitoring telephone intercepts were shocked when, only hours after a double murder, a lawyer told a gangster – 'be careful, don't say anything on the phones'. Some police feel some lawyers do not offer legal advice but act like co-conspirators.

Detectives suspect a lawyer managed to identify a police informer by cross-checking court documents. Being identified as a police informer can be a death sentence.

Melbourne's gangland murders drew worldwide attention. In just one of many international reports, the English *Guardian* newspaper reported: 'The latest episode in a gangland feud that has shaken a community which sees itself as having a chic, European-style cafe culture'.

But the reality was that while many people were fascinated, few were shaken by the murders. Despite the fact that murders were being committed in the streets, at a children's football morning and in local pubs, there was a sense that the public was just watching a Tarantino movie. In fact, it was reality television of the most compelling sort, with the latest episodes broadcast almost nightly and published in endless newspaper stories.

Melbourne boy turned savvy national magazine editor, Garry Linnell, knew the story was bigger than a one-city crime story, and devoted the *Bulletin's* cover space to regular updates. It pulled record sales.

One effect of the war was a public sentiment that while the gangsters were shooting each other they were not harming anyone else. Many people privately said they thought it was a good thing, claiming gangsters were doing what the police couldn't – cleaning up the underworld.

Indeed, it is certain that at least six hitmen have been killed and a seventh, who was planning a murder, was also shot dead.

Even as the paid hits continued to pile up Melbourne was voted, for the second year in a row, as the world's most livable city, according to the international newspaper the *Economist*.

Part of the formula is based on crime figures and safety. The truth is that despite the gangster killings the overall crime rate remains low. But this disguises the real dangers of the deadly violence to the public at large.

The truth is, underworld murders cannot be conveniently boxed as 'baddies versus baddies' with no impact on mainstream society. The potential for death and injury to innocent bystanders – and police doing their duty – is always present.

On 16 May 2004, the bodies of Terence Hodson and his wife, Christine, were found in their East Kew home. They had been shot in the head, execution style, almost certainly by someone they knew.

Hodson had been a drug-squad informer and his information had assisted in about six major drug operations. But later he became an informer for the Ceja anti-corruption task force after he was charged (along with two drug-squad detectives) with drug-related offences.

In the weeks before the double murder a three-page confidential police information report had begun circulating in the underworld. It said that an informer had been offered a contract to kill one of the main players in the feud.

Detectives investigating the Hodson double murder want to know if leaking the document was designed to get the informer killed.

Information from the document appeared in a newspaper story on 14 May. The next day the Hodsons were dead. The charges against one detective were dropped because without Hodson's evidence there was no case.

But the sinister implications of who had motives for plotting the double murder stirred public opinion and the suggestion of police corruption created a political firestorm. Senior police and politicians promised to redouble efforts to hunt out bent police and wealthy gangsters. The reaction to the Hodson double murder could yet prove to be a turning point in the whole murderous episode – the psychological moment when the 'good guys' regained control.

For a while, two of the New Boys would chat regularly on the telephone and in moments of self-congratulation boast to each other: 'We run this fucking city.'

But after one of them was arrested by Purana, a senior investigator poked the suspect in his ample stomach and said: 'Just remember, *we* run this city.'

Only time will tell how long that commitment will last.

1) Gregory John Workman
Shot dead by fellow standoverman, Al Gangitano, in St Kilda on 7 February, 1995. *Motive: Unpaid debt.*

2) George Marcus
A crime figure with legal connections; he was shot dead after visiting a criminal's wife in Box Hill North on 20 April 1997. *Motive: Possible underworld hit.*

3) Alphonse John Gangitano
Shot dead in his Templestowe home on 16 January 1998. *Motive: Falling out with former friend, Jason Moran.*

4) John Furlan
Died when his white Subaru Liberty exploded as he drove it along Lorenson Avenue, Merlynston, on 3 August 1998. *Motive: Business debt.*

Underworld killings

5) Mad Charlie Hegyalji
Shot dead in the front garden of his South Caulfield home on 23 November 1998. *Motive: Possibly debt or drug related.*

6) Vince Mannella
Shot as he returned to his North Fitzroy home on 9 January 1999. *Motive: Possibly debt-related or connected with an underworld power struggle.*

7) Joe Quadara
Shot dead as he arrived at work at a Toorak supermarket at 3am on 28 May 1999. *Motive: Unknown, possibly armed robbery gone wrong.*

8) Vicki Jacobs
Shot dead as she slept with her six–year–old son in the Bendigo suburb of Long Gully on 12 June 1999. *Motive: Payback for giving evidence in murder trial.*

9) Dimitrios Belias
Found by cleaners in a pool of blood below a St Kilda Road office on 9 September 1999. *Motive: Failure to pay gambling debt.*

10) Gerardo Mannella
Shot dead as he left his brother's North Fitzroy home on 20 October 1999. *Motive: Possibly pre-emptive strike because the killers believed he would avenge his brother's murder.*

11) Frank Benvenuto
Shot dead in Beaumaris on 8 May 2000. *Motive: Debt related.*

12) Richard Mladenich
Shot dead while visiting a friend in a St Kilda motel unit on 16 May 2000. *Motive: Drug related.*

13) Mark Moran
Shot dead outside his luxury home near Essendon on 15 June 2000. *Motive: Possible payback for earlier shooting.*

14) Dino Dibra
Shot dead outside his Krambruk Street, West Sunshine, home on 14 October 2000. *Motive: Payback.*

15) George Germanos
Repeatedly shot in an Armadale park on 22 March 2001. *Motive: Drug related.*

16) Victor George Peirce
Shot in his car in Bay Street, Port Melbourne, on 1 May 2002. *Motive: Drug related.*

17) Paul Kallipolitis
Shot dead in his West Sunshine home. Body found 25 October 2002. *Motive: Payback.*

18) Nik 'The Bulgarian' Radev
Shot in Queen Street, Coburg, on 15 April 2003. *Motive: Drug related.*

19) Shane Chartres-Abbott
The 28-year-old male prostitute was gunned down on 6 June 2003, in Howard Street, Reservoir, as he left home to defend charges in the Victorian County Court that he raped and attacked a female client. *Motive: Possibly to silence him from exposing elements of vice industry.*

20) Pasquale Barbaro
Shot in car park of the Cross Keys Hotel, Essendon North, on 21 June 2003 *Motive: Wrong place at the wrong time.*

21) Jason Moran
Shot in car park of the Cross Keys Hotel, Essendon North, on 21 June 2003. *Motive: Drug related or payback.*

22) Willie Thompson

Shot dead in his car in Waverley Road, Chadstone, on 21 July 2003. *Motive: Unknown, suspected underworld related.*

23) Mark Mallia

Charred body found dumped in a drain in West Sunshine on 18 August 2003. *Motive: Debt related or connected with Radev's murder.*

24) Housam 'Sam' Zayat

Shot during a late night meeting with a friend in a paddock in Tarneit on 9 September 2003. *Motive: Underworld related.*

25) Steve Gulyas

Shot with partner Tina 'Bing' Nhonthachith in their Sunbury weekender on 20 October 2003. *Motive: Business related.*

26) Tina 'Bing' Nhonthachith

Shot with her partner Steve Gulyas in their luxury Sunbury weekender on 20 October 2003. *Motive: Business related.*

27) Michael Ronald Marshall

Shot outside his Joy Street, South Yarra, home on 25 October 2003. *Motive: Underworld related.*

28) Graham 'The Munster' Kinniburgh

Shot dead outside his Kew home on 13 December 2003. *Motive: Underworld feud.*

29) Andrew 'Benji' Veniamin

Shot dead in the back of a Carlton restaurant on 23 March 2004. *Motive: Disputed story of self-defence.*

30) Lewis Moran
Shot dead in the Brunswick Club, Sydney Road, 31 March 2004.
Motive: Payback.

31) Lewis Caine
Shot dead and body dumped in Brunswick on 8 May 2004.
Motive: Was alleged to have accepted a contract to kill and was murdered first.

32) Terence Hodson
Shot dead in his Kew Home with his wife on 15 May 2004.
Motive: Drug related or to silence a prosecution witness.

33) Christine Hodson
Shot dead with her husband, Terry, on 15 May 2004. *Motive: She knew her husband's killer and could not be allowed to live.*

TWO

WORKING
CLASS MAN

*He has an air of confidence
and a touch of class.*

IN his 30 years in the underworld Gregory John Workman earned
a name for himself as a man who didn't blink when facing danger.

Like most of his breed he had a lengthy police 'docket'. It had
begun when he was a teenager, way back in 1966 when Sir
Robert Menzies was Prime Minister and imperial currency was
being replaced with dollars and cents.

Workman's record included convictions for assault, theft,
burglary, malicious wounding, abduction, illegal possession of a
firearm, armed robbery and escape.

He began to build a reputation as a tough teenager in a tough
place – the working-class Melbourne suburb of Preston. It was an
area and an era in which many teenagers joined gangs – either
the Mods or the Sharpies. Most of the kids moved on, but
Workman used street violence as work experience in his chosen

field. He was a diligent delinquent and eventually graduated from gang member to gangster. Workman's reputation in the northern suburbs grew and, like many others, the young standover man turned to dealing drugs as he moved into middle age.

But when he was young he was just a big, good-looking kid from Preston East State School with a ready smile and an early eye for the girls.

One of his first girlfriends remembered: 'All the girls had a crush on him. He had nice parents. I don't really know what went wrong for him.'

His family lived in a Housing Commission house in busy Albert Street – a few houses from a young policeman who would one day become the head of the Australian Bureau of Criminal Intelligence and one of the country's few real experts on organised crime.

Even then there were rumours around the teenage Workman that an older relative was dabbling in marijuana – a drug virtually unheard of in Melbourne suburbs in those days.

But years later there was no doubt that Workman was into crime full time.

'He was one of the better crooks in the area,' a policeman who locked him up more than once recalled more than 20 years later.

'He would stay in the background and wouldn't do stupid things to bring police attention on himself. He had an air of confidence and a touch of class.

'He was rumoured to be behind some good stick-ups in the area, but he wasn't convicted over them.'

He was a good crook but he wasn't always a good bloke. Just ask his family. One of his close relatives became a manager at a successful Melbourne clothing manufacturer. Police later found a boot-load of clothes stolen from the factory. Workman was said to have stood over his relative to make him the inside man in a stolen clothing racket. The relative lost his legitimate job and gained a criminal record. It would have been an interesting Christmas Day at the Workmans' that year.

Workman was successful by his own lights but in underworld terms he was a middleweight and was to be finally caught fighting out of his division. It would not be the police who would stop him, but fellow criminals. One in particular.

On February 6, 1995, Workman and a crew of heavy criminals, including Alphonse John Gangitano, met for a wake at a Richmond hotel before heading to a party to celebrate the release of Mark Aisbett, who had been bailed on armed-robbery charges earlier that day.

The party was already in full swing in a flat in Wando Grove, St Kilda, when the team from Richmond arrived about 1am.

After another three hours of drinking the mood turned ugly. Gangitano was seen arguing with one of his old mates, Martin Felix Paul. According to a confidential police report: 'Gangitano was identified by an independent person as being in possession of a pistol and arguing with another male. It was apparent that Gangitano was being restrained by another person and was highly agitated.'

One of Australia's most experienced investigators into gangland murders, Detective Senior Sergeant Gavan Ryan, was later to tell the coroner that someone at the party overheard a conversation between Workman and another man, in which the issue of Workman's gambling debts was raised.

The witness later told another man at the party that Workman was about to be 'bumped' over the debt.

The argument was loud enough for neighbours to call the police. Several said they heard the name 'Harry' being used – a nickname for Alphonse used by his closest friends.

Police arrived to the noisy party, unaware that a Who's Who of the underworld had gathered. They were told that the two men who had been arguing in the driveway had left and they were assured there would be no further problems.

It was an overly optimistic call.

When Workman walked out the front door on to the porch he was immediately shot eight times.

The woman who lived in the flat and had organised the party drove Workman to hospital, but he died without regaining consciousness. Eight .32 calibre slugs will do that just about every time.

If Gangitano had planned to kill Workman over a debt he picked a stupid time and place to do it.

A woman later told police she saw Gangitano standing near the body holding a small silver pistol and he was led away by another man.

A coroner, Wendy Wilmoth, later found that a witness 'stated that she heard gunshots, went to the porch and saw Gangitano and Martin Paul standing almost at the feet of the deceased. She heard someone say "get him out of here" and saw Martin Paul lead Gangitano away.'

Ms Wilmoth said another witness, 'saw Gangitano run from the porch holding a gun in the air, soon after she came out of the front door, and saw the deceased collapse, injured, on the porch'.

It should have been an open and shut case. But it wasn't.

Two sisters who saw the shooting were whisked into a witness-protection programme to keep them away from the gangsters.

It seemed a huge breakthrough. The man who had become the public face of organised crime in Victoria was in deep trouble. His lawyer contacted homicide-squad detectives and said his client was prepared to be interviewed.

Police said they were in no hurry. They were calling the shots.

But they made the mistake of not protecting what they had. They took their star witnesses for granted.

The sisters made statements implicating Gangitano and were then put under police protection and sent beyond Gangitano's influence – or so the theory went.

But it was not like the movies. Almost immediately, the sisters began to have doubts.

One was not allowed to visit her doctor for arthritis medication. They spent days in Carlton and were driven down Lygon Street several times, despite it being the area where Gangitano and his henchmen spent most of their time.

The witnesses were not allowed to collect clothes on layby at a department store and were forced to live on takeaway food. The witnesses told one detective they were 'made to feel like we're the criminals, not him'.

They were shunted into a cabin in a Warrnambool caravan park in western Victoria with a promise that their protectors were only a phone call away.

But when they tried to contact their police protectors three times the supposed 24-hour number rang out.

Increasingly anxious and annoyed, the women felt they had been left for dead – not a comforting thought when you were about to help police jail a ruthless gunman. 'The witnesses formed an opinion that their safety was no longer a priority of the Victoria Police and that the police were not in a position to adequately protect them,' according to a confidential police report.

Isolated, alone and frightened, they rang one of Gangitano's closest associates, Jason Moran, who arranged to meet them in Melbourne the next day. It was exactly two months after the murder.

Moran was a negotiator. His opening gambit, according to police, was to advise one of the women that if she gave evidence she and her family would be killed. He then took the sisters to his solicitor, Andrew Fraser, and to another lawyer's office where the witnesses made an audio tape recanting their original police statements.

Gangitano paid for them to fly out of Australia on May 20 to England and the United States. The murder case collapsed.

Eventually, Gangitano's lawyer billed police for $69,975.35 over the failed prosecution.

But Coroner Wendy Wilmoth was able to investigate the case even though the key witnesses had 'flipped'.

'It is beyond doubt that Gangitano was at the premises where the shooting occurred, at the relevant time, that he was in possession of a gun and that he was in an agitated state of mind. The retraction of their statements by the (sisters) can be explained by their extreme fear of Gangitano,' she said.

'Having considered this evidence, and taking into account the required standard of proof, I find that Alphonse Gangitano contributed to the death of the deceased by shooting him.'

In other words, he got away with murder. But, a few years later, it would be his turn. Another example of the truth of the saying 'What goes around, comes around', which would make a fitting epitaph for most standover men.

WORKMAN. — Greg Feb. 7 1995 (tragically). Memories of you are like stars that shine. they last until the end of time. Shine on you crazy diamond Sympathy to Patrice and family. especially Taylor. XX. With love as always. — Wendy (Mouse) Jackson Jake and George.

THREE

FRIENDS FALL OUT

*Many quickly paid – others
were slow learners.*

IT was just after midnight when the two men in the green hire car cruised over the almost deserted Westgate Bridge, heading away from Melbourne's city skyline.

The driver took little notice as his passenger casually picked up a McDonald's paper bag, apparently containing the remnants of their late-night snack, and casually threw it out the window.

It was only later that the driver would wonder why the bag wasn't sucked behind the fast-moving car and, instead of fluttering on to the roadway, flew straight over the railing into the mouth of the Yarra River, 54 metres below.

And it would be months before police would conclude that the weight in the bag thrown from the bridge equalled that of a .32 calibre handgun – the one used to kill one of Australia's most notorious gangsters less than an hour earlier.

Alphonse John Gangitano was still lying dead in the laundry of his home with two bullet wounds in his head and one in the back when the two men crossed the bridge, but it would take four years before the events of that night were exposed.

GANGITANO was not Melbourne's best gangster, but he was the best known and certainly one of the best dressed. Glamorous, charming and violent, he played the role of an underworld identity as if he had learned it from a Hollywood script. Which, to some extent, he had. He watched a lot of films. Too many, maybe.

The sycophants would call him the Robert De Niro of Lygon Street. His critics – and there were many – called him the 'Plastic Godfather'.

In a business where attention can be fatal, Gangitano was a publicity magnet, first as a boxing manager, photographed with world champions such as Lester Ellis, and then as a crime figure whose court appearances were routinely followed by an increasingly fixated media.

Some gangsters are born into the underworld, driven there by a cycle of poverty, lack of legitimate opportunities and family values that embrace violence and dishonesty. But that was not Gangitano's background. He came from a hard-working, successful family. His father had run a profitable travel agency and invested astutely in real estate.

Young Alphonse was given a private school education – at De La Salle, Marcellin and Taylor's College – but struggled to justify his parents' investment. He was remembered as a big kid with attitude, but not much ability and no application.

He was quick with his fists but not with his wits, though he was cunning enough to fight on his terms, usually king-hitting his opponents. He was charged with offensive behaviour when he was 19 and, over the next five years, he graduated from street crimes to serious violence. Along the way he started to gather a group which for two decades was known as the Carlton Crew.

Most young men eventually grow out of being fascinated with violence. Gangitano didn't. He was 24 when police first found him with a gun.

A confidential police report warned of Gangitano and his team: 'They approach [police] members and assault them for no apparent reason. They are all extremely anti-police and are known to be ex-boxers. They often frequent in a group numbering approximately 15. They single out up to three off-duty police and assault them, generally by punching and kicking them. On most occasions in the past, members have been hospitalised due to injuries received from these persons.' Gangitano was described as 'extremely violent and dangerous'.

In the early 1980s, Gangitano worked as a low-level standover man using an old tactic. He would walk into a club with a small group and tell the owners that he expected protection money or he would begin bashing patrons. Many quickly paid – others were slow learners. He was making more than $1,000 a week. Not huge money, but enough for a young man on the make.

He was charged with hindering police, assault by kicking, assaulting police, resisting arrest, and other crimes of violence. Each time, the charges were thrown out. The fact he was able to beat charges helped build his reputation. Some suggested he had influence inside the police force.

Before long, he started to take on the trappings of a crime boss – wearing expensive clothes, reading biographies on Al Capone as if they were DIY manuals and watching videos such as *The Godfather*. He didn't seem to grasp that in Hollywood, the good guys almost always win and the bad guys end up behind bars. Or dead.

Before poker machines and government-sanctioned casinos, the illegal gaming business was the underworld's most consistent money maker. Gangitano might have been bored at school, but he was a quick learner on the street. He bought into a profitable baccarat school in Lygon Street and, some say, either part-owned or ran protection on Victoria's then lucrative two-up school.

Police intelligence reports listed him as a big punter and suggested he was a race-fixer in Victoria and Western Australia. He allegedly sold guns at an old Brunswick nightclub.

In the early 1990s, many police were confused about Gangitano. They were not sure if he was just another try-hard bash-artist or a man building a serious criminal network. Their informer network reported he was a big underworld player yet several investigations found he was more style than substance.

If the aim of crime was to make big money, Gangitano was still an apprentice. But still the rumours continued that he was on the way to being 'The Godfather' of Melbourne.

He was seen with experienced and respected criminals. One of his new friends was Australia's best safebreaker. He also grew close to three brothers who controlled much of Lygon Street.

It perplexed police. Why did the big names of crime tolerate the dangerous and unpredictable new boy?

Gangitano brought publicity and the headlines made senior police demand reports from their organised-crime experts. It was not good for business. In the underworld, fame rarely brings fortune.

Most major crooks need a semi-legitimate veneer. Like the American gangsters he mimicked, Gangitano chose boxing and aligned himself with the Lester Ellis camp. But Gangitano could not grasp the fundamentals of lawful business – even if it was only a front. He bashed and bit the well-known boxer Barry Michael, a professional rival to Ellis, in a city nightclub in 1987. More headlines followed.

Around the same time, Gangitano went into partnership to build a casino in Fitzroy with a well-known Lygon Street identity, investing $300,000 in the project. Unfortunately for the entrepreneurs, police raided and closed the club two days after it opened.

It was a classic police sting. Watching from a secret surveillance post in a building across the road, they allowed him to pour his money into the project before they moved.

Gangitano was handsome, smooth and liked to think he was well-read. He could quote Oscar Wilde, John F. Kennedy and Adolf Hitler. Or, at least, he got away with it. In his crowd, no one would check if the quotes were accurate. And even if they did, they would be too tactful to mention it.

On one occasion an off-duty detective was dining in Lygon Street with a woman other than his wife. He heard a group of men at a table behind him swearing and laughing. He turned and curtly told them to improve their manners – before he realised the head of the table was Gangitano. The policeman expected trouble. Instead, the group finished their meal and filed out. The waiter came to the detective's table with an expensive bottle of wine and an apology from Gangitano.

Yet he could also be short-tempered, irrationally violent and tactically naïve. He often needed associates or his expensive team of lawyers to help clean up the messes he made.

A group of criminals, headed by Mark Brandon 'Chopper' Read, once planned to use land mines to kill Gangitano at his eastern suburbs house, but scrapped the plot because of the likelihood of others being killed.

Shortly before Read was released from prison in 1991, an associate of Gangitano went to Pentridge with a peace offer. But police say Gangitano had a back-up plan. He had placed a $30,000 contract on Read's head.

When Read was released, Gangitano produced yet another plan ... he took his family to Italy and did not return until January, 1993, after Read was back in custody on another shooting charge.

Gangitano should have learned from Read's carelessness with pointing guns. For, just over two years later, he had his own problems. It was in February 1995 at a party in St Kilda where Gangitano murdered fellow standover man, Gregory John Workman.

Two sisters at the party made statements implicating Gangitano, but later changed their stories when they felt abandoned in the police witness protection.

This was lucky for Big Al, but his good fortune came at a hefty price. The grateful mobster sent the sisters to Europe on an extended overseas trip and picked up all the bills.

Gangitano may have been hit with the foreign exchange rate, but he was compensated over legal expenses.

Gangitano's lawyer billed police for $69,975.35 over the failed prosecution.

Police were incensed that they had to drop the charges and, while they couldn't get Gangitano on the big pinch, they decided on a campaign of death by a thousand cuts. His Eaglemont house was raided. Police said he resisted arrest and that is why he suffered nasty head injuries.

Over a period of months, he was charged with assault, refusing a breath test and possession of firearms. He spent time in jail and was bailed on a night curfew. The myth that he was untouchable began to fade.

When reporting for bail, Gangitano saw an unflattering police Polaroid picture on his file. He paid for a professional portrait shot and took it to the station to replace the Polaroid mugshot. In September 1997, a crime report on radio 3AW stated Gangitano had fallen out with old friends and would be murdered. Gangitano scoffed at the suggestion. Police found a transcript of the report in his home the day after he was killed.

A television reporter contacted Mark 'Chopper' Read in late 1997 when the standover man was about to be released from jail.

She wanted to organise an interview with Gangitano and Read.

'Not possible, darling,' Read said. 'He'll be dead before I'm out, I'm afraid.'

IN many ways Graham Allan Kinniburgh and Gangitano were the odd couple of the underworld.

Kinniburgh was wealthy, but tried to hide it – Gangitano was struggling but deliberately cultivated an image of affluence.

Kinniburgh kept a low profile, preferring to conduct his business in private. Gangitano loved the headlines, although his profile meant he was always the target of police investigations.

Kinniburgh's criminal record understates his influence on the Melbourne underworld. It lists crimes of dishonesty, bribery, possession of firearms, escape, resisting arrest and assaulting police. But criminal records list only an offender's arrest history – his failures. Successful criminals learn from their mistakes and don't get caught.

Police became convinced that Kinniburgh – known as 'The Munster' – was close to the infamous magnetic drill gang, responsible for many of Australia's biggest safe break-ins.

Right up until the day he was killed Kinniburgh lived in a double-storey house in the affluent Melbourne suburb of Kew.

His occupation seems to be a mystery. Interviewed by police after Gangitano's murder, he struggled to remember how he paid the bills. When asked by the astute Detective Sergeant Gavan Ryan of the homicide squad what he did for a job, Kinniburgh eventually suggested he might be 'a rigger'.

But while employment was not at the top of his priorities, life had been kind to 'The Munster'. When police searched him outside the scene of Gangitano's murder he was carrying some change, keys, cigarettes and just over $3,000 in $100 notes.

While Kinniburgh could afford imported suits, he preferred the casual clothes of an off-duty dock worker, but in middle age he had acquired expensive tastes and was a regular at the world-renowned, budget-blowing Flower Drum restaurant in Chinatown.

But the master criminal planner made a big mistake. He didn't see that Gangitano was a magnet for publicity and trouble.

ALPHONSE John Gangitano didn't look like a worried man as he stood on the steps of the Melbourne Magistrates' Court after round one of his committal hearing.

Despite facing serious assault charges over a brawl in a King Street bar, he told friends he was confident he would eventually be acquitted.

He bragged that he was not concerned about the police case and his legal team would 'blow them away'.

He had every reason to be confident – having beaten so many charges before. But one of two co-accused, Jason Matthew Patrick Moran, was not so confident. After the assault on December 19, 1995, which left 13 people injured, Moran was recorded on a police listening device saying he had to 'shower to wash the blood off' and 'to cut a long story short, I started it'.

Moran and Gangitano were long-time associates whose relationship was starting to fray. Moran was secretly taped saying of Big Al: 'He's a fucking lulu ... if you smash five pool cues and an iron bar over someone's head, you're fucking lulu.'

But on the morning of January 16, 1998, as they left court together, they seemed as staunch as ever. They shook hands before moving off with a group, including four defence lawyers, to the Four Courts Cafe in William Street, for coffee.

Later, Gangitano and his solicitor, Dean Cole, walked to George's Cafe in Lonsdale Street for a light lunch before going to a small bookies for two hours of punting. Gangitano placed bets on seven races before he was picked up and taken back to his Templestowe home by his regular driver, Santo.

Soon after arriving home in Glen Orchard Close, Templestowe,

Gangitano rang Cole to say he was tired and would have a nap. It was 4.45pm. He promised to ring back later but didn't.

Gangitano was alone in his 30-square double-storey house. His wife and their two children were visiting a relative in St Kilda.

Gangitano removed the expensive, imported grey suit he had worn in court and placed it on the banister before heading upstairs for a four-hour sleep.

Gangitano had bought the house four months earlier for $264,000, but still had a mortgage of $200,000. The house was large, comfortable and suited his purposes.

It was in a dead-end road. From the upstairs windows Gangitano could see any friends, enemies – or both – as they entered the street. The sloping block meant the ground floor was not visible from the road, making police surveillance difficult. A four-camera security system was used when Gangitano was not at home.

The crime boss was not so much concerned about other criminals; he wanted the video system to deter police – the secret 'tech' branch – from breaking in and hiding listening devices in his home.

For a self-made crime headline, Gangitano valued his privacy. He tried to protect his family from his working life. Many of his closest crime contacts had never been to his home.

Those who had been there found themselves in the back garden. Gangitano's fear of listening devices meant he didn't like to talk business inside the house.

He did not tell his wife about his work and she did not ask. Her job was to care for the children. His was to pay the bills. He had a full-time mistress who was more aware of his work, but she was just as coy when asked questions at his murder inquest years later. She said she thought he might have been some sort of a property developer.

Alphonse seemed attracted to women who weren't curious.

GANGITANO rose from his sleep just after 9pm on January 16, 1998. Years of working as a night-time gangster left him with a nocturnal body clock. As part of his bail conditions, Gangitano had to be home after 9pm, although he did not always stick to the letter of the law.

While he liked to be seen after dark in Lygon Street, the bail restrictions meant his nationwide network of criminal associates knew where to find him.

Gangitano's unlisted number had found its way into the contact books of established and would-be criminals around Australia. In the hours before he died, Gangitano made – and received – many calls.

One was from his wife, telling him she was at her sister's house and would be home before midnight. An inmate from Fulham Prison rang, wanting a chat and some racing tips. A friend in Brunswick called and colourful West Australian personality, John Kizon, also rang.

Kizon was to Perth what Gangitano was to Melbourne. Big, charismatic and seemingly bulletproof, both men protested that they were not crime bosses, yet seemed to enjoy their public notoriety. They even shared the same lawyer, Croxton Park Hotel bouncer-turned-courtroom-fighter George Defteros.

Kizon was a convicted heroin trafficker, nightclub owner and entertainment promoter. Like Gangitano, he claimed to be misunderstood. His range of associates included Rose Hancock (he once dated her daughter, Joanna, before she was mysteriously bashed and fled to England), jailed businessman the late Laurie Connell, and Andrew Petrelis, a man who went into witness protection before being found dead in bizarre circumstances in Queensland.

Police believed Kizon had been involved in trafficking large amounts of cannabis from Western Australia to the eastern states.

It was just before 11pm Melbourne time when Kizon rang

Gangitano from a Chinese restaurant in Perth. They talked about how the court proceedings had gone that day. Gangitano chatted easily and sounded confident. He had a visitor who took the phone for a brief conversation. It was his long-time friend Graham 'The Munster' Kinniburgh.

The phone call lasted less than 10 minutes. Kizon said he would ring back. He didn't get the chance.

Kinniburgh had a drink with Carlton identity Lou Cozzo at the Laurel Hotel in Ascot Vale. Around 10.30pm, he slipped into his red Ford and drove across town to visit Gangitano.

'The Munster' was one of the few men in Melbourne who could drop in on Gangitano without an invitation. According to Kinniburgh, the big man was on the phone when he arrived and told him to clear off for about 30 minutes as he was waiting for another visitor to arrive for a meeting. But those who know them both doubt that the younger man would be so dismissive of 'The Munster'.

So what really happened?

Gangitano was sitting downstairs at a round kitchen table. From this spot he could see down the hallway to the wooden front door, which was open to let in the cool night breeze. Through the mesh of the second security door he could see out but no one could see in.

It was 18 degrees at 11pm and Gangitano hadn't bothered to change from his pyjama top and blue underpants. Judging from the time of Kizon's phone call, Kinniburgh was already in the house.

When Gangitano opened the door for a second visitor he didn't bother to put on clothes.

Detectives believe he would have grabbed a robe or dressed if he was about to have a business meeting. They say the man at the door was either a close friend or a subordinate — someone he had no need to impress.

Forensic evidence suggests the killer was standing in the kitchen to his victim's left and Gangitano ran towards the laundry to his right as shots were fired from close range. He was shot in the back, nose and head, before collapsing.

Kinniburgh said he had slipped away to a Quix convenience store in Blackburn Road to buy a packet of Benson & Hedges cigarettes. He was recorded on the store's security camera at 11.45pm and left a minute later.

Coincidently, Gangitano's de facto wife stopped at the same shop eight minutes earlier to buy the children ice-creams and drinks on the way home. Kinniburgh said he was gone for 30 minutes. He has not yet explained what he did for the other 25 before he returned to his friend's home.

When he pulled up at the house, Gangitano's de facto wife was already inside. She had found the body and dialled 000. The emergency tape recorded her call as she desperately tried to keep her children from seeing their dead father. Kinniburgh attempted to help, rolling the body over and trying to administer first aid, but Gangitano had already bled to death.

Kinniburgh must have known the big man was already gone. Did he go through the masquerade of trying to revive him to strengthen his alibi, or was it to ensure there was a logical reason for his DNA to be found on the body?

Police believe the second visitor and Gangitano had argued. The man pulled a gun and shot him three times. They think Kinniburgh was shocked, ran to the closed front security door and tried to burst through, cutting his hand on the strong mesh.

They say he calmed down – then slipped upstairs to check the security video system – and found it was turned off. Blood matching Kinniburgh's was found on the upstairs banister.

So who pulled the trigger?

RUSSELL Warren Smith was a dangerous man until the drugs beat him. In 1988, when he was more than halfway through a 10-year term for killing a man, he noticed a 20-year-old who turned up in Geelong jail.

The new kid was Jason Moran, born into a crime family and brought up with gangsters. When gunman Brian Kane was shot in the bar of a Brunswick hotel in 1982, the teenage Jason placed a respectful death notice in the paper to his 'Uncle Brian' from 'Your Little Mate'.

In prison, there are few loners. You team up with a gang, known as a crew, or you can be picked off.

'When Jason came into the jail he joined up with the crew I was running with,' Smith would later tell police.

'I found him to be a good bloke, but he was wild. He was always big-noting himself and I remember his big line, "Do you know who the fuck I am?"

'Jason was only a young kid and nobody in jail had heard of him [but he] could look after himself. Jail is a very violent place and Jason had to fight to protect himself.

'Jason would always be threatening people, it was his nature.'

They lost contact when they left jail but six years later they met again, through mutual friend Lou Cozzo, son of Melbourne furniture identity Frank.

In 1995, the three had been drinking in the Depot Hotel in Richmond. Cozzo and Smith were on day leave from the Odyssey House drug clinic and were not worried that a bellyful of beer would be a problem on their return – 'we always found it easy to get through the tests they would give'.

It was just after 11pm on a Saturday when Moran generously offered to drive them back to the clinic to beat the midnight curfew.

Like his long-time associate Gangitano, Moran was a hot-head who would act first and think later. Consequences were for others to worry about.

Another driver cut in front of Moran without using his indicator. The lights turned red and so did Moran. At one of
Melbourne's busiest and best-lit intersections, the corner of
Bridge and Punt Road, Moran grabbed a wheel brace, smashed
the other motorist's windscreen, dragged him from the car and
beat him severely. No one stopped to help.

'Jason got back in the car and was laughing,' Smith said later.

'Lou and Jason were part of the Lygon Street crew and that is
where I met Alphonse Gangitano. Alphonse would have been
the leader of this crowd, some people called him the Lygon
Street Godfather. All that crowd wanted to be known as
gangsters. They all cultivated tough reputations. I don't know
why they did this. It was just in their nature.' Smith said that
Gangitano 'always seemed to keep his family separate from the
Lygon Street crowd'.

On January 16, 1998, Smith was drinking at a hotel in
Campbellfield watching the lunchtime strip show when he saw
Moran. The two talked and smoked some marijuana.

They went back to Smith's Preston flat to smoke some
more. Moran promised to return that night to pay $500 for a
marijuana debt.

He returned at 9.45pm. They smoked, talked and then Moran
suggested a drive. Moran threw him the keys of his late-model
green Commodore sedan.

Moran was no longer the new kid on the block and Smith was
no longer the more experienced man. The pecking order had
changed. When Moran suggested something, it was done.

The car had a no-smoking sticker on the glove box. Smith
believed it was a hire car.

'I didn't know where we were going and I didn't ask.'

It was about 10pm when they left Preston and Moran told
Smith where to drive – 'Jason was talking and seemed calm.'

They pulled up in Templestowe. One of the first things Smith the career criminal noticed was that 'most of the houses had alarms or sensor lights on them'.

Moran opened the passenger door and said 'You can't come in. Just wait here and I'll be back in five or ten minutes.'

But Moran didn't walk into the double-storey house next to where they had parked but behind the car and down the street. Smith knew too much curiosity could be fatal, so he 'lost interest'.

After about 15 minutes Moran jumped back into the car and told Smith to drive. They went to a 24-hour McDonald's drive-through in South Melbourne.

Moran told him to drive to Williamstown. As they crossed the Westgate Bridge in the left-hand lane Moran casually picked up the McDonald's bag and threw it out the passenger window. Smith saw it clear the railing and fall towards the water far below. It was only later he wondered how a paper bag didn't fly behind a car travelling at more than 80kmh and instead went almost straight over the railing.

And it was only much later that he thought that Moran may have slipped his gun into the bag and thrown it into the river. Or so he was to say.

'I knew Jason always carried a gun. I don't know why he carried them, but he seemed to like guns.'

More than three months later, police divers spent a week trying to find the gun. Police threw paper bags with weights about the size of a .32 handgun off the bridge.

Detectives offered a bottle of malt whisky to the diver who could find the murder weapon. But tidal currents and the Yarra's permanent silt made it impossible.

A well-known underworld gun dealer lives in the Williamstown area. Police believe Moran made the trip to pick up a new gun after he threw the one used to kill Gangitano into the river.

Next morning, Smith was woken by radio reports that a

'gangland figure' had been murdered in Templestowe. 'I started to get nervous. I didn't know if Jason had anything to do with it but I started to think he may have.' When he found out the victim was Gangitano he become increasingly worried. 'To say I was shocked was an understatement.'

Two days later, Moran turned up at Smith's flat at 7am. Despite the hour they shared a bong and, according to Smith, Moran said: 'Alphonse has been put off … don't talk to any of the crew, especially Lou (Cozzo) and don't tell anyone you were driving me the other night.'

A few days later Cozzo rang and asked him if he knew anything about the murder and asked 'if Jason was involved'.

Police arrested Smith for stealing cars more than three months after Gangitano's murder.

He then decided to tell them what he knew because he wanted a fresh start and was 'sick of always looking over my shoulder for Jason Moran'.

His evidence may well have been compelling in any future murder trial but Smith committed suicide by hanging himself in jail – eight months to the day after Gangitano's death.

WITHIN 48 hours of the murder, a freshly-showered Moran arrived with his long-time lawyer, Andrew Fraser, to be interviewed by homicide-squad detectives in their St Kilda Road office.

Many would have expected a close associate of a murder victim to be visibly upset and want to help detectives. But Moran feigned indifference and refused to answer questions.

More than two years later, on June 15, 2000, Jason's brother, Mark Moran, was murdered in the driveway of his luxury home near Essendon. The killing remains unsolved.

Some in the underworld believe that Jason was not the only Moran in Gangitano's home that night. They say Kinniburgh tried to organise a peace meeting between the Morans and Gangitano, assuring Big Al there would be no weapons.

The theory goes that one of the Morans produced a gun and killed Gangitano in an ambush that shocked Kinniburgh – hence his reaction to the murder.

But if it was true then it raised the possibility that allies of Gangitano took their revenge for the double cross years later.

Jason Moran was eventually sentenced to jail for the King Street brawl where Gangitano was a co-accused. In September 2001, Moran was granted parole and released from prison. In an unusual move, the National Parole Board allowed him to leave Australia with his family because of fears for his life. But he was too stubborn and arrogant to stay away. Despite advice from his own family he returned to Melbourne on November 20.

On June 21, 2003, he was shot dead with his friend, Pasquale Barbaro, while they watched a junior Auskick morning in Essendon North.

On December 13, 2003, the man who wanted a low profile, Graham Kinniburgh, made headlines when he was murdered outside his Kew home.

Criminal lawyer Andrew Fraser knew many secrets. His clients believed they could tell him anything and their conversations would remain confidential.

Fraser knew the value of silence. His first advice to his many clients was that if questioned by police, refuse to talk. He would tell them to provide their name, age and address, but to respond to every further question with a standard 'no comment'.

Private school-educated Fraser prided himself on his ability to talk to his clients using the language of the underworld.

In September 1988, his private language became public knowledge when a conversation with a murder suspect was recorded in a city watch-house cell.

He was representing Anthony Farrell, one of four men

charged with, and ultimately acquitted of, the Walsh Street ambush murders of young police constables Steven Tynan and Damian Eyre.

Fraser said to Farrell: 'All you've got to do is fucking keep your trap shut. So say fucking nothing. And don't consent to anything.

'So just keep your trap shut, mate. This is the rest of your life here, because, don't worry, if you go down on this you're going to get a fucking monster, and we all know that, right?'

Fraser's tough-guy talk and his 24-hour-a-day availability made him popular with some of Victoria's best-known crime families. Drug dealer and killer Dennis Allen always used Fraser and the Moran family swore by him.

But Fraser was a braggart and a drug-addicted one. He refused to take his own advice to keep silent and by 1999 he was reduced to cocaine-fuelled rambles in his city office. In December 2001, Fraser was sentenced to a minimum of five years' jail for cocaine trafficking.

A key piece of evidence was a conversation secretly recorded in his office by police on August 16, 1999, when he plotted the importation of cocaine valued at almost $3million. But five days earlier, on August 11, drug-squad police from Operation Regent recorded another fascinating conversation.

Fraser, the lawyer who always told his clients to remain silent, could not shut up. He told a colleague that one of his clients, Jason Moran, was 'crazy'.

The colleague asked the lawyer, who always claimed to know many of the criminal secrets of Melbourne, who killed Gangitano.

Whether Fraser really knew or was just spreading underworld gossip is not known, but he responded with one word: 'Jason.'

THE fact and fantasies of Gangitano's life and death will never be separated.

He gave the impression of wealth, but he had serious debts; he appeared unworried by constant police investigations and court appearances, yet his autopsy showed traces of the prescribed anti-anxiety drug – Diazapam.

He owed his lawyer George Defteros $100,000 and had about $2,000 in a bank account. He was a paper millionaire, with assets valued at just over $1.1 million, but with debts of more than $300,000. Most of his wealth was in his late parents' property in Lygon Street that he and his sister had inherited. Most crooks use dirty money to invest in legitimate business. He used good money to try and build a crime empire.

There were more than 200 death notices for Gangitano. As has become an underworld tradition, hundreds packed the St Mary's Star of the Sea church for the funeral. It made the headlines and led the television news. He would have liked that.

Gangitano referred to himself as a property developer, although the occupation listed in his Will was 'gentleman'.

But the myth did not die with his murder and he proved to be more famous dead than alive.

The theatre continued at his inquest, four years later. Deputy Coroner Iain West heard that a musician had composed a song to Gangitano and the crime boss wanted Hollywood star Andy Garcia to play his role in a proposed movie.

Kinniburgh and Moran attended the inquest but both chose not to give evidence on the grounds of self-incrimination. Kinniburgh wore casual clothes befitting a man who didn't want to be noticed. Moran wore an expensive pinstripe suit and a flash diamond ring.

Observers noticed a large scar running down the side of his head left there after his skull was broken when he was arrested by police a few years earlier – an action which the trial judge said was 'remarkably heavy handed'.

Mr West found that both Kinniburgh and Moran were in

Gangitano's house and 'implicated in the death' but he did not have sufficient evidence to conclude who fired the gun.

GANGITANO. — Alphonse.
In loving memory of a loyal
friend that we now entrust to
God. Together now with your
dear parents.
— Partners and Staff Pryles &
Desteros.

FAREWELL THE BLACK PRINCE

*His ankles are tattooed almost
solid blue and green.*

OUTSIDE, the Mercedes and BMW coupés circle in the afternoon sun like sharks, cruising for parking spots among shoals of lesser vehicles jamming the usually quiet streets in West Melbourne. They're late models in dark colours, mostly black or midnight blue, and run to sharp personal number plates and mobile phone aerials tilted rakishly, like dorsal fins on sharks.

The whiff of menace and money – fat rolls of cash money – wafts from the drivers, their hard faces blank as they join the silent crowd gathered at the church door next to a big black Cadillac hearse parked near a pile of wreaths banked against the bluestone wall.

Not everyone here is a big shot and many mourners are clearly not from Melbourne's underworld, but they dress the part. There's a generic quality about the gathering that strikes a watcher. There are men old enough to be grandfathers who move confidently through the crowd, escorted by leggy young blonde women who are not their granddaughters.

There are young men, with their hair cropped short, tied back in tight ponytails or slicked back, hard and shiny. They mostly wear dark suits, gold jewellery, lightweight slip-on shoes and sunglasses. Many are heavily muscled, with the bulk that comes from weight-lifting, and perhaps steroids. They tend to favour permanent scowls, and would look at home on nightclub doors, as some no doubt do. If they don't smoke, they chew gum. Some do both.

One hard-boiled character dragging on a borrowed Winfield has on the compulsory dark suit, but with fawn slip-on suede loafers. He wears no socks, but it doesn't matter much. His ankles are tattooed almost solid blue and green.

Across the street, marooned on a traffic island, the cameras of the media contingent are trained on the crowd. Those who hold the equipment keep their distance, perhaps remembering the ugly scenes at the funeral of Robert 'Aussie Bob' Trimbole in Sydney in the 1980s, when angry mourners attacked cameramen and journalists.

This is the scene at St Mary's Star of the Sea Catholic church around 1.15pm on Friday January 23, 1998, as the minutes crawl towards the start of a funeral service for a man who died a week earlier the way he had lived: violently and fast.

His name is, or was, Alphonse John Gangitano, and he is one of the few criminals in Australian history to be known – even by people he'd never met – simply by his first name. Like Squizzy. Like Chopper. Like Neddy.

Alphonse, also known as Al, was shot several times in the laundry of his Templestowe home by an assassin officially unknown, though his identity is no secret, who must have been well known to his victim.

An assassin trusted enough, it would appear, that he was let into the house unchallenged before he produced a weapon and squeezed the trigger at close range.

Some details of the shooting are a mystery. So is the question of how a boastful schoolyard bully, who left school more than 20 years ago with nothing more useful than a bad reputation, managed to support himself and his family in relative luxury most of his adult life.

Gangitano often claimed he was a 'property developer', but that was probably just another example of the mischievous sense of humour his friends and supporters claim for him, exemplified by the fulsome praise heaped on him by one of his more unusual friends, bail justice Rowena Allsop, who addressed the packed church at the funeral.

Ms Allsop, who has been heavily criticised for her close association with Gangitano, was asked to speak by the dead man's family.

She delivered a ringing tribute in which she compared his wit with Oscar Wilde's, gushed about his silk ties, cashmere overcoats and 'the lingering scent' of his Dolce & Gabbana aftershave, and noted his consuming interest in John F. Kennedy and Napoleon.

She said her friend had been 'like a king commanding a court, with his friends laughing at his old jokes'. She said she was touched by him turning up at Melbourne's Royal Children's Hospital last Christmas with a bag of toys for the children in the cancer ward.

Others, however, detected a darker side to Gangitano's gregarious character.

He might well have developed properties, they say. And no doubt he sometimes arranged for holes to be dug – but not always to pour foundations.

If the man in the coffin wasn't a gangster, he acted like one. And he was certainly buried like one.

A fitting exit, some might say, for the Black Prince of Lygon Street.

MELBOURNE is Australia's Chicago, but with a touch of London's old East End 'manor' tradition about it. A tradition of almost feudal loyalty to local 'crime lords' going back to the solidarity of the old working-class inner suburbs in John Wren and Squizzy Taylor's day.

Unlike the criminal subculture in other cities, Melbourne's underworld has a tradition of big-occasion funerals, preceded by an avalanche of newspaper death notices. Many of these are effusive and ostentatiously long, implying that money is no object. Some are 'crocodile tears'.

A few are downright tongue-in-cheek, and contain coded jokes and messages. Police searching for clues to gangland slayings are known to comb the death notices carefully. Indeed, some are rumoured to write the occasional contribution themselves.

Gangitano wasn't the only one with a mischievous sense of humour. One notice read: 'The impression you left on me will stay eternally in my heart. Jim Pinarkos.' Pinarkos's headless body was found at Rye beach in July 1989. He died from an arrow through his heart. The murder was never solved.

Whatever the reasons, Gangitano's farewell was one of the biggest underworld funerals in Melbourne since the murder of master bank robber Raymond (Chuck) Bennett in the magistrate's court in 1979 and of Bennett's arch enemy, the notorious gunman Brian Kane, in a Brunswick hotel some time later.

The ritual ran over a week, starting with 22 death notices for Gangitano in the underworld's favourite newspaper, the *Herald Sun*, on the Monday after the murder.

The number of notices more than doubled to 48 on Tuesday, led by a joint tribute from Gangitano's widow and their daughters, and his sister Nuccia, and including several from prominent underworld figures.

It peaked on Wednesday, with 68 notices, including one from Charlie Wootton, a reclusive but well-known and much-respected gaming identity whose past links him with the blood-spattered history of the painters and dockers union.

As a teenager in the 1950s, Wootton reputedly disposed of the empty shotgun shells left when an 'unknown' gunman shot Freddy 'The Frog' Harrison on the wharves.

Dozens of men saw 'The Frog' get croaked, the legend goes, but it was never officially solved. Like the others, young Charlie Wootton developed amnesia, a condition that still affects police investigations today, including this one.

In the seven days before his burial there had been 209 death notices for Gangitano. This was a bonanza for Rupert Murdoch's classified-advertising coffers — and a measure of the generous underworld protocol that makes a hero of a man dismissed by some as a thug who didn't have the brains to be a 'Mr Big'.

Criminal groupies who hardly knew the dead man put notices in the paper as though they were great friends. But columns of newsprint aren't the only measure of Gangitano's posthumous popularity. At least 800 people, and possibly 1,000, turned up to the funeral service, filling the church and spilling outside.

So why the big deal?

One reason could be that Gangitano was, in his own way, a 'crossover' criminal. He was from a respectable Italian family — not one, according to police sources, that automatically connected him with organised crime from birth, as with some Calabrian and Sicilian peasant clans for whom kidnapping, extortion and violence are facts of life.

Gangitano went to school with other middle-class boys, and could just as easily have become a lawyer or an accountant if he'd studied, which he didn't. Schoolmates recall that he was always aggressive but that his father was outraged when he secretly tattooed his arms and forced him to have skin grafts to remove them.

When forced to leave Marcellin College, he did his last year of school at Taylors' College. Classmates there remember that even then, he was lazy, manipulative, on the make and constantly accompanied by the first member of what was to become his gang.

The picture that emerges is of an egotistical young bully whose nature made him gravitate towards a life of crime. His charm and his looks attracted attention. So did his vanity and appetite for extreme violence, especially when the odds were in his favour.

But whereas more traditional Italian organised-crime figures kept largely to their own, the more urbane Gangitano slipped easily between the Calabrian and Sicilian crime syndicates, other ethnic crime groups, and mainstream Australian criminals connected with the painters and dockers union. In the end, this willingness to deal with all comers might be what got him killed.

A former associate from the boxing world – who did not attend the funeral because of a violent disagreement many years ago – recalls being present when Gangitano spoke at length to the notorious Sydney standover man Tom Domican, with whom he evidently had a warm relationship.

Others describe Gangitano's links with one of Perth's heaviest criminals, the convicted heroin trafficker John Kizon, who has been named in connection with the late Laurie Connell, millionaire race-fixer and the most ruthless of the 'WA Inc.' corporate robber barons.

Domican and Kizon were reportedly among several interstate criminals who flew to Melbourne to attend Gangitano's funeral. They were joined, rumour has it, by an Asian contact who counted Gangitano a close enough friend to travel to Australia for the service.

In his private life, Gangitano was unlike the strictly controlled members of the traditional Italian groups, where marriages are often arranged, often between distant relatives from the same region in Italy. He did not marry, but lived with his de facto wife, a private-school girl who was not Italian. Her sister, a handsome and distinguished-looking woman, added a touch of class to the funeral proceedings by giving one of the readings during the service.

But, for all his wide-ranging contacts, Gangitano was best known and – at least on the surface – most admired in Melbourne's little Italy, Lygon Street.

There, according to one of the many death notices placed by people who had met him, he was 'an icon' in certain sections of the community.

All of which has a bearing on the huge turn-up at his funeral. It seems St Mary's Star of the Sea in West Melbourne, close to the Victoria Market, is the church of choice for Melbourne's mafia.

It was a case of history repeating itself. Hairstyles, hemlines and cars change, but among the older people in the congregation were some who have attended more than one big mafia funeral there.

When one of Victoria's earliest godfathers, Domenico 'the Pope' Italiano, died in 1962 he was buried at St Mary's. So were Vincenzo Muratore and Vincenzo Agillette, killed little more than a year later in the power struggle caused by Italiano's death.

They were all given elaborate funerals, early proof of the potency and loyalty of the Italian organised-crime groups that had taken control of Melbourne's fruit-and-vegetable markets.

But none was more elaborate than Gangitano's. From the taped music to the singing of *Ave Maria* by his friend, Simon Pantano, it was a lavish production from start to end.

Of course, not everyone present was in mourning. Apart from a core of family and close friends, the crowd comprised mostly those who felt obliged to be there, and hangers-on attracted by the publicity.

One reason for the big crowd, joked a well-known criminal lawyer afterwards, was the number of undercover police there to execute outstanding warrants on elusive criminals drawn from cover for the occasion. Another, he said, was the number of lawyers trying to collect overdue fees for court appearances for some of the colourful identities in the congregation.

A former detective who first ran against the young Gangitano in nightclubs in the early 1980s, and was respected by him, injects a sombre note.

'I hope a war doesn't go on over this, because the biggest losers are their kids,' he says. 'I have seen the toughest men, but all their lives consist of are a series of battles with the law and with their criminal counterparts. No kid deserves to have their father taken away like this.

'But it's happened to Alphonse's kids, and now there's probably someone out there scheming to kill some other kids' father.'

So, whodunnit? There were rumours. That the Albanians did it. That the Lebanese did it. That the Lebanese rumour was started by someone wanting to cover the real killer's tracks. That it was an inside job, performed with the blessing of people close to him. Any, or none, of these theories could be correct, although the smart money is on the inside job.

Rumours spread at the funeral that the mystery man who was at the house the night Gangitano was killed was a criminal well known on racetracks. And he wasn't the only visitor Gangitano had that night.

Police have their job cut out to sort the red hot from the red herrings.

A cryptic message from a well-informed underworld source says the shooting granted the dying wish of an old man ... and that the process of spreading disinformation about who and why it was done began 'before the gun was chosen'.

A postscript. In August 1992, another man called Al — Alfonso Muratore — was shot dead outside his Hampton home, 28 years after his father Vincenzo was shot outside his house in the same way, less than a kilometre away. Afterwards, a potential witness told police why he couldn't cooperate with them. 'You can put me in jail,' he said, 'but they can give me the death sentence.' Nothing's changed since then.

GANGITANO. — Alphonse.
I will never forget the fresh faced 17 year old that came into the Gym and watched us sparing and training. All the good times we had together and the long discussions will be sadly missed.
Goodbye true friend
Rest in peace
— Your friend Dave Hedgcock.

FIVE

THE MYSTERY PHONE CALL

*That someone was hired to kill
him remains a possibility.*

'MAD' Charlie Hegyalji was always security conscious – those in the illegal amphetamine industry usually are.

He filled books with the registration numbers of the vehicles he believed might be following him, was always discreet on the telephone and chose a house that he believed offered him the greatest protection.

His comfortable brick home in Caulfield South was shielded from the traffic noises of busy Bambra Road by ten mature cypress trees that form a six-metre high hedge so thick it has been cut back to allow pedestrians access to the footpath.

The tall horizontal plank timber fence acted as another buffer to noise and, more importantly for Hegyalji, as a screen to stop possible police surveillance.

Near the front door a small white surveillance camera trained down the six-metre garden path. From inside the house anyone entering or leaving the property could be safely observed on a video screen.

'Mad' Charlie lived in the house relatively secure in the knowledge he had done all he could to protect himself and his business from the untimely interruption of police or possible competitors. But, in the end, it wasn't enough.

Charlie was killed by a lone gunman who used the criminal's own security fetish against him. The killer crouched under the first tree inside the fence line, confident he could not be seen from the street, and waited until Hegyalji came home.

It was just before 1am on November 23, 1998, and it had been a long night for Charlie Hegyalji. A business associate had picked him up about 6pm and they visited the London Tavern, in Caulfield, the Grosvenor Hotel in Balaclava and the Newmarket Hotel in St Kilda. They met up with two other men for their night of drinking.

To an outsider it would seem like an old-fashioned pub crawl, but people like Hegyalji are always on the move, conducting business in pubs and clubs, avoiding set routines that would make him easy to track.

He drank beer and brandy and cokes with his friends. But he wasn't happy with just a night on the booze.

At one point he disappeared with a man and when he returned his friends thought drugs affected him. They were right. An autopsy would later show he had taken cannabis and amphetamines.

While in one of the hotels he made a call from a payphone. Police traced the number and found he had rung Dino Dibra, a violent drug-dealing try-hard who has been listed by police as a suspected hitman.

As with most of the underworld hits those who were likely to have important information refused to talk and Dibra would not share with police the contents of the phone call.

Detectives believe Dibra may have killed Charlie, but it is now a moot point because Dibra himself was murdered in 2000. Charlie and one of the men went back to a unit off Inkerman Street, St Kilda, just after midnight. He called a yellow cab from his friend's unit to take the short trip home around 12.40am.

When the driver rang the doorbell rang Charlie got up to go, leaving half a can of beer.

Instead of being dropped off outside his house he ordered the taxi to stop about a block away from home. It was another security habit he had developed. The theory was that if someone was waiting for him he could sneak up unheard. It was 12.50am.

Hegyalji opened the wooden gate and took two steps along the stone path inside when the killer, armed with a handgun, opened fire. One shot missed, but Charlie had nowhere to run. He was shot four times in the head.

A bullet wound was also found on his left hand – a defensive wound that was sustained as he tried to protect his head from the gunfire.

Neighbours heard the shots and called the police, but Charlie's obsession with privacy, in the form of the hedge and the fence, concealed his body from the police torches. The patrol car drove off.

Not that it made any difference. He had died instantly and the killer was gone in seconds, running past nearby Freeman Street. About seven hours later Hegyalji's de facto wife, Ellie, was about to prepare breakfast for their two children when she glanced up at the security screen, focused on the front path and saw his body.

The security camera remained operational and should have provided the biggest clue in the case. But, for all his security precautions, Charlie had grown lazy – there was no tape in the machine. The sensor light at the front of the house had also stopped working and Charlie had not bothered to get it fixed.

It is almost certain the killer knew he would not be filmed or illuminated. The odds are he had been a guest in the house or had been told by someone who had.

Either way, it was an inside job.

WHEN Hegyalji, then aged 13, arrived at Station Pier as a European refugee he said to his mother in Hungarian: 'Where is the Statue of Liberty?' He eventually got over his disappointment at not being in New York, but never forgot the gangster dreams of his adolescence.

According to his long-time friend and underworld associate, Mark Brandon Read, Charlie always wanted to be a mobster. 'All he ever wanted to be was an American gangster in New York. Through his fantasies he ended up becoming everything he wanted to be, except it was in the wrong country,' Read said.

According to Read, Hegyalji flew to New York and waited outside an old nightclub reputed to be a meeting place for members of the Gambino crime family. 'He stood in the snow for a week before he finally was able to say hello to Carlo Gambino. He pinched Charlie's cheek and said hello back. It was the best moment of his life.'

But he was to become more than just a tourist in the crime world. Hegyalji became a violent young standover man involved in rapes and robberies on massage parlours.

In the 1970s he began to call himself 'The Don' and modelled himself on the image of the US crime figures he revered. But by the 1980s he found there was more money to be made by being involved in the amphetamine trade than robbing fellow criminals.

In the 1980s a bright chemistry student, Paul Lester, quit university once he knew enough to produce the best amphetamines in Australia. He was a sought-after 'speed' cook who was more interested in tinkering with electronics as a hobby than making money from illegal drugs.

But Charlie was the sort who wouldn't take 'no' for an answer. He abducted Lester at gunpoint from a Rosebud street, and then drove him, blindfolded, to a Gippsland property where he forced him to produce amphetamines.

In another cook in Carlton, the process didn't work according to plan and Hegyalji poured the sludgy, volatile substance out on a tarpaulin, allowing the sun to evaporate the liquid and leaving the amphetamine powder. 'He called it "sun-dried speed",' Read said. In fashionable inner-suburban Carlton, it went with sun-dried tomatoes.

Police who dealt with Hegyalji said he was funny and, when it suited him, charming. 'He was always jovial but he was always trying to run you. He would ask more questions than he answered,' one said.

According to one detective he bought a book on police informing from the US in the hope he would be able to keep the upper hand when being interviewed. 'He was prepared to inform, but only out of self-interest. He would give information to expose his enemies and to keep himself out of jail.'

There was no sign of him ever working and he saw no pressing need to collect unemployment benefits.

But if his quick wit failed he had alternatives. When police raided a Narre Warren farmhouse in 1995 as part of an amphetamines investigation they found a hidden armoury behind a false bedroom wall.

Inside they found almost 20 pistols, machine guns and shotguns, six cans of mace, false drivers' licences and silencers. They also found a computer printout from a national security firm that listed alarm systems used throughout Melbourne. A pink highlighter had been used to identify the systems used in police stations.

Hegyalji's fingerprints were found on the list.

Read said Hegyalji was called 'Mad' Charlie after he bit off the nose of an enemy when he was still a teenager, but when another criminal was given the nickname 'Machine-gun Charlie' he became jealous and tried to persuade people to give him a more glamourous title.

'But to everyone he was still Mad Charlie,' Read said.

In the 1990s he was a semi-regular at the specialist Prahran bookstore Kill City, where he would pull copies of Read's books from the shelf and demand to know from the owner if the author had made 'a million dollars'. All the time one of Charlie's minders, a giant of a man, would stand in the doorway of the shop, silently watching his increasingly eccentric boss make a nuisance of himself.

He once stood in a bar next to some of the biggest names in Australian television, poured a white powder on the bar, either cocaine or amphetamines, and snorted it.

'He just stuck his nose in it, then punched himself in the chest and started to shadow box. We decided it was time to leave,' one prominent television and radio identity said later.

He made a lot of money at times, but there was no gain without pain.

In 1989 Hegyalji was shot in the stomach outside a house in South Caulfield and he later shot a man in the car park of a St Kilda hotel as a payback.

In 1997 he was involved in a gun battle with another criminal associate outside a panel beater's workshop in Prahran. Both men were unhurt.

Hegyalji was charged with attempted murder and kept in custody for just over a year until he was released in July 1998. The charges were dropped because, as in so many cases involving the underworld, witnesses refused to testify.

Charlie went back to his old patch of St Kilda and Caulfield, expecting business to return to normal but, according to police, others had filled his place. The people who had been left to run his business were not keen to relinquish control.

He had to flex his muscles and, when he was drinking, loved to wave his handgun around in hotels, playing up to his gangster image. But Hegyalji was forced to stop carrying his revolver with him at all times because, inconveniently, he was increasingly being stopped and searched by police.

In the drug business it can be as dangerous to be owed money as to be in debt.

Charlie was owed more than $100,000 when he was killed but the debt lapsed with his death. It is not a financial arrangement that can be listed on Probate documents.

Detective Senior Sergeant Rowland Legg, prone to the sort of understatement that comes from years of dealing with underworld murders, said: 'There was a little bit of business friction and there had been some ongoing discussions over the debt.'

In the world 'Mad' Charlie inhabited all his adult life, business deals were never committed to paper and some contracts could only be enforced with a gun.

Police do not like to use the term 'professional hit', believing it adds glamour to a gutter business, but Legg concedes: 'That someone was hired to kill him remains a possibility.'

Six days before his murder Hegyalji rang Read to wish the former standover man a happy birthday. 'I asked him how he got my number [it is unlisted] and he said, "You know me, Chopper. I've got everybody's number."'

What Charlie didn't know was that his own number was about to come up. He told Read he had a small problem with a mutual friend, but he said it was nothing he couldn't handle.

'He seemed anxious and I knew he had some sort of problem,' Read said.

Soon after Charlie's murder, Read found that his then wife was expecting their first child. It was a son. He named him Charlie in honour of his murdered mate.

HEGYALJI. — "Charlie".
Always in my heart. So many
treasured memories. With love
— Michelle Newman.

SIX

AMBUSH

He was arrested when he
was 21 for carrying a dagger.

VINCENZO Mannella was nearly everyone's friend – outgoing, generous and funny – but sometime during his life of wheeling and dealing, he managed to make at least one serious enemy. And Mannella moved on the fringes of a world in which it doesn't pay to rub the wrong people the wrong way.

His last night on earth started as a pleasant summer evening. It was January 9, 1999, with the sort of balmy weather that encourages socialising, and Vince Mannella didn't need many excuses to get out on the town.

He spent the evening with three friends in a coffee shop in Lygon Street, Carlton, and, later, at a restaurant in Sydney Road. Then, though it was almost midnight, the group decided to kick on to a wine bar in Nicholson Street.

Mannella, 48, and married with two children, drove his blue Ford Fairlane sedan back to his weatherboard house in Alister

Street, North Fitzroy, from where he was to be picked up by one of the friends to go on to Elio's Wine Bar. He parked the car in the front driveway next to his wife's BMW and walked towards the front door. The sensor lit the front landing and a security camera pointed from the roof, but this would prove to be no help, as the camera had never been connected.

He carried a plastic bag filled with leather belts he had just bought, a packet of Peter Jackson cigarettes and his car keys. It was 11.45pm.

A gunman, who either waited outside the house or followed Mannella's car, walked up behind him and shot him repeatedly with a handgun.

Mannella fell forward, his head resting on the welcome mat at the front landing.

As with so many of the Melbourne hits, police found that Mannella's killer had carefully planned his escape route before doing the deed.

Police are confident that the killer ran about 800 metres along nearby Merri Creek and then up Albert Street to an agreed pick-up point. He obviously did not want any potential witnesses to connect his distinctive getaway car with the sound of gunshots.

MANNELLA was the sort of criminal who was big enough to make a good living but small enough to avoid constant police attention.

Detectives who investigate organised crime knew of him, more because he associated with some of the biggest names in the underworld than as a result of his own activities.

According to police, he was an associate of crime figure Alphonse Gangitano, shot in his Templestowe house almost a year before. He also came to attention as a possible source of amphetamine chemicals during the drug-squad operation, code-named *Phalanx*, into Australia's speed king, John William Higgs.

When Gangitano opened an up market illegal casino above a restaurant in Carlton in 1987 he invited many of Melbourne's major crime figures for the launch. When police raided the place at 1.30am they found Mannella, Higgs and another major amphetamines dealer in the crowd. When asked by police why he was there Mannella said 'I come here to eat' while Higgs said he was 'having a feed'.

Police say Mannella was a middle-level crime entrepreneur who was always looking to turn a profit, and wasn't too bothered what product he had to move – or steal – in order to make one.

In late 1998 he became involved in a gang that specialised in stealing huge quantities of foodstuff. Police believe the gang hit two regional targets and Mannella was the man with the contacts to sell the produce.

Detectives have found he was a heavy gambler, and had owned or part-owned nightclubs and coffee shops.

While he was well liked in his own circle and, for a man who didn't work or receive unemployment benefits, extremely generous, there was an element of violence in his nature.

He was arrested when he was 21 for carrying a dagger in his pocket and six years later was found carrying two pistols.

In 1981 he displayed a savage temper. It happened when the owner of a small coffee shop in Nicholson Street, North Fitzroy, told Mannella that he was no longer welcome to play cards there because he was 'acting tough', carried a loaded pistol and drove a Mercedes even though he didn't work'.

Mannella drove to the coffee shop on February 20, 1981, and three times called the owner outside to try and persuade him to change his mind. But the man wouldn't budge. Mannella then pulled out a pistol and, from a distance of less than a metre, opened fire. The wounded man ran down Nicholson Street while Mannella shot him a total of seven times. Miraculously, he survived, having told hospital staff in

Italian that if they didn't save his life he would come back and haunt them.

Mannella was later sentenced to nine years with a minimum of seven over the shooting. Like 'Mad' Charlie Hegyalji, Mannella went back to what he knew when he was released from prison and, like Charlie, he was owed a six-figure amount when he was murdered.

One of the difficulties police face in an investigation into the murder of a man like Mannella is that 'friends' can be enemies and that business deals are never documented.

Arrangements are confirmed with a nod, plans are hatched in the back rooms of coffee shops and interested partners tell no one of their schemes for fear they will be leaked to the police – or, worse, competing criminals.

Mannella was definitely owed money and may have, in turn, owed others big amounts. For a man who drifted in and out of the lives of some of Australia's most dangerous criminals, either situation could have cost him his life.

'We are exploring possible motives including his criminal associations and debt matters, but nothing has been discounted,' says veteran homicide investigator Rowland Legg.

Mannella had $500 in his pocket when he was murdered. The killer didn't bother to take it. He would be paid much more by the person who ordered the hit.

VINCE Mannella's brother Gerardo would have known in the last few seconds of life the answers to questions homicide squad detectives are still trying to solve.

As he left the house of his brother, Sal, in inner-suburban Melbourne on October 20, 1999, Gerardo saw two men walking out of a lane 15 metres away. Police say he immediately yelled 'No' and ran about 50 metres, dropping a power tool and mobile phone he was carrying. It was likely Mannella recognised the men or saw the guns and knew they had come to kill him.

He ran from the footpath out to the middle of the road, but they caught him, shooting him repeatedly in the head.

Mannella, 31, had been to work as a crane supervisor at the City Square project and to a union meeting before going to his brother's home in the middle of the afternoon. He had not been in trouble with the police for years and his last problem had been for carrying a pistol seven years earlier.

Police don't know if he was followed to the house or the killers had been tipped off, but they were waiting when he left to go to his Avondale Heights house about 8pm.

A third man, driving a dark Ford station wagon, picked up the killers moments after the hit.

As in the case of his brother's murder the killers had done their homework. Mannella, the father of three, gave no indication when he left the house that he thought he was in danger, but one career criminal with a history of providing solid information said Gerardo had repeatedly said he intended to find and kill the men who shot his brother, Vince.

'It is most unwise to speak openly about these matters because if people take you seriously they will be forced to get in first.' Dead men can't hurt anybody.

RISING early was no problem to Joe Quadara – after all, he had been getting up before the sun for as long as he could remember.

Horse trainers, newsagents and people in the fruit-and-vegetable industry don't bother grumbling about early starts because they are a fact of life. And death, sometimes. Early risers do make tempting targets. For Quadara, last his trip to work would take only a few minutes on the empty streets from his unit in Toorak, one of Melbourne's most expensive suburbs, to the Safeway supermarket in nearby Malvern Road.

After more than 30 years in the fruit-and-vegetable industry,

Quadara had gone from being a millionaire to a bankrupt. He had once owned a string of big fruit shops and was a popular and generous patron of the Collingwood and Frankston football clubs, but interest rates and an over-committed line of credit brought him crashing down.

He had to sell his shops in Frankston and Mornington, his lavish Mt Eliza house and virtually everything he owned to try to pay off his debts, but there were still at least 60 creditors when he closed his doors.

He owed various creditors from $2,000 to $50,000, although they would admit he hadn't run away from his debts and had battled to try to make good.

Even though his business reputation may have been in tatters, he was still acknowledged to be a perfectionist in fruit and vegetables, presenting only the best produce and providing the warm personality that makes customers want to come back.

By then aged 57, he had become the produce manager at the Toorak supermarket and when it was taken over by Safeway he kept the job. He had worked at the wholesale market and in shops almost all his adult life and was known for his boundless energy and enthusiasm.

But recently he had not been feeling well and had yet another doctor's appointment for later that day. He had already been told he might need surgery for cancer. What he didn't know was that his problems were terminal.

At 3am on May 28, 1999, he drove his green Commodore into the rear car park and stopped behind the Crittenden's liquor shop. Two men, armed with handguns, ambushed him and shot him repeatedly before he could get out of the car. People heard screaming and yelling before the shots.

A Safeway truck driver found the body about 90 minutes later.

It was seemingly a murder without motive and police are yet to find the answer to a series of basic questions such as:

- Why would two men execute a seemingly harmless fruiterer in a deserted Toorak car park?
- What was it about Joe Quadara that would drive other men to kill him?
- And why, at his funeral a few days later, did three of Melbourne's most notorious gangsters – Alphonse Gangitano, the main suspect on the shooting, a man who was at Alphonse's house when the murder was committed and Gangitano's former right-hand man – all turn up to pay their last respects?

Police have now established the two killers were seen in the car park the previous day in a dark-coloured Toyota Camry station wagon. The trouble is, 32,000 cars fit that description.

It is possible the killers believed Quadara had the keys to the safe and the yelling seconds before he was shot was part of a failed robbery bid.

But Joe Quadara wasn't even the purchasing officer at the supermarket so he didn't carry company funds or have access to the safe.

Detectives said he was a good fighter when he was younger and had a strong survival sense developed from three decades in an industry with more than its share of seemingly unexplained murders.

'If someone had put the squeeze on him the pressure would have been put on gradually and he wouldn't have been parking in a dark car park at work,' one detective said. If robbery was not the motive then the killers checked the scene the day before as part of their plan to execute Joe Quadara.

But was it the right Joe Quadara?

There is another Joe Quadara, also aged in his mid-50s, also with connections in the fruit-and-vegetable industry – and with a more colourful past.

This man was named in an inquest as having prior knowledge of the murder of Alfonso Muratore, who was shot dead in 1992. He denied the allegations.

Muratore was the son-in-law of Liborio Benvenuto, the godfather of Melbourne who died in 1988. If it was a payback, it seems the wrong man paid the debt. It would not be the first time.

MANNELLA. — Vince Died (tragically). Vince. sorry to see you go this way. you were a good friend, always trying to help everywhere you could. You will be sadly missed. Deepest and sincere condolences to your wife. children, and also your brothers and respective families. Rest in peace my little mate, until we meet again. — **Mick Gatto.**

SEVEN

SILENCING
A WITNESS

*It's lucky kids sleep
through anything.*

VICKI Jacobs was no angel, but even in her darkest times others saw in her a spark of something better. Even in jail, where she ran with the meanest women in a mean system, she showed glimpses of the character that later allowed her to turn her life around.

It was no temporary 'conversion' calculated to win parole, sympathy or a job. Soon after the birth of her son, Ben, in 1993, she left her career-criminal husband and the life he represented.

From then on the only false thing about the petite blonde woman was the surname she took by deed poll to make a clean break with her dirty past — and the evil people in it.

It wasn't enough. On the Saturday morning of July 12, 1999, some of those people reached out and destroyed the life she'd reclaimed for herself and her son.

In an act as callous as it was careful, a killer who'd almost certainly watched her for days slipped into her unit in Wood Street, Long Gully, on Bendigo's outskirts, and shot her in the head as she slept on a fold-down settee with her Ben. The killer held his small-calibre weapon so close, police believe, that the shot was muffled by the bedding.

The head of the homicide squad, Chief Inspector Rod Collins, looked close to tears when he called a media conference to appeal for information about a crime that rocked the state.

'It's lucky kids sleep through anything,' he said later. Amazingly, Ben wasn't woken by the shot that killed his mother. The chilling suggestion is that anyone who could murder a mother with her child wouldn't hesitate to kill the child too, if there was any chance he might identify the shooter. By the same reckoning, it's lucky that the murdered woman's 13-year-old niece, asleep in the next room, wasn't a witness. Otherwise, the teenager's life could have been ended as brutally as her aunt's.

Detectives are sure the murder had nothing to do with Vicki Jacobs's recent life in Bendigo, where she had enrolled in a university computer course and was involved in the church.

The killing is almost certainly the result of Jacobs following her conscience by giving evidence the previous year in a case in which her ex-husband, Gerald Preston, and another man were convicted of a brutal underworld double execution in Adelaide.

She refused witness protection before and after the trial, instead changing her name. For a while she lived secretly in a small central Victorian town before deciding to break cover by moving to Bendigo to be nearer friends and family. It seemed to her that it was worth the risk. It was a gamble she lost.

So who was Vicki Jacobs?

Born Vicki Joy Solomon, she was one of four daughters and two sons of a respectable couple who have lived for many years in a quiet street overlooking paddocks on the edge of Ballarat, one of Victoria's bigger provincial cities. Vicki's father is a strict Christian, a lay preacher. The family closed ranks after her murder. They kept the private funeral in Ballarat a tightly held secret, trying to avoid the possibility of their grief being turned into a media 'event'.

What isn't a secret is that Vicki was an intelligent but rebellious teenager whose life up to the age of 30 was proof of the dangers of falling into bad company.

Involved, as police say, in 'drug-related' offences, she was jailed in Fairlea Women's Prison in the early and mid-1980s. There, she associated with a group of hardened offenders including Lisa Lewis (now dead), Robyn Barwick and Ricki Dewan, who were among 28 'troublemakers' transferred to Pentridge as punishment after a fire at Fairlea.

Although not a model prisoner in other ways, Vicki Solomon was a keen jailhouse student who shone at mathematics and computers. She was, recalls a former Fairlea officer, 'the black sheep of her family, but I honestly feel she was too good for most of the prisoners.'

She was also 'a comedienne, full of vim and vigour and practical jokes', he says. Once, when authorities were concerned about people throwing contraband into the prison, Vicki lampooned the situation by sticking a pair of gumboots upside down in the lawn to make it look as if someone had dived head first over the wall.

Another time, she was part of a group that 'found' a visiting prison governor's radio transceiver and broadcast embarrassing messages that questioned his motives for coming to Fairlea. A lawyer who knew Vicki Solomon and her friends recalls the women stealing a mobile telephone and pulling a hoax with media and police that there was a 'mass riot' at the prison. Even the new name Vicki chose revealed a subtle sense of humour.

Like Solomon, Jacob is a Biblical name, and it means 'He will supplant'. It also means 'One that trips up'.

There's nothing funny about the way she died, or the reasons behind it. In her past, Vicki Jacobs was no angel. But the odds are that those who ordered her killed were. Hell's Angels.

A HOMICIDE investigation begins with the obvious. When a woman is murdered the first suspect is usually her husband or lover.

So when Vicki Jacobs was shot dead next to her six-year-old son in their Bendigo home, detectives automatically made inquiries about her former husband.

At first, it seemed more than promising. The husband looked a prime candidate for organising the murder. After all, he was a convicted criminal who had suffered a bitter separation.

And police knew exactly where to find him: in his high-security cell in Adelaide's Yatala Prison — where he is serving 32 years for a double murder. And his former wife had given evidence against him – four days of it, in the South Australian Supreme Court.

Gerald David Preston had, as the court heard in 1998, accepted $10,000 to kill an Adelaide garage proprietor as a favour to a Melbourne Hell's Angels member.

This is what happened. On August 15, 1996, a man wearing a fine-mesh mask over his face entered the business known as Les's Auto Repairs in Adelaide's southern industrial area of Lonsdale. He was solid, wore shiny trousers and carried a distinctive semi-automatic pistol, a rare wartime German model stolen in Victoria long before. He entered an office to the left of the repair shop and confronted two men working there.

Pointing the pistol at one of them, Tim Richards, the gunman said: 'Are you Les?' When Mr Richards replied 'no', the gunman shot him. Then the gunman turned to Les Knowles and asked him the same question. When he gave the same answer, he, too, was shot.

A third man, mechanic Kym Traeger, didn't wait around to answer any questions. But he didn't get away quickly enough to avoid being shot in the wrist before the gunman escaped in a car driven, the Crown later alleged, by Preston's friend, Kevin Wayne Gillard. The operation was as clumsy as it was cold blooded. As a hitman, Preston made a good stamp collector. Although he'd dabbled in crime for 20 years, he was a thief, marijuana dealer and occasional armed robber, not a contract killer.

Preston, the eldest of six children of a Scottish migrant couple, had graduated from being a teenage stamp collector to running a second-hand shop called Money For Nothing before turning to crime, becoming connected with the notorious Melbourne Hell's Angel when he met some of them in prison in the 1980s.

Soon afterwards he met Vicki Solomon, as she was then known. They married in 1992, and split within two years, after the birth of their son, Ben.

Vicki had a chequered past, but she wanted to put it behind her. She changed her name by deed poll to Jacobs.

Despite the split with Preston, they kept in touch. After the Adelaide murders, he came to visit, and talked. In hindsight, it would have been better for both of them if they'd made a clean break.

His confession to Vicki implicated him — and drew her into a murder case as a key witness. Ignoring the advice of her closest friend, Colleen Hunter, and the hard lessons learned behind bars, she agreed to give evidence against her former husband. She also ignored the South Australian police's offer of witness protection, preferring the stability of a home in Long Gully to the lonely, secretive life of the protected witness.

The cruel irony was that after a lifetime of wrong turns, her courageous decision to do the right thing and tell the truth probably signed her death warrant.

While homicide investigators were to look at all possible

motives for the murder of Jacobs, it took them only a few days to decide to go to Adelaide to speak with her former husband.

One thing the police knew for sure was that Gerald Preston didn't pull the trigger, because he had the perfect alibi of being locked in a high-security cell. But who did?

ON the surface, Preston could have wanted his former wife dead because, in his eyes, she had betrayed him. He had every reason to blame his 32-year sentence on her four days and 500 pages of unwavering testimony. He has maintained his innocence of the Adelaide double murder and, in sworn evidence, blames his brother. But Jacobs's version of events destroyed his story. And any homicide detective will tell you that revenge is high on the list of the eight key reasons for murder.

But to assume that Preston organised the murder from his cell is to assume that he had the contacts, the money and the will to do it.

The fact is, he is not an organised-crime figure, nor a feared standover man; he was a marijuana salesman with a taste for computers and stolen cars.

On the evidence, he didn't graduate to being a successful hitman. Firstly, he couldn't identify his victim, let alone catch him alone. Secondly, he used a rare and easily identified weapon — a vintage 9mm Luger pistol stolen from a South Gippsland collector whose armoury was rifled during a break-in that resulted in several weapons entering the flourishing criminal black market for guns. He broke the gunman's cardinal rule: he didn't dispose of the weapon properly after the crime; instead, he gave it to a family member, who still had it when police came searching. Finally, he chose as his accomplice a man who confessed to police.

But, if Preston were involved in Jacobs's murder, there's one more thing to consider. That is, for someone with all the time in the world, he couldn't have chosen a worse moment to have his former wife killed.

Preston and Gillard were granted leave the previous March to appeal against their convictions. They were due in the Supreme Court just six days after the murder. This was lousy timing — even for a man who in matters of life and death had proven to be less than a master tactician.

While the appeal was to be judged on six points of law, including the claim the two accused should have been granted separate trials, the violent death of a star witness is hardly calculated to win sympathy for his case from the appeal court.

Days after Vicki's death, Preston was interviewed by Melbourne police in Yatala. Their discussions remained confidential but police did say he was not 'formally interviewed'.

In other words he was not 'officially' a suspect ... at least not yet, although it seemed certain that detectives would be back, this time with more pertinent questions.

Preston did place a death notice in the *Herald Sun* for his former wife. His notice read: 'Soulmates once, you gave us a beautiful healthy son and blossomed as a proud, devoted mother. Truly. And while we grew apart I always admired your strength and never stopped missing you ... You will always be in our hearts.'

But even if Preston wasn't involved in his wife's death, the motive behind the murder might well arise from the evidence she swore before the Supreme Court in 1998.

The prosecution case in the double murder was that Preston took $10,000 from a Melbourne Hell's Angel. The trial judge, Justice Mulligan, said: 'They were cold-blooded, pre-planned executions of two men for money and as a personal favour by you, Preston, to a friend or friends. You [Preston] acted in a callous disregard for human life in order to achieve your purpose of killing Mr Knowles.'

In sentencing Preston to 32 years and Gillard to 25, Justice Mulligan described the evidence against the pair as 'overwhelming'.

Preston said: 'I don't accept the jury's verdict. I steadfastly maintain my innocence.'

Although a motive was not established in court, police believe the Hell's Angel wanted Knowles dead because of a dispute over amphetamine distribution. Police found $70,000 in the Lonsdale garage after the murders, confirming that Knowles, a well-known criminal, was a heavyweight drug dealer encroaching on the Hell's Angels' territory.

Police know that the Hell's Angel who ordered Knowles killed has got away with it so far … mostly due to Preston's silence. Preston testified he knew the biker through trading marijuana but he did not implicate him in the murder.

It is possible, even likely, that the biker ordered Vicki Jacobs killed in a twisted attempt to avenge Preston's conviction, and to reward his silence in the dock. Either way, the unmistakable message was to warn potential witnesses not to give evidence.

In Vicki Jacobs's evidence, she said her husband had made admissions to her about the two murders. But she went further, implicating the Hell's Angels in the plot, giving evidence of going to the clubhouse with Preston after he had told her about the Adelaide murders. What Melbourne homicide detectives want to know is if Jacobs was killed not on the orders of her former husband, but for pointing the finger at the Hell's Angels.

An even more sinister theory (if that is possible) is that the timing of the murder of Jacobs was deliberately linked to her former husband's appeal — not to help him win, but to stack the odds against him.

For the fact is that if Preston was granted a retrial, the issue of who ordered the Adelaide hit would become alive again.

He could fight the case in a fresh trial, blaming his brother and hoping a new jury believed him, or he could be prepared to cut a deal in the hope of a greatly reduced jail sentence. He would then have one great bargaining chip — the name of the person who hired him. Jacobs's murder could have the effect of silencing a potential witness — while making any further legal examination of the murders of Knowles and Richards unlikely.

The murder would also send a message to the other 104 witnesses: silence is golden.

Preston remains a prime suspect in the homicide investigation. But he's not the only one.

THE Nomads chapter is the fourth arm of the Hell's Angels established in Australia. The Nomads, formed in Melbourne in August 1980, is reputed to be among the most violent of all outlaw motorcycle gangs.

Organised-crime investigators say that in the past decade most bikers have made efforts to conceal their criminal activities. But the man who police allege paid Preston to kill in Adelaide remains steeped in a tradition of violence.

Aged in his 30s, he is from a well-known Melbourne crime family. One of his close older relatives was considered one of Australia's best safebreakers.

On May 13, 1995, a festering dispute erupted between biker gangs after Bandidos members were bashed and their colours stolen by the Nomads. During the war, Gerald Preston's biker friend was repeatedly identified by police as a Nomads enforcer.

On June 1, 1995, uniformed police on a routine patrol checked a car parked near the Nomads' Thomastown clubhouse. They found four members of the Ballarat Bandidos gang, armed with firearms and other weapons. An official police report stated they 'probably had intentions of committing some sort of armed raid on the Hell's Angels Nomads' clubhouse'.

Two months later, members of the organised crime squad arrested two men from the Nomads, the sergeant-at-arms and the enforcer — the man who allegedly offered Preston the murder contract on Knowles.

They found firearms and a book that contained personal profiles of 14 Bandidos members. 'It is possible the Hell's Angels had these details for use when targeting the Bandidos members with violence,' a confidential police intelligence report noted.

On November 29, 1995, a Bandido biker was run over while riding his bike from the gang's Ballarat clubhouse. The car that hit him had been rented by the girlfriend of the Nomads' enforcer. The enforcer has consistently shown a propensity in two states for interfering with witnesses and perverting the course of justice — apparently successfully.

He was investigated for attempting to intimidate witnesses in the Adelaide murder trial. The case against him failed when witnesses refused to testify about the intimidation tactics used against them. In 1995, he was involved in a minor traffic altercation in the Melbourne outer suburb of Campbellfield when another motorist blew his horn after he was cut up. The Nomad followed the second driver and started a fight, but the man who tooted his horn fought back, giving as good as he got.

Police allege the Nomad then pulled out a pistol, firing five blanks while threatening to kill the motorist.

Police say that after the motorist made a statement to police, the Nomad hired a champion kick-boxer and another man to intimidate him. The victim told police that three men approached him and one said: 'If you go to court and give evidence you may as well go to the Fawkner Cemetery and reserve a grave for yourself.'

The Nomad was committed for trial, but the Director of Public Prosecutions dropped the charge when the witness refused to testify.

The Hell's Angels culture is littered with examples of potentially damaging witnesses being intimidated — and killed.

Mothers of young children are not treated differently. In the early 1980s, members of the Hell's Angels arrived at the Melbourne County Court in their gang colours in an attempt to influence jurors and witnesses.

In 1976 a woman called Margo Compton cut her ties with a Californian chapter of the Hell's Angels and moved north to a small Oregon village with her six-year-old twin girls. She began to write an autobiography, claiming the gang forced her into prostitution, kept her drugged and beat her. She also made a statement to police about the outlaw motorcycle gang's involvement in the vice industry.

Compton, her little girls and a 19-year-old visitor were all shot dead, just two weeks after she gave court evidence against the Angels.

Police later found that gang members intercepted a letter she wrote to a relative in which she had naïvely included her return address. Vicki Jacobs went to the trouble of changing her name, but she wasn't hard to find.

Police believe that whoever killed her probably stalked her and knew the layout of her unit. It had all the hallmarks of a professional hit … unlike Preston's botched Adelaide job.

Meanwhile, Preston's mysterious friend, the pistol-packing Nomads enforcer, could not be contacted by the authors. He was in Rio de Janeiro at an international Hell's Angels conference.

EIGHT

DIGGING YOUR OWN GRAVE

He was a loser who always
backed the wrong side.

THE Esquire Motel had about 40 rooms and most nights almost all of them were occupied by people who wanted cheap accommodation close to Fitzroy Street in the busy heart of St Kilda.

The fashionable suburb, where millionaires and professionals now rub shoulders with street people, still has a few hangovers of its seedier past – and the Esquire is one of them, a 1970s building in Acland Street that has packed a lot of low life into its three decades.

Drifters, backpackers, runaways, prostitutes and drug dealers could all get rooms. Some just stayed the night; others stayed for as long as they could afford the tariff, not having the security or the confidence to look for something more permanent.

Late in 1999 a man moved in to room 18 and made himself at

home. He showed no sign of wanting anything better. For him the location was perfect – and at $50 a night the price was right.

And it was positively roomy compared with the prison cell he had vacated only a month earlier. He was a drug dealer and he turned the room into a 24–hour–a–day business address. There was no need to advertise. Word of mouth in the street is all a pusher needs.

Local police say that for six months he worked 'red-hot' and built a strong customer base. The dealer had visitors at all times of day and night. One of them was Richard Mladenich. The fact that it was 3.30am, that one man was asleep on the floor, a woman was asleep in a bed and a third person was also in bed would not have fazed the man, who loved to talk.

When the door of room 18 swung open a little later to reveal an armed man, it was one of the few times in his life that the standover man and serial pest was caught short for words.

The assassin didn't need to break down the door – underworld murders are seldom that dramatic. The door was unlocked and all he had to do was turn the handle slowly enough not to forewarn the victim. Before he walked in he yelled the name of the resident drug dealer – almost as a greeting – to show that he was no threat.

By the time Mladenich realised he was in danger it was too late. When he stood to face the young man in the dark glasses and hood, he saw a small-calibre handgun pointing directly at him.

His experience of more than 20 years of violence would have told him that only luck could save him. It didn't. Before he could speak the gun barked and the man holding it was gone, leaving Mladenich fighting a losing battle for life.

MLADENICH was a drug dealer, a standover man and a loudmouth. He was also funny, outrageous, a showman and a jailhouse poet with a sense of theatre. When Mladenich, 37, was hunted down by a hitman on May 16, 2000, detectives had a big problem. It was not to find suspects who wanted him dead, but to eliminate potential enemies from the long list of possible gunmen.

If he was followed then the killer did a professional job, as Mladenich had visited several other rooms at the Esquire before he reached room 18 just before 3am.

But after an extensive investigation police believed the killer knew his quarry's movements because he was close to him. He was either someone who made money in the same business as Mladenich and decided to eliminate him – or, more likely, he was working for somebody who wanted him out of the way. In the underworld it is almost always associates, rather than strangers, who finally pull the trigger. The rivals just provide the bullets.

There was more than one reason why Mladenich's days were numbered. As well as being a prolific drug dealer, he had another gig. The big man with the bigger mouth was a minder for drug dealer Mark Moran. Moran was murdered outside his luxury home in June 2000 – a month after Mad Richard.

It is possible that Mladenich was simply killed to eliminate protection for the ultimate target of a rival drug syndicate. Police believe his killer was Dino Dibra, who was himself also killed later that year. Dibra's name is also listed as a suspect in the Mark Moran killing.

If the theory is right it adds a black postscript to the recurring theme of Mad Richard's short, brutal and wasted life: that he was a loser who always backed the wrong side.

According to former standover man Mark 'Chopper' Read, Mladenich was 'a total comedy of errors' and 'without a doubt the loudest and most troublesome inmate in any jail in Australia'.

In 1988 Read and a then young Mladenich were both inmates in the maximum security H Division of Pentridge Prison during the so-called 'Overcoat War' between prisoner factions.

'Poor Richard fell over and hit his head on a garden spade, but he told the police nothing and dismissed as foul gossip and rumour suggestions that I had hit him with it.' Read was never charged with the attack, but Mladenich carried permanent reminders of it in the form of scars on his forehead.

Rumours that prison officers, who were tired of Mladenich's dangerous ways, stood by when Read allegedly attacked him were never substantiated.

But there is no doubt that he earned enemies wherever he went. One night in jail Mladenich grabbed his plastic chair and banged it against his cell bars from 8.30pm until 4.20am – not as part of a jail protest, but simply because he thought it was funny.

'He was never short of a word,' Read explains. 'Once, he went to Joe the Boss's place and stood outside yelling threats. This was not wise and a short time later he was shot in the leg in what was an obvious misunderstanding. He kept yelling abuse before he limped off. He could be flogged to the ground and then he would say, "Now let that be a lesson to you."'

Mladenich was 14 when he was charged with stealing a car in Footscray. He was to end with a criminal record of more than nine pages and 24 aliases, including Richard Mantello and John Mancini.

But while he considered himself a smart criminal his arrest record is filled with offences involving street violence. He was no master gangster.

His lengthy police file included a large number of warnings, including one that he had 'violent rages that can be triggered off at any time … he will attempt to kill a [police] member or members'.

One entry read: 'According to prison officers with years of experience they stated [Mladenich] was one of the craziest and most violent offenders they have seen. [He] is a mountain of a man who has a very violent and unpredictable nature. He must be approached with caution and extreme care. A tough cookie.'

Read said Mladenich had a fierce heroin habit from the mid-

1980s. 'He would come into jail looking like a wet greyhound and then he would pump iron and build up while inside.'

More than 10 years ago Read predicted that Mladenich would die young. 'The drugs will kill Richard and it's sad to see.'

Read, now a best-selling author and artist, says many of his old friends and enemies were being murdered because they refused to accept they were too old to dominate the underworld.

'The barman has called last orders, but these people won't go home and they just hang around to be killed. I have found that the writing of books is a far better way for your middle-aged crim to spend his winter nights, well away from excitable types with firearms.'

Former drug squad and St Kilda detective, Lachlan McCulloch, said Mladenich was one of the more bizarre criminal identities he had investigated in his 16 years in the job.

McCulloch said that during a drug raid in Albert Park armed police were searching a house when there was an amazing scream. 'Mladenich jumped out into the lounge room pointing a gun at everyone and going "Pow Pow!" He had this toy laser gun and was running around shooting all of us with the flashing red light. The trouble was we all had real guns with real bullets. We could have blown his head off.'

McCulloch said that while Mladenich was eccentric and violent ('He was as crazy as they came') he lacked the planning skills to be successful in the underworld.

The former detective said Mladenich, who liked to be known as 'King Richard' but was also known by others as 'Spade Brain' and 'Mad Richard', had ambitions to run a protection racket. He stood over prostitutes and drug dealers, but wanted to broaden his horizons. 'He wore this black gangster's coat and a black hat and walked into a pub in South Melbourne. He said he wanted $1,000 a week for protection money and he would be back the next day.'

When he came back 24 hours later he didn't seem to notice a group of detectives sitting at a nearby table, sipping beers. He was arrested at his first attempt at a shakedown.

Read said one detective tired of dealing with Mladenich through the courts. He said the detective walked him at gunpoint to the end of the St Kilda Pier, made him jump in and swim back. 'Would have done him good, too,' Read said.

As a criminal he was a good poet, reciting his verse to a judge who was about to jail him. He once was waiting in a Chinese restaurant for a takeaway meal when he started a friendly conversation with the man next to him, complimenting him on a ring he was wearing.

When the man left the restaurant, Mladenich was waiting outside to rob him of the ring. 'He nearly pulled the finger off with it,' a detective said.

He had a long and volatile relationship with many Melbourne barristers and judges. He was known to have stalked a prosecutor, Carolyn Douglas (later appointed a County Court Judge), to have disrupted Supreme Court trials and to abuse lawyers who had appeared against him.

He once chested a respected barrister, Raymond Lopez, in the foyer of Owen Dixon Chambers. 'It is the only time I have felt under physical pressure in that way. I thought he was as high as a kite,' Lopez recalled. 'He calmed down but he struck me as the type who could turn quickly.'

He walked into the office of one of his former lawyers, locked the door and asked for money. At the same time he noticed the barrister's overcoat on the back of the door and started to go through the pockets. This was an outrageous breach of protocol – it is acknowledged in the legal fraternity that it is the barrister's job to fleece his clients, not the other way around.

One member of the underworld said many people would be happy that Mladenich was dead. 'He was a hoon, a pimp and lived

DIGGING YOUR OWN GRAVE

off everyone else. He never did one good job, but he would come around looking for a chop out.'

But the death notices in the week after his death included some from many well-known criminals, including career armed robbers and an underworld financier dying of cancer.

It is believed that Mladenich had run up drug debts with at least two major dealers who were prepared to write off the money. Neither was likely to order his murder.

Richard's mother, Odinea, said society should take some responsibility for the criminal her son became. She said he was bullied by his step-father and was eventually sent to a state institution.

'They took my little boy and they gave me back a zombie. He was a victim of this rotten society.'

She said he was the second youngest inmate sent to the notorious top-security Jika Jika section in Pentridge. 'He had to become like he was to survive,' she said.

Mrs Mladenich said many children who went to boys' homes had their lives destroyed – and there is evidence to support her claim. Many of the worst names in crime can trace their criminal beginnings to what happened in boys' homes, some of which were deservedly notorious.

Mrs Mladenich said that the same families she saw at boys' homes 'I would see later at Pentridge'.

Elder brother Mark said: 'He was 16 when he was in the hardest division in an adult jail. He wasn't allowed to be soft. He had to be hard to survive.

'I know about his record, but when he was with his family he was different. He was good-hearted.'

Mladenich was released from prison only a month before his death and told friends and relatives he was determined to keep out of trouble. But as usual, Richard wasn't telling the whole truth.

Within weeks of his release he was trying to establish a protection racket by standing over restaurants in Fitzroy Street.

In May 2003, three years after the murder, Coroner Lewis Byrne concluded: 'Richard Mladenich lived at the margin. He had friends and acquaintances who lived outside the law. He had quite an extensive criminal history and had only shortly before his death been released from prison. I only include this aspect of Mr Mladenich's personality to make the point that some of his friends, associates and indeed enemies are part of a subculture where violence and death are not unknown. Although comprehensive investigation undertaken by the homicide squad has been unable to identify the killer of Mr Mladenich the file remains open and should it be warranted, if further information comes to light, this inquest can be reopened.'

Don't hold your breath.

MLADENICH. — Richard.
Sorry to see you go this way
Condolences to the family.
Rest in Peace
Mick Gatto

NINE

SET-UP

*Sometimes it can be more
dangerous to goad a snake than
to leave it alone or kill it outright.*

THREE generations of Morans have knocked around in Melbourne criminal circles and their reputation was not earned with a pacifist philosophy.

But Mark Moran, 36, had seemed to be the white sheep of the family, the one who stayed in the background and kept a low profile. However, as stock breeders will tell you, blood in the end will tell. Mark Moran was bred for trouble and it was only a matter of time before it found him.

His mother, Judith Moran, was attracted to gunmen all her life. Mark's natural father was one of them. His name was Leslie John Cole and he was ambushed and shot dead outside his Sydney home on November 10, 1982.

History repeats itself. Mark went the same way as his dad when he was shot dead outside his million-dollar home in the Melbourne suburb of Aberfeldie on June 15, 2000. He was the latest victim in the underworld war that had claimed up to nine lives in less than three years – and would, by late 2004, have a death toll over 30.

Within 24 hours of the murder, the homicide squad's Detective Inspector Brian Rix said police were receiving little help from the Morans. The family might not have known then that they had been targeted and were to be hunted down by an underworld faction as if they were feral animals. A family that had built a reputation as criminal hard men was to find out what it was like to be the intimidated.

But that was in the future. Back in June 2000 Rix would state the obvious when he said the Mark Moran murder had 'all the hallmarks of an underworld slaying'.

'The indications are that he was out of his car at the time of the shooting, which means that perhaps his killers laid in wait,' Rix said.

Sometimes you can guess more from what police don't say.

What Rix didn't mention was the reason why Moran had left his house for less than half an hour on the night he was killed.

He had gone to meet someone, but who?

Did the killer know Moran would go out and then come back that night?

It is fair to conclude that a killer would not sit outside a luxury house in an affluent street all night on the off chance the target would venture out. He had to have some inside knowledge.

The killer would also have known that his target was at his most vulnerable. Mark's half-brother, Jason, was behind bars and his minder, 'Mad Richard' Mladenich, had been shot dead in a seedy St Kilda hotel a month earlier.

So the real question became: who set him up?

As Rix said: 'Mark fancied himself as a bit of a heavy. I would think the underworld will talk about this to somebody, and I'm sure that will get back to us in some way.'

He was right, they did talk but the talk remained a long way short of admissible evidence. No one knew then that Mark Moran's death would be just one in the most savage underworld war in 100 years.

Moran left his home in Combermere Street, Aberfeldie, for just over 20 minutes. When he returned someone shot him as he got out of his late-model Commodore.

The shotgun blast knocked him back into the car, killing him instantly.

It was no surprise when it became known that a Moran had been murdered. The surprise was that it was Mark and not his elder half-brother, Jason, the notorious gangster who was serving two years and six months over an assault in King Street, Melbourne.

While Jason Moran was seen as wild, violent and erratic, Mark was calmer and tried to keep a lower profile.

'Jason was out of control, Mark was the brains,' said one policeman who has investigated the family.

But as Jason became increasingly restrained by court action and stints in jail, Mark began to take a higher profile.

About 18 months before his death he took offence when an associate made a disparaging comment about a female relative.

'He went around to the guy's house, stuck a gun in his mouth, took him away and seriously flogged him,' a criminal source said.

In 1999, he was involved in the assault of a policeman at Flemington racecourse on Oaks Day – not a good business move. Neither was the falling out the Moran brothers had with a crew of new players.

The dispute, about six months before Mark's death, began over a failed venture that cost all concerned a lot of potential earnings. When words failed a firearm was produced.

A women heard an argument followed by a man crying out: 'No, Jason.'

The incident was a warning, not an attempt to kill. But

sometimes it can be more dangerous to goad a snake than to leave it alone or kill it outright, as the Morans were to find out the hard way.

It is not certain which brother pulled the trigger that did the damage to the other crew's frontman. Either way, it wasn't just his feelings that were hurt. But, although the shot was undoubtedly from close range, the wounded man could not help police with details. Muzzle flash from guns can do that: temporarily blind people and cause memory loss and confusion.

On February 17, 2000, police noticed Mark Moran driving a luxury car. When they opened the boot of the rented vehicle, they found a high-tech handgun equipped with a silencer and a laser sight.

They also found a heap of amphetamine pills that had been stamped in a pill press to appear as ecstasy tablets.

The day after Mark's murder, police raided an associate's home and seized another 5,000 tablets similar to those found in the boot of the rental car.

Months before, Mark Moran had been ejected from the County Court after he tried to use a false name to get access to the plea hearing after his half-brother was found guilty over the King Street assault. AFL footballer Wayne Carey gave character evidence for Jason Moran, which was a case of history repeating itself.

A high-profile Carlton footballer of impeccable credentials once gave character evidence for Moran's maternal grandfather over a stolen-property charge.

Not surprisingly, the property had been stolen and hidden at the grandfather's place by the teenage Moran boys and the old man was obliged to shoulder the blame for his delinquent descendants.

Police described Moran as one of a new breed of drug traffickers known as the 'Bollinger Dealers', who associated with minor celebrities and the new rich.

They wore designer suits and used a pill press to stamp their amphetamine-based products to look like party drugs, such as ecstasy.

Mark was a former professional chef and a 'gym rat' often seen at the Underworld Health and Fitness centre beside the Yarra in the central city. He once listed his occupation as personal trainer. But like so many of his class he had not worked regularly for years and police say his high-income lifestyle and expensive home could only have been supported through illegal activities. He refused to speak about business on telephones and rarely spoke with associates in his house because he feared police had the place bugged.

He was proud of his fitness and physique and was described as 'extremely narcissistic'. He liked to be well dressed. When he was shot he was wearing a huge diamond stud in his left ear.

Mark Moran was young, good looking, rich and fit. But in the months leading up to his murder, he was depressed and at one point was hospitalised when he told friends he was considering suicide. In the end, someone beat him to it.

The day before Moran's murder, police conducted a series of raids on a sophisticated amphetamines network and a number of criminals, including one known as 'The Penguin', were arrested.

One theory police are looking at is that someone connected with the network wrongly blamed Mark Moran for having informed on them to try to remove a competing drug syndicate. A second underworld rumour was that the murder was a payback for Jason's alleged involvement in the death of Alphonse Gangitano and that Mark was considered an easier target because the dangerous Jason was in jail.

A third source suggested that a gangster had a personal grudge against Mark and that Moran was warned to back off. When he didn't, the gangster ordered the murder.

But the favourite early theory and the one that firmed to a

near certainty a few years later was that it was a payback from the aggrieved team of new players.

However, the 'favourites' had alibis for the night. While this may have impressed the police it left associates of the Morans unconvinced. Within days of the murder there were reports of shots fired near the North Fitzroy home of one of the the main suspects.

One name mentioned as the possible gunman who killed Moran was Dino Dibra, a try-hard young gangster from Melbourne's west. Police believe he shot Moran's minder, Richard Mladenich, on May 16 and then may have gone after Richard's boss five weeks later. But Dino can no longer assist police with their inquiries as he was also shot dead a few months later.

'It is not the right time to be taking sides,' a detective said after Mark's funeral. He was right, as the murders continued for years, with people who took sides getting killed.

In accordance with underworld union rules, the *Herald Sun* was filled with death notices to a 'lovely gentleman' after Mark Moran's death. There were many from former league footballers including one from a former Carlton captain who fondly remembered them running a victory lap after a premiership in the 1980s.

There was one falsely placed under the nickname of a drug-squad detective.

Police suspect it was placed to give the appearance Moran was talking to police when he was killed.

The funeral was the usual procession of real friends, hangers-on and crims in black suits who refused to remove their sunglasses, even though it was a cold winter's day.

Jason Moran was allowed day leave from prison to speak at the funeral. Mourners said the brother spoke with real emotion but his death notice worried police. It read: 'This is only the beginning, it will never be the end. REMEMBER, I WILL NEVER FORGET.'

It was an empty boast. Within three years Jason would join his brother as an underworld victim.

Because the funeral was going to choke local streets, a request was made for uniformed police to control traffic, but a senior policeman vetoed the plan. He didn't want media images of police holding up traffic for half of Melbourne's gangsters.

While Mark Moran had a low public profile, he had a long and violent criminal history. Career criminal Raymond John Denning once told an inquest Moran was one of three men involved in an armed robbery in which a guard was shot dead.

He said the three men involved were Russell 'Mad Dog' Cox, Moran and Santo Mercuri. The robbery was on July 11, 1988, in Barkly Square, Brunswick. Two armed guards were leaving a Coles warehouse with a cash tin when they were held up at gunpoint. A struggle followed and one of the guards, Dominic Hefti, 31, was shot in the chest and the leg. He died two days later at the Royal Melbourne Hospital.

Denning said the three men planned to kill a woman whose car Mercuri had stolen for his getaway. Denning said: 'It was decided among the three of them that they try to find her home address and knock her because she was the only one that Sam believed had identified him.'

In a chilling postscript to the story, when the armed robbery squad later raided the Doncaster home of Russell Cox, they found that the page of the telephone book carrying the woman's name and address had been torn out.

Hefti's murder sparked another spate of killings. Police wrongly believed that armed robber Graeme Jensen was responsible and he was shot during an apparently clumsy attempt to arrest him on October 11, 1988.

The following day two young uniformed police, Constables

Steven Tynan and Damian Eyre, were murdered in Walsh Street, South Yarra, as a payback.

Detectives on the Moran case have also looked at another intriguing possibility. They have investigated a possible link between the murder of Mark Moran and the unsolved killing of Frank Benvenuto, who was shot dead in Beaumaris on May 8, 2000.

The pair were known associates.

Benvenuto was the son of the former 'Godfather of Melbourne', Liborio Benvenuto, who was fortunate enough to die of natural causes on June 10, 1988.

Moran was killed with a shotgun, the preferred weapon in Italian payback killings. But he was also shot with a pistol, the weapon of choice for Australian gunmen.

Either way, he's dead. Just like his father ...

LES Cole didn't think lightning could strike the same place twice. He was wrong. The former painter and docker was shot dead in the same garage in which a gunman had ambushed him and seriously wounded him just two months before.

That was on November 10, 1982, at Cole's heavily fortified Kyle Bay home in Sydney. It was to prove eerily similar to the death of his biological son, Mark Moran, 18 years later. Each was shot dead as he returned home. Each was living well above his legitimate means at the time. And each almost certainly knew they were in danger.

Cole managed to live one more year than his son. He was 37 while Mark made it only to 36.

It was the second attempt on Cole's life. He had been shot just two months before by a man he described as 'a bad loser'. But if the gunman was a bad loser then Cole was a fatally slow learner.

He was still recovering from the first attack, and was returning from a physiotherapy appointment for treatment for his injuries, when he was killed.

In the first shooting he had been wounded in the right foot, right knee, midriff, right shoulder and twice in the forearm.

But the second time the gunman left nothing to chance, shooting Cole twice in the chest and once behind the right ear.

When police interviewed him over the first shooting he said: 'I don't want to say anything. I will sort it out myself.'

Police said Cole knew the Kane brothers and the senior Moran brothers Lewis and 'Tuppence' and had visited Melbourne the day before his death. 'He was not a bad little bloke, a bit of a knockabout,' one policeman recalled.

His widow, Jennifer Ann Cole, told the inquest into his death she had never bothered to ask her husband what he did for a living. 'He always said what I didn't know wouldn't hurt me.'

Cole was supposedly a security officer at Sydney's Sea Breeze hotel, but he failed to sniff the winds of change. He didn't realise until too late that someone had a terminal grudge against him.

Like the Kanes, Cole was heavily into protection and debt collecting and moved to Sydney to advance his career. Police at one stage believed he was killed by a Melbourne hitman flown in for the job, but the whisper was that a Sydney gangster called Mick Sayers pulled the trigger. Sayers was later murdered.

Cole had installed state-of-the-art security. He had electronically operated doors, a video surveillance system, floodlights, steel bars over windows, steel mesh over the backyard and he kept two guard dogs.

But even though he had been shot once before he became slack and left the garage door open, allowing the gunman the perfect position to hide. It wasn't the action of a prudent man – but if he were prudent he wouldn't have been a career criminal.

MORAN. — Mark.
Deepest and sincere
condolences to Antonella,
Lewis, Judy, Jason, Trisha and
their respective families.
Thinking of you all at this sad
time.

Rest in Peace

— Mick Gatto.

TEN

A YOUNG MAN IN A HURRY

On the walls of his house were framed posters from Hollywood gangster films.

TO be a top gangster you need to be ruthless, dangerous and cunning — but most of all you need to be born with a survivor's instinct.

Dino Dibra didn't live long enough to find out that the first three without the fourth was a fatal combination.

Certainly he was ruthless, let alone dangerous. Take the case when he and three of his gang kidnapped a man — punching, kicking and pistol-whipping him before throwing him into the boot of a car.

According to police reports the team grabbed the man in the Melbourne western suburb of Ardeer, on August 2, 1999.

Dibra and his soldiers were seemingly unworried that successful abductions were usually carried out under the cover of darkness. They chose to grab their man in broad daylight.

Despite his injuries the kidnap victim wasn't cooperative. As they drove off he popped the boot, jumped out and ran. The gang simply chased him down and, in front of shocked witnesses, dragged him back into the boot. Even *The Sopranos* brains trust would think it was a bit rich.

They took him to what they believed was the privacy of Dibra's Taylors Lakes house. Sadly for the kidnappers they may as well of taken him to the set of *Big Brother*.

Police technicians had been to the house much earlier to install listening devices and a small video camera because Dibra was the main suspect in an earlier shooting outside a popular nightclub.

The kidnap team demanded $20,000 from the victim's brother but, being practical men, were prepared to settle for $5,000.

The listening device caught Dibra and loyal deputy, Rocco Arico, discussing their negotiations.

Arico: 'Hey, if I'd have known he's only gonna get five grand, I would have put one in when he tried to jump out of the car.'

Dibra: 'You're an idiot. Listen to you.'

Arico: 'I would have just went fucking whack. Cop this slug for now. I would have slapped one in and I would have said, "Hold on to that for a while, don't give it to anyone and jump in the coffin."'

The tape was damning but there was another key piece of evidence: the kidnap victim was still in the boot when police arrived.

There can also be no doubt that Dibra was dangerous.

On July 15, 2000, he and Arico were driving in separate cars on their way back from a nightclub when they cut off another motorist in Taylors Lakes. It was 7am.

The motorist spun his car 180 degrees at a roundabout and narrowly avoided a smash. Understandably enraged, he followed the two cars a few streets then, seeing three men, continued to drive on – but two of them, in one car, decided to chase him.

When they stopped, a discussion of road etiquette followed. Arico asked the motorist: 'So what do you want to do about it?'

He unwisely replied: 'Well, I wanted to put his head through the windscreen.'

Arico pulled an automatic pistol and fired six shots – five hit the driver – before the man could even unbuckle his seatbelt. He was struck on his forearms, abdomen, right elbow and shoulder but, against the odds, he survived.

Police arrested Arico two days later at Melbourne airport as he was about to board a flight to Perth. He was alleged to have $100,000 of cocaine in his pocket at the time. He later claimed police planted the drugs.

He had a business-class ticket and although he had no luggage he told police he was heading west for a three-week holiday.

Later, police said the road-rage victim and his family were offered hush money to say he had incorrectly identified Arico.

But Dibra would not have to worry about the subtleties of the legal system.

He would be dead before the trial.

Dibra was well known at nightclubs and not because he liked to dance. He was a drug dealer who moved pills and powders, but he wanted more than money. He wanted respect and a reputation in the underworld.

Before he became well-known in the drug field, Dibra ran a lucrative stolen car racket and became an expert at car re-birthing, buying damaged cars and 'repairing' them by stealing identical models and transferring identification details.

But if he needed wheels in a hurry he would intimidate nightclubbers into handing over their keys and then simply drive off in their car.

Dibra seemed to think he was above the law from a young age. As a teenager he would ride his unregistered motorcycle past police patrols, trying to goad them into a high-speed pursuit.

When he was jailed in 1996 for 18 months, and had his licence cancelled for five years in 1996, the presiding magistrate commented Dibra had 'one of the worst driving records I have seen'.

When his dog was impounded after biting a woman Dibra organised an escape plot to get the dog out. When a policeman came to the door as a result of a complaint that the dog was dangerous Dibra told him to 'fuck off'.

Sometimes he did his own dirty work, but as he rose up the criminal pyramid he found others eager to please.

He stood by and watched as some of his team shot two bouncers outside the Dome nightclub in 1998.

He was also an associate of 'Mad Charlie' Hegyalji, who was shot dead outside his Caulfield South home on November 23, 1998.

Police had Dibra on the top of a very short list of suspects for Mad Charlie's murder. They found that hours before the death Mad Charlie contacted Dibra from a hotel pay phone. Dibra refused to tell police the content of their conversation, but it was unlikely to have been about stamp collecting.

Perhaps Dibra had a problem with criminals with the nickname 'Mad' because police believe he pulled the trigger on standover man 'Mad' Richard Mladenich, who was shot dead in a room in the seedy St Kilda Esquire Hotel on May 16, 2000.

They believe Arico may have accompanied Dibra to the hotel. Mladenich acted as a minder for Mark Moran and Dibra's name was also mentioned as a possible suspect for the murder of Moran, who was shot dead outside his home on June 15, 2000.

Dibra was living his fantasy. On the walls of his house were framed posters from Hollywood gangster films – *Pulp Fiction, Scarface* and *Goodfellas*.

In August 2000, he told a *Herald Sun* reporter outside the

Melbourne Magistrates Court during one of the many days he had to attend court: 'Mate, I've just watched *Reservoir Dogs* too many times.'

He probably thought the title of Quentin Tarantino's ultra-violent signature film referred to the northern Melbourne suburb of Reservoir, near Preston, and that it involved pit bull terriers and police informers.

He would have been better off studying the classics. Then he might have learned the wisdom of the saying that 'he who lives by the sword dies by the sword'. For, just as the young gunman filled with steroids and bad manners was getting the reputation he craved as a serious gangster, he was himself shot.

The man suspected of pulling the rug, and the trigger, on Dibra was a fellow drug dealer, Paul Kallipolitis.

Present with Kallipolitis was Andrew 'Benji' Veniamin, a hitman who appeared to love his job. Some say he was a workaholic.

They would both later see the other end of an assassin's gun.

On Saturday October 14, 2000, Dibra, then 25, was shot dead outside a house in Krambruk St, Sunshine.

Detective Inspector Andrew Allen, of the Purana task force, said much later: 'The homicide investigators have established that three people are involved in this execution murder and someone out there holds the key to solving this violent crime.'

Two of those men are now dead.

A $100,000 reward has been offered in connection with the murder. Dibra may have lived like a millionaire but court documents listed his only asset as a half share in a block of land. His estate was valued at $60,000.

Which made it official ... Dino Dibra was worth more dead than alive.

ELEVEN

FRIENDS AND ENEMIES

*As a joke, he once chased her around
the house waving a dismembered toe.*

WHEN all the forensic checks were done and the police finally returned her murdered husband's 1993 Commodore to her, Wendy Peirce immediately slid her fingers under the front ashtray with practised ease.

The grieving widow found what she was looking for – almost $400 in cash. She was pleased but not surprised at this small legacy. 'It was his favourite spot to stook [hide] money,' she shrugs.

Her husband, Victor – one of Australia's most notorious gangsters – was shot dead in the car in Bay Street, Port Melbourne, almost six months earlier, in May 2002.

Once police finished with the maroon sedan, Wendy had it detailed – which included patching a nasty bullet hole, replacing the shattered driver's side window and fitting seat covers.

It looked as good as new.

She sits opposite Station Pier in a trendy part of Melbourne recently favoured by tourists and the new rich. She sips a café latte in the afternoon sun, discussing her husband's fatal bullet wounds with forensic detachment. Her ten-year-old son sits by listening, until boredom and loose change draw him to a nearby amusement machine.

She has studied the autopsy report and knows that Victor was shot twice from point-blank range. A third shot missed, lodging in the pillar between the doors.

She also knows he probably used his right arm to try to block the shots as he sat in the driver's seat. Both shots travelled through his arm into his body, causing fatal wounds to his liver, diaphragm and lungs.

'They revived him twice there but he was unconscious and they couldn't save him,' she says with little emotion.

Later, in the car, she re-enacts the crime, draping herself theatrically from the driver's seat to the passenger's side, in the position her husband finished when he was shot. Her teenage daughter sits in the back seat.

The mother of four speaks calmly about her Victor's murder. She says people misjudge her if they think she is callous. It is just that violent death has always been part of her adult life. It's not welcome, but it comes with the territory, the way farmers accept drought.

Wendy's brother-in-law, Dennis Allen, was the suspect in 11 killings before he died in 1987 from heart disease. Allen's wife, Sissy, who had on occasions been left chained to the family washing machine, had earlier committed suicide.

Another brother-in-law, Jamie Pettingill, died from a drug overdose in 1985. Pettingill was involved in an armed robbery in a Clifton Hill hotel where a barman was shot and later died.

Wendy Peirce spent her life surrounded by career criminals, including Mark Militano, Frank Valastro, Jedd Houghton,

Graeme Jensen and Gary Abdallah, all shot dead by police. Other friends and associates, including Frank Benvenuto, also died from bullet wounds.

As Benvenuto lay dying, he managed to press the speed dial on his mobile phone to ring Victor. But he could not give the name of his killer – he could only gasp and moan.

Victor Peirce, his half-brother Trevor Pettingill and friends Peter David McEvoy and Anthony Farrell were charged with the murders of Constables Steven Tynan and Damian Eyre, who were shot dead in Walsh Street, South Yarra, on October 12, 1988. They were acquitted.

At one time Wendy was to be the star witness against her husband and was put in police protection before she reunited with him and changed her story. She was later jailed for perjury.

She now says that, in between long jail terms, Victor was a devoted family man. 'There were two sides to him,' she says, but she doesn't try to hide that one of them was chilling. She has a bent little finger on her left hand, a legacy of her husband's temper. 'He said it would be the nose or the finger: I passed out with the pain.' He once fired shots around her feet to encourage her to dance: 'I didn't move. I wouldn't give him the satisfaction.' As a joke, he once chased her around the house waving a dismembered human toe. She failed to see the humour. 'It was disgusting.'

But there was romance. Earlier in 2002 he gave her a Valentine's card that read: 'You are now and always will be the only woman in the world for me.' He took her to Port Douglas for a five-star second honeymoon.

The couple had spent one New Year's Eve at a Port Melbourne restaurant before returning to their nearby double-storey townhouse. Come midnight they went into the backyard to let off about five shots from his handgun to welcome in 2002.

According to Wendy, her husband was more than just a

gangster. 'He was devoted to his children and loved his grandchildren.'

But detectives say Peirce was a standover man, armed robber, killer and drug dealer who had plenty of enemies. He was hated by many police and despised by almost as many in the underworld.

So who killed him?

One theory, and there are several, is that an old friend – one who once shared the criminal dock with him during a trial – set him up.

As the story goes, the old friend worked for a South Yarra drug dealer whose supply of ecstasy was ripped off by Peirce. The associate was given three choices: kill Victor, get the drugs back, or die.

He took the first option.

On the evening of Wednesday May 1, 2002, Peirce was relaxed and chirpy. Forensic tests later indicated his good mood was chemically induced. His autopsy revealed residues of ecstasy, Valium and amphetamines.

He had played football with his son, Vinnie, and then kissed Wendy and daughter Katie before saying 'he had to meet a bloke'.

'He told me to go home and put his coffee machine on for his short black,' Wendy says. 'The last thing he said to me was, "I love you, darl."'

As he sat in his car, waiting for the meeting, two men in a stolen Commodore pulled up, walked over and shot Peirce. They then hopped back in the sedan and calmly drove off.

Detectives found that Peirce, 43, was unarmed. They also found he had two mobile phones in the car – one rigged by a friendly technician from a telecommunications company so that it operated without charge. 'He had one for home and the free one was for business,' Wendy says. She doesn't expand on what that business was.

GANGSTER. Drug dealer. Gunman. Cop killer. Victor Peirce was called all these things before his death.

But when he was buried eight days later he was just someone's father, someone's son. The grief of those who loved him was as real as anybody else's, a sobering thought for the most hardened observer.

There were plenty of those at St Peter and Paul's Catholic Church in South Melbourne, where mourners mingled with plain-clothes police, reporters and at least one known gunman; a prime suspect in another unsolved gangland slaying.

It wasn't, however, a huge funeral by underworld standards.

Whereas almost 1,000 people had jammed St Mary's by the Sea in West Melbourne to farewell Alphonse Gangitano four years earlier, perhaps a quarter of that many went to Victor's.

And whereas Gangitano – a 'celebrity' gangster known by his first name – cultivated a Hollywood image, Peirce lived and died on a smaller stage.

Gangitano was a middle-class private-school boy who turned his back on respectability to become the black prince of Lygon Street. Peirce, by contrast, wasn't so much working class as underclass, condemned from birth to a sordid life cycle of crime and violence. The wonder was not that he died violently, but that he survived as long as he did.

His mother, Kath Pettingill, once a notorious thief and brothel madam dubbed 'Granny Evil', had seven children by several men. She has now buried three of the children and must wonder how many more family funerals she will attend. She narrowly escaped death years ago, when a bullet blinded her in one eye.

The mourners gathered well before the service, under a sky the colour of lead. Most of them looked as sullen as the weather. The men tended to mullets or close-cropped hair, the women were mostly bleached blondes, tattoos half-hidden under dark stockings. Sunglasses and cigarettes were compulsory for both sexes, chewing gum and earrings optional.

In the church, many shied away from the pews, preferring to stand together at the back of the church, as deadpan as the inmates of a prison exercise yard. Which many undoubtedly had been.

Father Bob Maguire, whose inner-city flock has included many a black sheep, conducted a service, as he called it, 'designed by the family'. Instead of hymns, popular songs were played. Instead of a formal eulogy, the dead man's children and friends read out personal tributes that were clapped, like speeches at a birthday party.

Katie Peirce said her father was a 'strong, kind, family man' who had hired a double-decker bus for her sixteenth birthday and taken her out to get her drunk as a treat. His pet name for her was 'Pooh Bum'.

His youngest son, Vinnie, named in honour of His Honour Justice Frank Vincent after Peirce's acquittal in the Walsh Street murders, said he would miss his dad picking him up from school, buying him lollies and driving around.

'I remember when he used to go fast in the car with me,' he said.

The first line of the opening song, 'Soldier Of Love', began with the words 'Lay down your arms'. The song chosen for the exit music was 'When I Die', by the group No Mercy. It sounded like a portent of funerals to come. One of the mourners was Jason Moran. He could not know that his funeral would be held across town just over a year later.

Outside, it had begun to rain. A guard of honour — or maybe dishonour — lined the street, blocking traffic. It stretched about 20 metres. At Steven Tynan's police funeral, after the Walsh Street tragedy more than 13 years earlier, the honour guard stretched for kilometres.

But there was real sadness. As the hearse took the outlaw Victor Peirce for his last ride, hard faces softened briefly.

Under a tree in the churchyard, a homicide detective watched and wondered if the killer was in the crowd … and how many more were destined to suffer the same fate.

SOME in the criminal world say the homicide squad would not be overly concerned if its clean-up rate was spoiled by the unsolved murder of Victor George Peirce staying that way. The death of a suspected killer of two young police is unlikely to fill many detectives with a sense of outrage.

But, according to Wendy Peirce, homicide investigators worked huge hours on the case. 'Dean Thomas and his crew [the investigating team] have been fantastic. I ring them every day. I know they haven't hit a brick wall yet. I expect I will get a call in the middle of the night from them saying, "Wendy. We've got them."'

But the phone calls between Wendy and the police sometimes come at inconvenient times. For instance, one day she was having a dispute with a man over the ownership of a vehicle when Thomas rang to update her. She was sitting on the car trying to persuade the driver that she was the rightful owner by stabbing him in the neck and arms with a screwdriver. 'Dean rang and I had to say I would ring him back because I'm in the middle of stabbing someone.'

Police were called and Wendy had to be handcuffed to a lamppost while matters were sorted.

She had a second dispute with the man, in which the car he was driving was sideswiped and the windows smashed with a cricket bat.

Unknown assailants later attacked him, causing injuries that required his spleen to be removed.

There have been raids and disputes. She was accused of firing shots at a house, a charge she says is false. Police found hydroponic gear in the ceiling of her home, but she asserts it must have been left by previous tenants. You can be unlucky like that. Landlords should be more careful about what is left behind by tenants.

In August 2002, police conducted raids and interviewed five men, who were associates of Peirce, over the murder. Inquiries are continuing.

Wendy Peirce believes an associate of her late husband hired the killers. 'It had to be someone he knew who paid for it. The two dickheads who did it had to be paid. He must have been frightened of Victor and got in first.

'I know there are people who know what happened. I hope they will come forward for the sake of his kids. They deserve better than this.'

Wendy says she lost almost 20kg after the murder. 'Sometimes I can't believe he's gone. I think when the phone rings that it will be Vic. I can't eat and I can't sleep. One week I'm sort of okay and then I have a relapse.'

The two met when she was a teenager. She was then an office worker from an honest family and he was an apprentice crook in a crime dynasty and had already served time in Pentridge. Wendy does not ask for sympathy. 'I chose this life – I have been the black sheep,' she admits.

She has applied for crimes compensation after being advised by detectives that her family was eligible.

'People get upset about that because they say I have been living off the money Victor was supposed to have made from crime. But what about the kids? What have they done wrong?'

When Wendy arrived at the Alfred Hospital after the shooting she wasn't concerned. 'A neighbour told me he was just shot in the arm. But about ten minutes later they told me he was dead. He was already cold. The nurses had to drag me away from his body.'

She told staff to remove his gold wedding ring. 'I told them not to break his finger, but I wanted it.'

As she tells the story she plays with the ring on a gold chain around her neck, next to a crucifix. The ring's inscription reads: 'Victor, Yours Forever, Wendy.'

She regularly put flowers on the lightpole next to where Peirce was murdered but, just as regularly, they were ripped down. She approached the local council and now is allowed to place a floral tribute and cards there on the first day of every month.

She says she has seen strangers with tears in their eyes when they see the home-made memorials. They are more concerned, she says, with her loss than his past.

One day she went outside to see a blue ribbon flag (to commemorate the death of police on duty) attached to the aerial of her car. She is convinced detectives with a grudge left it as their calling card.

Victor Peirce always hated detectives, referring to them as 'The Enemy'.

The funny thing is, now they are the ones Wendy hopes will solve his murder.

More than a year after the killing police held a press conference with her to announce a $100,000 reward for information leading to the arrest and conviction of her husband's killers. Wendy Peirce says she can understand why people who see murder in the underworld as an occupational hazard may lack compassion for her loss. She admits that her husband and some of her in-laws have killed on a whim.

Wendy says the death of her husband has left her with a new-found disgust for gangland violence. 'I have seen bodies and I have known people who have been killed. I've treated it all like a bit of a joke. I found it hysterical.

'But I didn't understand what it was really like until Victor was killed. Now I know but I wish I didn't.

'I lived around drugs and murders in those days. I don't want to live that life any more.'

Wendy says she doesn't expect sympathy because she has made her own life. 'But what about our children and six grandchildren? They have lost a father and they are heart-broken. Someone has to help me put smiles back on their faces.'

PEIRCE. — Victor.
Our sincere thanks for your kindness and love. You will never be forgotten. Our prayers are with you.
Rest in Peace
Love — Victor Brincat and Tommy Ivanovic.

TWELVE

THE LAND OF OPPORTUNITY

It was just a power thing for him.
He wanted to be like Al Pacino in Scarface.

NIKOLAI Radev, a young Bulgarian wrestler, arrived in Australia in 1980 without any assets, but he was welcomed by his country of choice and granted refugee status. It would prove a fatal mistake.

In 1981 he married Sylvia, a teenage hairdressing apprentice in Melbourne.

He worked at a Doveton fish-and-chip shop owned by his in-laws and then opened a pizza shop nearby. But after about a year he decided there were better ways to make a crust than from pizzas.

From 1983 until his death 20 years later Radev did not work or pay tax, yet maintained the lifestyle of a millionaire.

Soon after arriving in Australia, Radev made contact with known members of Melbourne's flourishing Russian organised crime syndicates. His reputation had preceded him and he was already known as a ruthless young gangster from his early years in Bulgaria, yet Australian authorities were not aware of his record before granting him refugee status.

His former wife, Sylvia, says Radev always wanted to be a gangster. 'He had no fear and no shame. It was just a power thing for him. He wanted to be like Al Pacino in *Scarface*.'

When they were married he could be occasionally charming but more often brutal – and he would disappear for days. 'He would say he was going to the shop and then not come back.' She soon learned not to ask for an explanation.

'He told me later that he married me just to get Australian citizenship. He ended up just wasting his life. It was really sad.'

In 1985 he was first jailed in Victoria for drug trafficking. After experiencing prison in Bulgaria, Melbourne's jails were like weekend retreats for the hardened gangster. It was just another place to pump iron and plan his next standover campaign.

Radev's criminal record shows his life-long love of violence. His prior convictions include assaults, blackmail, threats to kill, extortion, firearm offences, armed robbery and serious drug charges.

A police report said: 'He is a dangerous and violent offender, well connected within the criminal underworld. He carries firearms and associates with people who carry firearms.'

In early 1998 Radev began a relationship with a Bulgarian woman 12 years his senior. She was financially comfortable, but that was not enough for Nik. Soon they were trafficking heroin in the St Kilda district.

When Radev was again jailed in 1999 the older woman sold drugs to try to pay his legal fees. She was caught and sentenced to prison. When he was released Radev was, in crime terms, upwardly mobile and began to flaunt his wealth. From 2000 he found a rich vein of crime and, according to associates, 'went up in the world'.

Radev told associates that he was now a businessman and involved in property development, a job description that covers a lot of ground. He started to deal with other gangsters on the move such as Housan Zayat, Sedat Ceylan and Mark Mallia.

In 1998, Radev and Zayat were charged over a home invasion in which a 71-year-old man was bashed and his five-year-old granddaughter tied to a bed and threatened with a handgun. Radev's friendship with Ceylan was short lived – and so might Ceylan himself have been if Radev had got his way.

Ceylan falsely claimed to have bought electronic equipment worth about $10million, resulting in a GST refund of almost $1million.

Radev thought it was an excellent scheme, but expected his cut. He abducted and tortured Ceylan, demanding $100,000. The GST fraudster fled to Turkey with his money and is still wanted in Australia.

Certainly Radev loved violence. He once firebombed the car of rival drug dealer, Willie Thompson.

Willie must have been delighted when he heard of Radev's death, although his delight, like a lot of Radev's friendships, would have been short lived. Thompson was shot dead in Chadstone just months after Radev's murder in remarkably similar circumstances.

The Bulgarian even threatened police who had the temerity to arrest him. He intimidated one of the arresting officers, Ben Archbold, who eventually resigned because of the stress. Archbold later gained some notoriety himself when he became a contestant in the television reality program, *Big Brother*.

In 2001, Radev the standover man had become big enough to employ his own protection, using a professional kick-boxer as his muscle. He rented a home in Brighton and had no trouble finding the $530 weekly rent, paying promptly in cash.

He showered his de facto wife and their child with expensive gifts, but chose not to live with them. He paid the rent on their flat and their substantial expenses.

Just weeks before his death he bought a 1999 Mercedes for $100,000. It was black, naturally.

For the one-time penniless refugee, Australia was the land of opportunity – even if nothing he did appeared legitimate.

He began to wear expensive clothes, preferring the exclusive Versace range. When he wanted his teeth fixed he paid a dentist $55,000 in cash for a set of top-of-the-range crowns.

Life was good for the wrestler-turned-gangster – so why was he shot dead?

Police know it was drug related. Perhaps he was in debt or a major player on the other side of town wanted to remove the potential competition. 'His attitude to personal accounting has always been cavalier,' said Mark Brandon Read, a keen observer of local criminal matters and manners. Or maybe Radev got big enough to be a danger to some people without being big enough to protect himself.

What police know is that, as in so many of the gangland murders in Melbourne, the victim was set up by his so-called friends.

On April 15, 2003, Radev left his luxurious bayside home and drove his black Mercedes to meet a group of friends and associates at the trendy Brighton Baths Café.

Detectives now suspect the hitman was at the café.

Radev and some of the men at the meeting travelled in at least three cars to Coburg. Police believe Radev, 48, was persuaded to drive there on the promise of a lucrative drug deal.

Radev left his car in Queen Street to talk to two men. He then turned and was walking back to his Mercedes when he was shot up to seven times in the head and body. He died next to the car he had bought with his hard-earned drug money.

Purana police have identified and interviewed one man who was at the meeting. It is believed he drove one of the cars.

They also have found a witness at the murder scene who saw a small red sedan, possibly a Holden Vectra, in Queen Street, near the intersection with Reynard Street. The car left the area moments before the shooting.

Police believe the car was one of the vehicles driven from Brighton to Coburg. They suspect that the two men in the car left after they saw that Radev had been successfully lured into the trap.

Police became particularly interested in the car when they learned that one of the main players in the underworld war – a man we can only identify as the frontman for legal reasons – had access to a red Vectra. A close relative owned a similar car, but is believed to have sold it some time after the Radev shooting.

Police also believe that another well-known player in the drama was supposed to have a meeting with Radev that day. This was none other than Andrew 'Benji' Veniamin, killed in a Carlton restaurant a year later.

After the Radev murder, Veniamin refused to help police with their inquiries. He was so uncooperative on principle that he even warned his own parents not to help the police if he were killed. He must have had a crystal ball. He knew he, too, was living dangerously and stood a big chance of being killed ... he just couldn't tell when and where.

When he was shot dead Radev was wearing a Taba-brand watch valued at $20,000 and a complete Versace outfit – including shoes.

His passing saddened not only friends and criminal associates. He owed one Versace outlet in Melbourne $8,000 at the time. It is unlikely to be paid. One well-known legal identity is also likely to write off Radev's substantial unpaid legal fees.

Although Radev was known to often carry several thousand dollars in cash, his Commonwealth Bank accounts remained dormant for months at a time.

He flew overseas five times in four years and always travelled business class. His last trip was to Israel the year before his murder.

He was a regular at some of Melbourne's best restaurants and often stayed in five-star hotels. After his death police found receipts for $400 bottles of Cognac and $50 cigars among his possessions.

But what they didn't find was cash. They believe his friends went to his Brighton home and took at least $200,000, claiming it was their share of the profits.

But Radev was living, and later dead, proof that money can't buy class. Several women have revealed that he had the word 'taxi' tattooed on his penis. It was one of several crude 'jail tatts' on his body.

Police have been told by several underworld sources that Radev loved his wealth so much he was buried with at least some of it. His casket was gold plated and said to be valued at $30,000.

Most of his associates lived similar lifestyles, driving luxury cars including Porsches, Jaguars and an Audi coupé.

But like Radev, Gangitano and the Morans, they were to find too late that money doesn't buy protection. Eventually the hunter becomes the hunted. Next to go was Mark Mallia, a close friend of Radev. Mallia, 30, was another standover man connected in the drug world.

Soon after Radev's death Mallia went to Nik's home to collect certain valuables, including an expensive watch, claiming that as the Bulgarian's best friend he was entitled to the keepsake.

It was a cunning move by a greedy man but he wasn't smart enough to work out that for him, time was also running out.

Mallia's charred remains were found in a drain near a reserve in West Sunshine on August 18, 2003.

While senior police were in the last stages of planning to expand the Purana gangland task force, another case emerged.

This one was yet another associate of Radev. Housam 'Sam' Zayat, 32, of Fawkner, went to a late-night meeting at a paddock near the junction of Derrimut and Boundary Roads in Tarneit, west of Melbourne, on September 9, 2003. It was a bad move.

Zayat was facing drug-trafficking charges, but had been released on bail only a week before his murder. His co-accused included suspended and former police. His committal hearing was due to begin the week after his death.

A suspended articled clerk, who managed to escape the ambush, ran 12 kilometres to the safety of the Sunshine police station. He had allegedly driven Zayat to the meeting.

In 1994, Zayat was charged with the murder of his 50-year-old lover in a Footscray house and the attempted murder of her teenage son. He was later convicted on the attempted murder charge.

His brother, Mohhamed Zayat, was found hanged in 1999 at Port Phillip Prison. Another brother also served time in jail.

For men like Moran and Radev the inexhaustible demand for amphetamines and ecstasy created a gold rush. Men too lazy to hold down a job on a factory floor found they could maintain the lifestyle of wealthy industrialists. But only for a while. Eventually, they screwed it up by killing each other.

RADEV. — Nikoli (Nick).
To our brother in our hearts
forever. Loving father to Raquel
and Monique. Dearly beloved
son of Radka.
Brother of all brothers

THIRTEEN

DEAD MAN WALKING

*He carried a handgun before
he was old enough to drive.*

EVERYONE in the underworld knew Jason Matthew Patrick Moran was a dead man walking.

Too erratic to be respected and too violent to be ignored, the drug dealer and suspected killer was always the popular tip to become a murder target in Melbourne's crime war.

At the funeral of Jason's half-brother, Mark Moran – murdered outside his luxury Aberfeldie home on June 15, 2000 – a well-connected crime figure gave a friend a two-word warning that he should distance himself from the younger Moran. 'He's next,' he whispered.

Not that underworld identities and a select group of police were the only ones to suspect that Moran's name was on a death list. It was Australia's worst-kept crime secret.

Standover man turned author, artist and renowned after-dinner speaker, Mark Brandon Read, released his tenth book, *The Popcorn Gangster*, in November 2001. On the back cover Read stands in an old Tasmanian cemetery near three weathered gravestones. The photograph has been digitally altered to show one headstone with the name 'Mad Charlie' (a murdered gangster friend) and the date of death; on the second is 'Big Al' (Alphonse Gangitano) with the date of his murder. On the third is simply 'Jason' with a question mark. The message was clear. The fact that Moran was to be murdered was no longer an issue. It was simply a matter of time.

Less than two years later that date was filled in: June 21, 2003. And so it had come to pass: Chopper Read was not just making a crime-writing profit but was also a crime-writing prophet.

But there were no jokes about the way the murder was carried out. It was unusually brutal, and smacked of a South American drug cartel killing in Miami or Colombia rather than the old painter and docker way of doing the business. For, while Moran's murder came as no surprise to police, criminals or true-crime devotees, the nature of the double execution shocked almost everyone.

Moran was with a group of children after a game of junior football when he was gunned down with his friend, Pasquale Barbaro, in front of up to 250 people in the car park of the Cross Keys Hotel on Pascoe Vale Road in Essendon North.

While murdering two men in front of hundreds of people might, at first, seem reckless, to the killer it made perfect sense.

Moran was no easy target. He had carried a gun since he was a teenager and was considered an expert in counter-surveillance. For added security he had repeatedly changed addresses in the previous year.

After selling his luxury home in Grosvenor Street, Moonee Ponds, he moved into his sister-in-law's house, before relocating to the large home of a friendly hotel owner. The standover man and drug dealer made sure he had a bodyguard with him when he travelled on business at night.

Months earlier, there was an incident where shots were allegedly exchanged near a pizza parlour. In James Bond style, Moran flicked the boot of his car to act as a shield as he sped away.

Three weeks before he was shot, Moran was told again he was a gangland target. Never short of guns, he made it known he wanted fresh stock and was prepared to pay $3,500 per handgun – well over the going rate.

The killer would have found Moran's unpredictable movements hard to track. But Moran did have a habit he was reluctant to break: he had a life-long love affair with football and regularly took his children, as well as others, to the Auskick clinic at Essendon North.

On Saturday mornings he would park his pale-blue Mitsubishi van at the Cross Keys Hotel overlooking the reserve.

To the killer, it was the ideal time to strike.

Moran was at his most vulnerable. On those mornings he appeared to be an average suburban dad rather than a gangster in survival mode – although associates say he always carried a gun, even at Auskick.

The gunman also would have known – as he almost certainly watched the spot on previous Saturdays to plan the murders – that no one would have noticed him, or if they had, he would have been mistaken for just another footy dad, or a punter heading to the pub.

A stranger in a quiet street sparks interest. A man in a busy car park is anonymous.

The spot also gave the killer a clean exit strategy – across a footbridge over the Moonee Ponds Creek to a waiting car.

On this Saturday, he rolled a balaclava over his face and blasted Moran through the closed driver's side window with a shotgun before his victim could draw his own gun. He then used a handgun to shoot Moran's mate, who was sitting in the passenger seat.

At least five children, including Moran's twin girl and boy, aged six, and Mark's fatherless children, were in the Mitsubishi van when the gunman fired. Several other kids were playing near the vehicle. 'I have just seen my uncle shot,' one of the girls from the van told an Auskick umpire moments after the attack.

Barbaro, known as 'Little Pat', was a long-time friend of Moran and a low-level criminal in his own right. Barbaro's criminal history included nine convictions for possessing cannabis and one for trafficking and using heroin. A major drug syndicate once used him as a trusted courier.

West Australian organised-crime-squad detectives arrested him at Perth Airport on May 11, 1999, as he carried a black bag containing 367 grams of amphetamines.

His choice of lawyer said much about his criminal connections. Andrew Fraser, who later that year was arrested in Melbourne and charged with cocaine trafficking, defended him. Fraser was also the lawyer of choice for the Moran clan.

Fraser told the court that Barbaro was paid $3,000 for carrying the drugs and was financially ruined after losing $100,000 at Crown Casino. He said his client was an alcoholic who drank Scotch and smoked marijuana as soon as he woke up in the morning.

When Judge Alan Fenbury sentenced Barbaro to six years' jail, he said the prison term 'might even save your life'. In reality it just postponed his death.

When 'Little Pat' was released in 2001 he returned to Melbourne and quickly re-established his links with Moran.

The killer selected his weapons with care. He used the shotgun to blast through the closed window. In the crime world the shotgun is considered the perfect weapon for close-range work. You don't miss from a metre with a 12-gauge and do not provide much for ballistics experts to work with.

The killer then dropped the sawn-off gun next to the van and used the pistol to shoot Barbaro up to five times.

The same types of weapons, a shotgun and handgun, were used to kill Moran's half-brother, Mark, three years earlier.

Coincidence or connection? Police were told the one man probably ordered the murders.

The 12-gauge shotgun used to kill Jason was a popular, and cheap, Miura model Boito brand imported from Brazil in the early 1970s.

An inscription engraved on the metal breech of the shotgun dated 22-4-56, reads: *'Mitch on your 21st ... from The Boys'*.

One of the first on the scene on the Saturday was, ironically, an ex-detective called Phil Glare, who was working at a scrap-metal merchant's across the road. He found Moran and Barbaro already dead in the van.

Glare, an old-style detective from the disbanded consorting squad, is no stranger to gangland wars and public executions. He was escorting Raymond Patrick Bennett to an armed-robbery hearing when Bennett, also known as Chuck, was shot dead by an unknown gunman inside the Melbourne Magistrates Court building in November 1979. Bennett's murder remains unsolved.

The City Court hit was a payback. Bennett was one of three men who had walked into the Wantirna unit of well-known gangster Les Kane and shot him in the bathroom, using modified automatic rifles fitted with silencers. The body was never recovered.

Les had been married twice. His daughter from his first marriage, Trish, went on to marry a young Jason Moran. Police insist the bald facts are that Kane's brother, Brian, was the gunman in the City Court who killed Bennett. In November 1982, Brian Kane was shot dead in the Quarry Hotel, Brunswick.

Days later the young Jason Moran placed a death notice in the *Sun* to 'Uncle Brian' from 'Your Little Mate'.

But the Moran family connection to underworld murders does not stop there.

Jason and Mark Moran were half-brothers. They had the same mother, Judy, but different fathers. Mark's father was a Sydney gunman called Les 'Johnny' Cole, originally a painter and docker from Melbourne who became a standover man for NSW gangster Frederick Charles 'Paddles' Anderson.

Cole was gunned down outside his luxury home at Kyle Bay in November 1982, in what was the first of eight murders in a Sydney underworld war.

Jason's father was Lewis Moran who, together with his brother 'Tuppence', was respected by Melbourne's underworld. Both were well-known figures at the racetrack.

But Tuppence's health had been failing for years and he was less active than he once was. He even indulged in the respectable hobby of breeding a few thoroughbred horses at a property near Melton, west of Melbourne. Lewis had his own problems and was on remand over drug charges when Jason was shot.

He was refused permission to attend the funeral on security grounds and declined to share his thoughts on the murders with homicide squad detectives who had spent long hours trying to solve the murders.

Besides crime and punting, the Morans' great love was the Carlton Football Club. Judy Moran's father, Leo Brooks, was the club's doorman and general assistant. Many star recruits, from rogues to Rhodes scholars, boarded with Brooks during the 1970s and 1980s.

For some, the bonds remained for life. Premiership star Wayne Johnston told a reporter he met Mark and Jason through Brooks. 'In those days a lot of the players, myself included, used to come down from the country and stay with Leo and that's where I first met the boys. I used to babysit them.'

JASON Moran came from a family of career criminals, but he had many opportunities to break free from his past. In the end, he loved the idea of becoming a gangster too much.

The death of his wife's father and uncle as well as the murder of his half-brother's father didn't seem to show him that it was a career with clear limitations. In the underworld, fringe benefits can be tempting, but the redundancy package is distinctly unattractive. It is small, made of lead and arrives suddenly. You don't even see it coming.

Educated at a solid middle-class private school, Moran excelled at sport but was not interested in taking advantage of academic opportunities or tertiary studies. Why be a lawyer when you could buy one?

Never too concerned about blood, he worked at the City Abattoir near the Newmarket saleyards for three years before the business closed. He then worked at a duty-free shop and later in the jewellery industry. But as his tastes for an expensive lifestyle increased, his stomach for honest work declined.

He carried a handgun before he was old enough to drive and was always prepared to let people know he was armed. Regular drinkers at the Laurel Hotel in Ascot Vale tended to give young Moran a wide berth. He once followed a family friend into the toilet after a minor argument, pulling a gun and shoving the barrel into his head with the accompanying threat to blow it off. Lightweight criminals were frightened of him while heavyweights did not react because of their respect for his father.

When Moran went to jail, his reputation for violence grew. One inmate who spent time with him remembers the new boy in the (shower) block would tell anyone who could be bothered listening that he was a force to be reckoned with. 'Do you know who the fuck I am?' he would ask. It was a rhetorical question.

An inmate at Geelong Prison said: 'Jason was only a young kid and nobody in jail had heard of him [but he] could look after himself. Jail is a very violent place and Jason had to fight to protect himself.

'Jason would start fights in jail. He would threaten people if they upset him ... [he] would always be threatening people, it was his nature.'

Moran became a staunch ally of Alphonse Gangitano, the self-proclaimed De Niro of Lygon Street. The two became heavily involved in protection rackets, illegal gambling and violence.

Some of the violence was premeditated – some simply mindless. He bashed a stranger with a wheel brace in Punt Road because he believed the man had not used his indicator when passing.

'Jason smashed a window of the other car and then dragged the other bloke out and hit him. Jason beat this man quite severely. After assaulting this man Jason got back in the car and was laughing,' one of his mates said later.

No one challenged him. Few ever did.

After Gangitano shot a standover man called Gregory John Workman after a wake in St Kilda it was Moran who helped get his then friend off the hook.

But in December 1995, Moran and Gangitano went berserk in a bar in Melbourne's nightclub strip of King Street.

They were charged and the court case dragged on for years. Moran was caught on police listening devices saying Gangitano was out of control and a 'Lulu'.

On January 16, 1998, Gangitano was shot dead in his home in Templestowe. Police say Moran was the gunman and the murder weapon was thrown from the Westgate Bridge. Despite the homicide squad's incentive of a top-quality bottle of Scotch, no police diver was able to find the gun at the bottom of the Yarra.

The Morans were to keep a cross in their front yard as a tribute to Gangitano.

The death of Alphonse should have shown Jason that

nobody was bulletproof. He failed to understand that his time would come.

In the underworld the hunter can become the hunted overnight.

Moran was convicted of the King Street assault even though the judge remarked that his arrest, in which he received a fractured skull, was 'remarkably heavy handed'.

Mark was murdered while Jason was in jail. He was given prison leave to attend the funeral. Many predicted he would plot the payback. His death notice in the *Herald Sun* strongly implied revenge.

But when he was released from jail in 2001, Jason applied to the parole board to travel overseas because of fears for his life.

Members of his family suggested he stay overseas, away from trouble.

He would receive regular payments from family enterprises, whatever they may be. But, against all advice, he returned to Melbourne within months.

FOR the homicide squad, all investigations start with looking for motive, means and opportunity. In most murder cases, the challenge is to find someone who wanted the victim dead. For homicide-squad crew two, which was originally assigned the Jason Moran case, there were too many to choose from. It was a matter of trying to discount some of his enemies.

And in the Morans social and business circles, enemies don't just cross you off their Christmas card list.

One theory is that Moran was killed as a payback for the murder of Victor George Peirce, who was gunned down in Bay Street, Port Melbourne, in May 2002.

The story goes that Peirce was a close friend of Frank Benvenuto, the son of former Mafia 'Godfather' Liborio.

Frank employed Peirce, a gun for hire, on a freelance basis when he needed protection. Benvenuto was shot dead in Beaumaris in May, 2000, and the theory goes that Peirce blamed the Morans and so shot Mark the following month as a payback.

Jason then shot Peirce to avenge his brother's murder, and the circle was completed with Jason's murder.

But Peirce's widow Wendy says the theory is just another fantasy. 'It's complete crap. Victor didn't kill Mark and the Morans had nothing to do with shooting Victor.' Police tend to agree.

Jason Moran was among the mourners at Victor Peirce's funeral. And, despite all the bloodletting, Wendy Peirce was still shocked at the way Moran and Barbaro were killed.

'It's a dirty thing doing it in front of all those kids.'

But Jason Moran himself had shown no remorse about leaving children without a father. Gangitano had two children and Moran left his former friend's bleeding body to be found by his wife and children when they returned home after visiting a relative on the other side of town. In 1995 police set up a video camera in the house of a family across the road from Jason Moran's home. When Moran found out he is alleged to have responded by telling the family he would bomb their home and harm their children.

They sold their house, allegedly at a loss of $19,000, and launched a writ against the police force.

But while there was no shortage of theories about Jason's murder, the strongest involved a feud between established gangsters and a group of criminals known as the New Boys.

The New Boys frontman was shot in the stomach and the Moran brothers were blamed (with ample justification because they had done it).

Jason Moran was effectively at war with the team that he blamed for Mark's murder (with ample justification because they had probably done it).

Associates of the Morans were to be dragged into the war as Melbourne gangsters were eventually forced to take sides. Some with no real interest in the feud would also end up as victims.

The hostility between the two teams began over a failed illegal business venture and soon became venomous.

Ironically, the children of the two feuding families attended the same private school.

The wife of one of the New Boys went to the police to complain that Jason had harassed her outside the school. She considered seeking an intervention order but later withdrew her complaint. But after Mark's murder, her husband complained to one of the authors because a story in the *Age* suggested he could be involved. 'You could get a man killed writing things like that,' he said.

Even before the bodies of Jason Moran and Barbaro were removed from the van the dogs were barking the name of a man declared the most likely to be the shooter – a career armed robber known for his cool head, a master of criminal brinkmanship but a victim of his own violent impulses.

He had a long and remarkable criminal history and was a former member of the police ten most wanted.

In March, 1990, he escaped from the Northfield Jail in South Australia where he had been serving a long sentence for armed robberies. The following month he was arrested in Melbourne and questioned over four armed robberies.

As he was being driven to the city watch-house he jumped from an unmarked police car and escaped again. He was arrested near Kingaroy in Queensland in January, 1991.

Police say he probably carried out 40 armed robberies in Victoria, South Australia and Western Australia over seven years. His trademark was to run into a bank, pull a gun, demand large-denomination notes and then run up to 500 metres to his getaway car.

In 1999 he was again arrested after he tried to rob a Carlton bank.

A fitness fanatic and vegetarian, the suspect is a friend of the man with the grudge against the Morans. They were seen together after Jason's murder.

This, coupled with the fact the killer ran from the Cross Keys Hotel car park after he murdered Moran and Barbaro, led some to think the man in the balaclava could be the armed robber who loves to run.

Homicide squad detectives interviewed the suspect and he said he could not help them. Detectives say he was one of many people who have been interviewed as part of the investigation and underworld rumours cannot be substituted for evidence.

But police did have one breakthrough in the Moran case. They had a videotape, shot from a hotel security camera, showing a balaclava-clad gunman running towards Moran's blue van moments before the murders.

The hotel video shows a white van parked near the car park just before Moran and Barbaro were murdered. It also shows a man running away. The camera overlooks the car park where Moran and Barbaro were parked that morning.

Police believe the gunman and his partner were in the van.

On October 25 two men were arrested in a white van in connection with the murder of Michael Marshall, shot dead in South Yarra only hours earlier.

JOHN William Moran was a good man and an upstanding citizen. He joined the army in 1941 during World War II to fight for his country. He died peacefully with his family on June 22, 2003. He was 81.

There was a handful of death notices for John William Moran from his family and the Glenroy RSL, where he was a respected regular. He was also a member of the Glenroy Lawn Bowls Club, having been a player, selector and coach for 30 years.

About 60 people attended the quiet and dignified service for the former bootmaker at the Fawkner Crematorium.

Jason Matthew Patrick Moran (no relation) died the day before John Moran. He also passed away in the company of members of his family – his six-year-old twins. But it was not peaceful.

For Jason Moran – gunman, drug dealer, standover man and killer – there were hundreds of death notices. In death he was accorded qualities he did not readily reveal in life. In the notices he was described as 'a gentleman ... a lovable rascal ... a special friend ... a good bloke ... a diamond'.

About 700 'mourners' attended his funeral at St Mary's Star of the Sea in West Melbourne – the same church where Gangitano was farewelled. Police were required for traffic control. Floral tributes worth thousands were sent to the church.

His mother, Judith, a big blonde woman compared in her younger days with the former film star Diana Dors, spoke at the funeral and gave a not-so-cryptic message to those present. 'All will be dealt with, my darling,' she said.

Jason Moran was loved by his family and their grief is every bit as real as anyone feels when they lose someone close.

But the assorted mates, associates, crime groupies and downright fools who have tried to suggest he was anything but a dim thug must have been sampling the amphetamine-based products Moran peddled.

He was described as a 'family man' – yet he pursued a violent criminal career that constantly placed him, his wife and children under threat, and he was always happy to wreck someone else's family.

He was warned at least three weeks before his murder that his card had been marked, yet he still drove around with his children as though he (and they) were bulletproof.

The truth is that Moran was born into a life of violence and crime – and revelled in it. He showed no signs of wanting to change. It is not just the criminal world that is fascinated with Moran and his type.

The view can be tragic: Two young children step from a funeral limousine. The boy, aged about six, is dressed in a little gangster suit and wears the mandatory gangster sunglasses, although the weather is bleak and overcast. The child looks directly at a press photographer and flips him 'the bird'. The next generation on display.

The fascination with gangsters is nothing new, nor unique to Melbourne – where, at least, crime tends not to rub shoulders openly with the judiciary, politicians and senior police. By contrast, gangsters such as George Freeman and Neddy Smith were given celebrity status in Sydney.

The Kray brothers and the Great Train Robbers were, if not respected, certainly recognisable characters in Britain. Mob restaurants in America are part of the tourist run; visitors eat pasta and veal while drinking bad Chianti, hoping to glimpse supposed Mafia figures.

But notoriety should never be mistaken for character. We live in a world where soap-opera stars playing television doctors appear on magazine covers while real surgeons saving lives remain anonymous.

Most people in Melbourne know the names of Gangitano and Moran, but few recognise the names of the detectives who originally headed the investigation into their murders (for the record, they were Detective Senior Sergeants Charlie Bezzina and Rowland Legg).

Ned Kelly may be Australia's most recognisable name but few can recall the police killed at Stringybark Creek – Michael Scanlon, Thomas Lonigan and Michael Kennedy.

American author Damon Runyon once wrote: 'Legitimate guys are much interested in the doings of tough guys, and consider them romantic.'

But there was nothing romantic about Jason Moran. Beyond his own family and friends, he was no great loss.

MORAN. — Jason.
Sorry Champ to see you go like
this, you changed a lot for the
better. My heart goes out to
Trisha and the twins Memphis
and Christian. Deepest and
sincerest condolences to my
good mate Lewis (keep your
chin up), Judy and all the Moran
families. — Mick Gatto, Ron
Bongetti and family.

Rest in Peace

FOURTEEN

INSIDE JOB

The hitman was either
incredibly lucky, or, more
likely, expertly briefed.

PEOPLE can strive all their lives to make money to guarantee their security. The irony for many Australian criminals is that as their illegal assets rise, so do the risks to their long-term future.

The maxim that money can't buy health or happiness applies especially to criminals. In the case of a Melbourne couple shot dead in 2003, the money they made through the lucrative vice industry couldn't give them good taste.

Steve Gulyas and his partner Duang 'Tina' Nhonthachith, also known as 'Bing', had all the trappings of wealth, but they were destined not to live long enough to enjoy them.

As with so many of the Melbourne underworld murder victims, they knew they were in danger, but not that they would be almost certainly betrayed by someone close to them.

Steve Gulyas didn't see it coming the day he was shot on the hobby farm he had bought with vice money. He and Tina had gone to their luxurious retreat near Sunbury for the weekend. He was lying on the couch, relaxed and secure, the remote control in his lap and a drink beside him when the killer placed the gun almost to his cheek and pressed the trigger.

Tina may have been able to get from her chair and run a few steps before she, too, was shot dead.

When the bodies were found on October 20, 2003, the television and the central heating were still on. Police believe a professional murdered them. They probably knew the killer, or invited him in.

They were security conscious. In their business they had to be. But the killer may have known that the couple's elaborate security systems would be flawed that weekend.

Electronic gates at the property were being installed, but were not yet operational, and their guard dogs had been taken back to Melbourne that day. The hitman was either incredibly lucky or, more likely, expertly briefed.

He would have known that vicious dogs, an iron fence and window shutters protected their home in Coburg. And that their 'introduction agency', Partner Search Australia, was also protected by a security system, including cameras.

But at their 30-hectare hobby farm in Wildwood Road the couple was vulnerable – until the gates and mesh fence were erected to make their weekender a mini-fortress.

Istvan 'Steve' Gulyas, 49, was born in Hungary, and Tina Nhonthachith, 47, in Thailand. Their bodies were found by an employee who went to the home after she became concerned for their safety. Police believe they had been dead at least 12 hours.

Partner Search Australia, in Sydney Road, Coburg, supposedly specialised in introductions to Russian and Asian women. But police say Gulyas had specialised in employing under-age Asian girls in the sex industry. Signs at the premises of Partner Search

Top left: Mario Condello – a man of means by no means.

Top right: Crown case – Nik Radev spent $55,000 on his teeth then had his head blown off.

Bottom left: Willie Thompson – Radev firebombed his car, then Willie bought a convertible. Go figure.

Bottom right: Detective Sen Sgt Stuart Bateson leads members of the Purana Task Force away from the Melbourne Magistrates Court after winning an order to interview a murder suspect.

Top left: Head of Purana, Detective Inspector Andrew Allen.

Top right: Experienced gangland investigator Gavan Ryan heads for court.

Bottom left: George Defteros – seasoned criminal lawyer charged by Purana Task Force with conspiracy to murder.

Bottom right: Dino Dibra – suspected hitman and later victim.

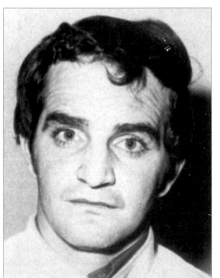

Top left: Alphonse Gangitano – accused killer and later victim.

Top right: Born Adrian Bligh, lived as Lewis Caine, died as Sean Vincent. Took a contract, but did not live to carry it out.

Bottom left: Brian Kane – shot dead in 1982. What goes around …

Bottom right: Pasquale Barbaro – shot dead with Jason Moran while surrounded by children at a junior football morning.

Mad Richard' Mladenich – Mark Moran's minder, shot dead in May 2000. Mark Moran (below) was shot one month later.

Mark Mallia – body dumped in West Sunshine in August, 2003.

Top left: Happier days – Victor George Peirce on vocals hamming it up with Jo Jo Zep in Pentridge.

Top right: Arrested by police – Peirce suffers superficial injuries. Later wounds from an unknown gunman were fatal.

Bottom left: Gotcha – the Special Operations Group arrests a suspected gunman on behalf of the Purana Task Force.

Bottom right: Graham Kinniburgh's funeral in leafy Kew – Mick Gatto (*back, right*) is one of the pallbearers.

Top left: Graham 'The Munster' Kinniburgh dresses down at Alphonse Gangitano's inquest.

Top right: Jason Moran dresses up for the inquest – it did him no good. He was still blamed for Al's murder.

Bottom left: The hitmen's stolen car – dumped and burnt out after Kinniburgh's execution? Police said they had done their homework.

Bottom right: 'The Munster' in his Crown Casino hat – a high roller used to five-star treatment.

Top left: Andrew 'Benji' Veniamin – police say he killed four before he became a casualty of the underworld war.

Top right: Mick Gatto invited 'Benji' to a Carlton restaurant and left Veniamin dead on the floor – he claims self-defence.

Bottom left:Veniamin's body leaves La Porcella restaurant in Carlton.

Bottom right: Last drinks – La Porcella closed permanently within weeks of the shooting.

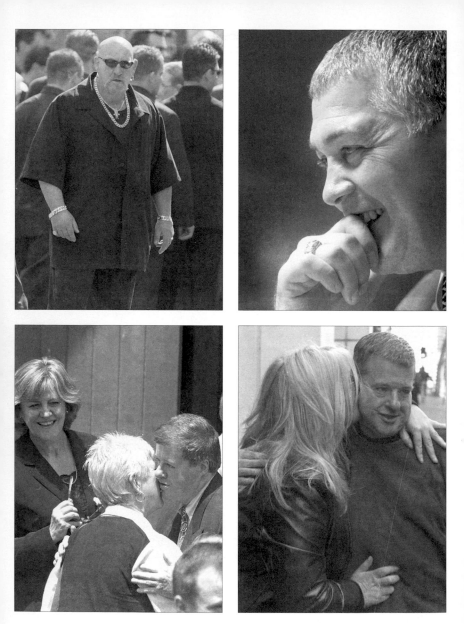

Top left: A mourner at Andrew Veniamin's funeral.

Top right: Big Mick – will he have the last laugh?

Bottom left: Paying respect – Lewis Moran at Graham Kinniburgh's funeral.

Bottom right: Lewis Moran is greeted after being bailed in July, 2003. Police said he was safer inside – they were right.

promote massage services – but it was unlikely the customers were looking for relief from bad backs.

It was well known in the sex industry that Partner Search was an illegal brothel as well as an introduction service. Tina Nhonthachith became a director of the business just two months before her murder.

The Partner Search sex workers were kept in a weatherboard house across the road from the office. Conditions were basic. Introductions were offered as face-to-face meetings in the business offices or a more relaxed approach at cocktail parties held in the business's in-house, licensed function room.

Gulyas had an extensive business history and a questionable reputation, with company links in Sydney and Queensland. He was once known as 'The Birdman' until he sold a pet-bird business, also based in Coburg. He also owned a successful truck business with his son.

Some of his former customers believed themselves to be the victims of an arranged-marriage scam and one complained that he had lost more than $10,000 after his 'bride' disappeared.

One customer looking for a wife was introduced to a woman he suspected was a prostitute. When he asked for his $5,000 back, he said later: 'They just laughed. It was a total rip-off.'

No one has been able to find one case where Partner Search helped anyone establish a meaningful relationship. When immigration officials raided the business in June 2000 they detained three Thai women who worked at the agency.

Tina Nhonthachith was a businesswoman in her own right and had her own fashion line, 'Tina's Trends'. But she and Gulyas ran the introduction agency for several years. Both often returned home: Gulyas to Hungary and Nhonthachith, whose three adult children live in Australia, to Thailand.

The house where the couple died is 500 metres from the road. It is well hidden and surrounded by hills. The couple kept to themselves and their neighbours liked it that way. 'They are not the type of people you would want to associate with,' one said.

Gulyas bought the Sunbury property about two years before his death, which proved he had plenty of money. He filled the house with his collection of stuffed animals, proving he had no taste.

In Melbourne, Gulyas had confided to neighbours he felt he was being watched. He was concerned about the Russian Mafia. His fears were well founded.

On the weekend of the murders, the couple had planned some hard work on the Saturday to be followed by a relaxing Sunday. On Friday Gulyas had picked up a stuffed polar bear from a Thomastown taxidermist to go with his lion and bison. On Saturday a neighbour saw Gulyas shifting earth on a bobcat – the small machine, not the large cat.

There was a barbecue on Sunday and a mechanic who worked for Gulyas picked up a bottle of his boss's favourite Hungarian Golden Pear liqueur at Dan Murphy's in Ascot Vale.

The mechanic stayed for lunch with business associates, but agreed to take the couple's dogs to Coburg that night. He knew the dogs usually snarled and growled at motorists from the back of his truck, and did not want them acting up on the Tullamarine Freeway in Monday's traffic, so drove them to Coburg on Sunday afternoon. With the dogs gone and the gates not yet erected the killer had open access.

If the dogs had stayed, there might have been no killing at all. Or a triple murder.

FIFTEEN

ON THE BOUNCE

*Police knew it was going to
happen. But they didn't
know what 'it' was.*

THE kilometre-square block in the middle of South Yarra is
one of the busiest in Melbourne. Traffic there regularly slows to
a crawl. No one would have noticed the late-model sedan that
cruised the choked streets for days.

No one, that is, except the police surveillance experts assigned
to help Victoria's gangland task force, codenamed Purana.

Police were tracking two of the suspects in some of
Melbourne's unsolved underworld murders. Both were known
to police.

They drove around the block bounded by Chapel Street and
Malvern, Toorak and Williams Roads, past the upmarket
boutiques that thrive near the 1960s housing commission flats.
They cruised by the 24-hour Prahran police complex in
Malvern Road, then turned left into Williams Road and past

The Bush Inn Hotel, a favourite with local police. They pulled over, checked the side streets and studied the area with the fastidiousness of town planners.

In one week in October 2003 they went to the block at least four times.

Experienced police believed these men were not sightseeing. They suspected they were there on business.

Detectives checked the area for likely targets and considered the possibility of a Spring Carnival raid on the Pub bookies at The Bush Inn. Two luxury car dealerships were also marked as susceptible. There was also a theory that the two suspects might have been planning an armed rip-off of a drug dealer in the area – but the investigators could only make educated guesses.

The detectives did have one big advantage – they had planted a tiny bugging device in the car being used by the suspects. But while it may have seemed that the men were researching a crime, they were not discussing details. Why would they? They knew what they were planning so there was no need to spell it out.

Police knew it was going to happen. But they did not know what 'it' was.

It is a scenario both frustrating and increasingly familiar. In recent years, tensions in Melbourne's underworld have spilled on to the streets. In the past decade, a violent underclass, fuelled by massive drug profits, have taken control of syndicates of unprecedented size. The syndicates have expanded rapidly until they have been competing in the same market.

Self-appointed crime generals, with virtually unlimited wealth but sometimes limited intellects, respond by sending out their soldiers to destroy the opposition.

In Melbourne, there have been more than 30 underworld murders in 10 years. While many of the murders appear related, police at first tried to treat each one in isolation. Earlier in 2003, Assistant Commissioner (Crime) Simon Overland decided on a new approach.

While gangsters killing each other hardly sparks public outrage, Overland knew that as killers became more brazen, the risks increased that a bystander would be caught in the crossfire.

One victim was shot dead in his convertible in Waverley Road, Chadstone. Bullets were found sprayed into a nearby building, shots that could easily have struck a passer-by. Without a breakthrough, the murders would continue and eventually affect the larger community.

Overland decided to form a task force to deal with groups of murders that appeared to be related. The Purana team grew to a strength of around 50 and, despite police budget cuts, Overland remains determined to resource the task force.

None of which was proving much help to the detectives sitting in an office, five kilometres from South Yarra, listening in on the muted conversations of their suspects. Police knew who they were. They knew they were up to something. But all they could do was wait.

Four months before this surveillance exercise, on June 21, 2003, Melbourne's underworld war intensified when a gunman wearing a balaclava ran up to a blue van parked at an Essendon North junior football clinic and shot dead crime identities Jason Moran and Pasquale Barbaro.

After shooting the men in front of a group of children, including Moran's six-year-old twin boy and girl, the gunman ran over a Moonee Ponds Creek footbridge to a waiting vehicle.

On the day of the murders, detectives were tipped that one of the men subsequently monitored in South Yarra was the likely gunman. Any chance of police having the advantage of surprise was lost when a television reporter rang the Moran family and nominated the suspect.

Detectives were confident the gunman was not working alone. The other man cruising South Yarra with the main suspect was also known to police as a 'person of interest' in the Moran-Barbaro investigation.

Detectives have a security video from the Cross Keys Hotel showing the gunman running towards the blue van parked near the Essendon football clinic just before shooting the two men. It also shows a white Toyota Hiace van parked near the bottle shop beforehand, then driving off.

It was the same type of van owned by the person of interest in the Moran-Barbaro investigation. An interesting fact but in evidentiary terms, hardly a smoking gun.

The two suspects had something else in common. They were both friends of a prominent member of the New Boys who knew many of the players in the underworld war.

The new player was the main suspect in the feud against the Moran family following a violent confrontation with them in the late 1990s.

The New Boy's wife claimed the confrontation was over a trivial matter. 'Jason wanted someone's phone number and [husband's name] refused to give it to him. Jason was humiliated and wanted to get back at him,' she said. Her husband was later shot but survived.

She denies that her husband was involved in the subsequent murders of Mark and Jason Moran.

'Even at school [her children and Jason Moran's children attend the same school] he would say "look away" when we saw Jason.'

The main suspect driving around South Yarra was particularly close to her husband and they were often seen together after the suspect was released from jail in 2003. Again, interesting but not evidence of a murder conspiracy.

Immediately after the Moran-Barbaro double murder, police

say the suspect began to behave as if he was under investigation, talking in code on telephones and constantly looking for
police surveillance units. This did not mean he was the killer,
only that he knew he was on the police list of suspects for the
double execution.

In October 2003, when the homicide crew had to return to
normal duties, the Moran-Barbaro killing was assigned to the
Purana team. While the main suspect knew he was a suspect, the
second target apparently was unaware he was a target of the task
force's investigation.

This let police slip the bug into his vehicle, unnoticed. Now
they could observe without spooking the pair.

But this created a dilemma.

The first job of police is to deter rather than apprehend. If
detectives know a crime is to be committed, they have a duty to
try to stop the offence. But intercepting a major criminal and his
sidekick because they appear to be driving suspiciously looks
more like harassment than deterrence.

Police had no evidence to lay charges, and pulling the suspects
over would only alert them to the electronic surveillance.

Investigators had no real choice but to let them run.

The head of the Purana task force, Detective Inspector
Andrew Allen, was at work on the evening of Saturday October
25, when he got the call from police monitoring the listening
post. The suspects were on the move but what they were doing
remained unclear.

Then police started to get calls from the public. There had
been a shooting in South Yarra. At gangland task force headquarters, investigators had a database of victims, suspects, potential
targets and associates. They had established a core of around a
hundred and a second ring of about the same number. The man
who was killed was not on the police list of possible targets – but
he was on someone's.

In underworld terms, Michael Ronald Marshall, 38, was a nobody with a minor criminal record – a former kick-boxer whose chosen occupation was self-employed hot-dog vendor, selling mainly around nightclubs.

The fast-food business can be lucrative, but Marshall appeared to be flying. He lived in a large double-storey home on the corner of Williams Road and Joy Street in South Yarra.

The hot-dog seller and his de facto wife had bought the house from a Melbourne surgeon in December 1991, paying off their ANZ mortgage in just three years.

A three-metre-high brick fence and an electronic security camera at the gate on Williams Road protected the house. But it was not enough.

The men who had come for Marshall had done their homework. The getaway car was parked in the next road, Howitt Street, facing Williams Road.

Marshall had been to a local bakery with his five-year-old son to buy hot-dog rolls for his busiest night, Saturday.

Joy Street is a narrow road filled with blocks of 1970s-style flats and architect-designed townhouses. Marshall parked his four-wheel-drive halfway down the short street, behind his hot-dog van.

Although his house had a double garage, he preferred to park in the street. His second security camera, looking down on Joy Street, was not working.

As Marshall stepped from the car, at about 6.30pm, and before he could open the back door to help his son from his harness, a lone gunman ran up and shot him at least four times in the head.

Just as in the Moran-Barbaro case, the killer seemed to have no qualms about shooting a man in front of his children and, as in the earlier case, the gunman had his escape route planned.

The killer ran down a partially hidden 50-metre path through a block of flats to Howitt Street. The driver had the motor going and took off in the classic getaway style, making sure there was no need to cross traffic flows, turning left into Williams Road and left again into the next main street.

Within hours, two men were arrested near the Elsternwick Hotel. They were in a white Toyota Hiace. At the time of the arrests, Marshall was still alive in the Alfred Hospital. He died about three hours later.

His de facto wife was understandably distraught. But, like so many vital witnesses in Melbourne's underworld war, she was reluctant to talk.

MARSHALL had an interesting circle of friends and business associates.

He trained at the same gym as Willie Thompson, another kick-boxer connected to the nightclub business.

Thompson sold lollipops for vending machines at nightspots – although police suspected he was also involved in selling more lucrative products to clubbers. He had been shot dead in Chadstone three months earlier, on July 21, 2003.

The lives and deaths of Marshall and Thompson were remark-ably similar. They were opportunists connected to the fringes of the nightclub industry – men who appeared to live well beyond their ostensible means and who paid with their lives when they finally alienated more powerful criminals.

Willie Thompson was shot dead as he sat at the wheel of his $81,000 Honda S-2000 sports car in Waverley Road, Chadstone, about 9.30pm. He was ambushed by two gunmen who approached him from either side of the car as he was about to pull out from his parking spot.

Thompson, 39, of Port Melbourne, had just left a martial arts class at the Extreme Jujitsu and Grappling gym when he was gunned down. The killers used their stolen car to block the sports car's possible escape route with a T-Bone manoeuvre.

Police found a bullet lodged in the wall of a bookshop in Waverley Road, two metres from Thompson's car. The killers were lucky not to have shot each other as they fired from opposite sides of the vehicle.

The two gunmen who ambushed Thompson's Honda had waited at a Red Rooster restaurant directly across the road for their target to leave the gym.

The gunmen's stolen Ford sedan was later found burned out in Port Melbourne – two streets from where underworld figure Victor Peirce was murdered on May 1, 2002.

It was clear the killers knew Thompson's movements and while the job wasn't as 'clean' as some, it still showed the prerequuisite planning.

Thompson was another victim of the underworld war without a big reputation, although he had big enemies.

Drug dealer Nik Radev firebombed Thompson's car about 18 months earlier. So in hindsight, replacing the destroyed car with a convertible was probably not one of Willie's better moves.

Radev was murdered in Coburg on April 15, 2003.

Police believe the murder of Thompson and Marshall and the killings of Jason Moran and Pasquale Barbaro could be linked. Thompson was a familiar face at some of Melbourne's biggest nightclubs and was a well-known bouncer for more than ten years.

Through his nightclub contacts he became involved in the film industry as a bit actor with roles in films partially financed by the owners of a city strip club.

He appeared in *The Nightclubber*, an alternative film shot at the Tunnel Nightclub and the Men's Gallery. It is a motion picture unlikely to be mentioned in dispatches at Cannes or even Cairns.

But none of these side interests could maintain Thompson's lifestyle.

Colourful Melbourne identity Mick Gatto placed a death notice in the *Herald Sun* for Thompson, a sure sign the dead man was connected in the underworld.

Friends said he was a 'gentleman' and well liked. But, apparently, not by everyone. Like many who were gunned down in Melbourne's gangland feud he lived like a drug dealer and ultimately died as one.

Another man who used his nightclub connections as a front for his drug activities was George Germanos.

Germanos was a power lifter with a mean streak. Immensely strong, he worked as a nightclub bouncer and was said to dabble in drug trafficking. He also made the mistake of using his own product.

Just weeks before his murder he took offence at a nightclub patron, lost control and beat the young man badly enough for him to be hospitalised.

It was a bad 'blue' by Germanos. The youngster was well connected to men who were not impressed with the beating.

A few weeks later Germanos, 41, went to a meeting in an Armadale park. It was late on the night of March 22, 2001.

After driving his early model V8 Valiant to the park in Inverness Avenue he was ambushed and shot repeatedly in the head and chest.

Coincidence? Maybe. But it certainly appeared to be another case where the victim must have known his killers.

GERMANOS. — George.
We will always have fond
memories of you at the St Kilda
Breakfast Club. Deepest
sympathy to the Germanos
family. — Brett Mason, Barry
Murray and Jason Banner.

SIXTEEN

SHORT LISTED

*He was at times seen walking
a small white, fluffy dog.*

GRAHAM Allan Kinniburgh was a modest man. Although considered by some as the most influential gangster in Victoria, he was always shy about acknowledging his achievements.

He preferred to conduct his business in private, though what that business was few really knew.

His criminal record understates his influence on the underworld. It lists offences of dishonesty, bribery, possession of firearms, escape, resisting arrest and assaulting police.

But criminal records list only an offender's arrest history – his failures. The definition of a successful criminal is one that tends not to get caught.

Many wondered how he prospered. Sometimes even he struggled to explain. When he was interviewed soon after the 1998 murder of his friend and fellow gangster Alphonse John

Gangitano, he was uncharacteristically tongue-tied. Asked by homicide investigator Gavan Ryan what he did for a job, he responded: 'Occupation at the moment? It would be – I'm a – well, I'm still, I'm still, I'm still a rigger. I'm still a rigger, yeah.'

It could have been a Freudian slip. Whereas a lay person might assume he was referring to rigging in the construction industry, it was whispered that one of Kinniburgh's talents was to be an extremely well-informed punter. Although it was never proven, or even widely alleged, that he was involved in rigging horse races, people on both sides of the law – including a former assistant police commissioner – loved to get a tip from the man they called 'The Munster'. He was a great and good friend to more than one leading jockey.

'Rigging' had been kind to Kinniburgh, 62, right up until he was gunned down in front of his double-storey brick home in Kew just after midnight on December 13, 2003. Ryan – a member of the Victoria Police Purana gangland task force – was immediately assigned to investigate the murder.

The shooting of 'The Munster' is the most telling – and probably the most ominous – of the underworld killings committed in Melbourne since 1995.

Nearly all the previous victims have been volatile and erratic men who saw violence as a weapon of first resort. There was an unspoken sense that they had it coming. But the older and wiser Kinniburgh was a tactician who saw gangland feuds as counter-productive.

While police are looking at a number of motives, two stand out as the most obvious. The first is that a man who is alleged to have ordered up to seven of the underworld murders has embarked on a campaign to kill all real and imagined competitors.

The second – and less likely – is that he was killed as a payback for the murder of Alphonse Gangitano. It was the relationship with Gangitano that first forced the reticent Kinniburgh from the shadows. He was a close friend of Big Al – a relationship that senior police found hard to understand.

Kinniburgh was wealthy but tried to hide it – Gangitano was often struggling but deliberately cultivated an image of affluence.

Kinniburgh kept a low profile while Gangitano loved the headlines, although that high profile meant he was always the target of police investigations. 'The Munster' went to visit the younger gangster on January 16, 1998, the night Alphonse was shot dead in his Templestowe home.

Police believe Jason Moran was at the house and argued with Gangitano. They say Moran opened fire on Alphonse without warning, killing him instantly.

The smart money says that a startled Kinniburgh ran to the front door of Gangitano's house, injuring his hand on the security mesh in his haste to throw it open. He then went upstairs, the theory goes, to check the security video to see if there was any compromising evidence – a blood-spot from Kinniburgh was found in the area.

Kinniburgh told police Gangitano was on the phone when he arrived and asked him to leave while he had a meeting. He said he went to get cigarettes and returned 30 minutes later to find Big Al dead. It was a fabrication.

Kinniburgh left the murder scene and went to the 24-hour convenience store in the hope the shop's security video tape could convince police he was not present at the killing.

He returned moments after Gangitano's de facto wife and children arrived home. Kinniburgh rolled over the body, claiming he was attempting emergency first aid, although he knew the big man had been dead for too long for any miracles. But he also knew that touching the body in front of a witness would enable him to explain at a later time why his DNA was on the victim. Kinniburgh didn't become a gangster heavyweight by losing his head when others (literally) lost theirs.

But Coroner Iain West didn't buy hastily built alibi of 'The Munster': 'I do not accept Graham Kinniburgh's version of events, as I am satisfied he was present at the time the deceased was shot.'

He said Kinniburgh went to the convenience store to be filmed on the security camera 'thereby attempting to establish an alibi of being absent from the premises at the critical time'.

'I am satisfied that both Graham Allan Kinniburgh and Jason Matthew Patrick Moran were implicated in the death.'

The difference between Moran and Kinniburgh could be seen at the inquest.

The younger gangster wore a flash suit while Kinniburgh dressed down for the occasion. He would do nothing to draw attention to himself.

While Kinniburgh could afford imported suits, he mostly preferred the casual clothes of an off-duty dock worker, even if in middle age he has acquired some expensive tastes and was a regular at the exquisitely expensive Flower Drum restaurant in Melbourne's Chinatown.

A regular at Crown Casino, he also enjoyed trips to Las Vegas to try his luck at the spiritual home of The Mob.

Kinniburgh lived in a large, tasteful house in a quiet street in one of the better blocks of the prestigious Melbourne suburb of Kew, the natural haunt of doctors, lawyers, stockbrokers and media executives. But he drove a second-hand Ford, the car he drove home on the night he was shot. While Kinniburgh didn't flaunt his wealth he managed to put his three children through private schools while not working in any legitimate job.

In 1994, his son married a girl from a well-to-do Melbourne family. After the wedding, it was just a short walk from St Peter's Anglican Church to the reception in Melbourne's grand old establishment hotel, The Windsor.

During the stroll, an alert observer might have noticed photographers taking pictures not of the wedding party but of the guests. The photographers were intelligence police looking to upgrade their files.

As is the case in many weddings, the groom's friends and family had little in common with the bride's group.

One friend of the bride was mildly startled when introduced to Kinniburgh, not so much by the man himself as by the four who were standing around him. 'They were all wearing *Ray-bans* and it was ten at night,' she said later.

Dressed in a dinner suit, Kinniburgh welcomed his 100 guests with a speech that left an impression. One guest, who didn't know the colourful background of 'The Munster', later said: 'He reminded me of Marlon Brando.'

Weddings are emotional times and this one was no different.

A guest of the bride, a millionaire property developer, was dancing with a woman invited from the groom's side.

A friend of the groom, released from prison days earlier after completing his sentence for biting a man's ear from his head, told the friend of the bride that he would be shot if he didn't immediately become a wall-flower.

The property developer lost interest in the music and retired to the bar. It was a sensible move.

Only a few months before Kinniburgh's death, his daughter married into a well-known Melbourne family with strong connections to Melbourne's legal and political establishment. The reception was held at the National Trust showpiece property, Ripponlea.

For three decades Kinniburgh has been connected with some of Australia's biggest crimes. Police say he was the mastermind behind the magnetic-drill gang – Australia's best safebreaking crew – that grabbed $1.7million from a NSW bank, a huge jewellery haul from a Lonsdale Street office and valuables from safety deposit boxes in Melbourne.

He was alleged to have been the organiser of a gold-bullion snatch in Queensland and was also once charged over receiving stolen property from a burglary on the home of the well-known and fabulously wealthy trucking magnate, Lindsay Fox.

When police raided Kinniburgh's home they found $4,500 in a drawer and a rare pendant owned by Mrs Fox in a coat pocket. He told police they could keep the money if they didn't charge him over the burglary. This time he appeared to be out of luck. The detectives were honest and added attempted bribery to the other charges.

While he was convicted of bribery he beat the theft charges by having an identical pendant made in Hong Kong to raise doubt about the unique nature of the jewellery.

In the 1990s he was charged over an attempt to import a record 15 tonnes of cannabis resin.

Police flew to Sydney for the initial court hearing where Kinniburgh was granted bail.

Detectives flew back in economy seats only to see Kinniburgh in first class. The case against him later collapsed.

In his younger days Kinniburgh usually carried a gun. He was charged in the early 1980s after a parking officer saw a gun sticking out from under the driver's seat. The grey ghost turned a whiter shade of pale and contacted police who arrested Kinniburgh when he returned to the car.

He was also charged after police found a gun stashed in a stormwater drain opposite his house when he lived in Balwyn.

He once punched a detective outside a city nightclub, breaking his nose. A well-respected detective later went to his injured colleague and said Kinniburgh was upset at what he had done and would give 100 pounds as a peace offering if the charges were dropped. But the only thing bent about the battered policeman was his nose. He refused the bribe and the case continued.

In his later years Kinniburgh saw no value in exciting police, and other members of the underworld, by carrying a gun.

But in the weeks before his murder he again began to carry a handgun. Friends say his mood became morose and they believe he knew he had been marked for death.

A few days before he died he dined in Lygon Street, Carlton, with five colourful Melbourne identities. It can only be assumed that none knew this would be the last time they would see their friend alive.

On the night of his murder he returned home to Belmont Avenue and parked on the street just past his drive shortly after midnight. He walked about six steps, carrying a bag of groceries, before he was ambushed.

A pistol was found next to his body and the bag of groceries he dropped. He had been able to fire just one shot before he died in front of the house that crime built.

Typically, the murder appeared to have been carried out by a hit-team of two – a gunman and a driver. Witnesses who heard the shots say one gunman fired at least two volleys of bullets before fleeing in a car just after midnight.

Ambulance paramedics called at 12.07am found Kinniburgh dead at the scene.

The killing appears to have been meticulously planned. Within seconds the hit-team was driving north along Belmont Avenue towards Parkhill Road before doubling back to cross Cotham Road.

They were using a blue Ford Falcon. Any chance of the killers leaving clues in the car appeared to be destroyed when it was found burning about one kilometre from the scene soon after the murder. Residents among the million-dollar houses of nearby Doona Avenue reported the car had been dumped and set alight in a hidden driveway down a narrow, cobbled service lane.

The killers had certainly planned the hit for at least a week. Police quickly established that the getaway car was stolen from South Melbourne the previous Saturday and hidden until the hit-team used it in the attack.

Police also believe the gunmen had carefully scouted the victim's street and the local area before striking. The fact that the Falcon was dumped and burned in a tiny lane not shown on any maps shows they had done their homework.

Detective Inspector Andrew Allen told the media that police would keep an open mind about motives but the fact that the murder was immediately referred to the Purana task force and not left with the homicide squad showed that detectives accepted the inevitable conclusion: 'The Munster' was the victim of an underworld hit.

'There's a number of things that may have been attributed to this man in his past which may or may not relate to why this has happened,' he said.

'The fact that there's another execution-style murder is obviously impacting on the community; it impacts on lawlessness and quite clearly we are pulling out all stops to investigate this to our fullest ability,' he said. 'This sort of behaviour and this type of lawlessness must stop.'

While several million law-abiding citizens agreed with the policeman's sentiments, the people who really mattered – a handful of Melbourne gangsters – took no notice at all, as subsequent events were to prove.

And Kinniburgh? Long-time residents of Belmont Avenue said they knew of his reputation but said he was 'a quiet man who kept himself to himself'. There were no surprises here.

They said he had lived for at least 15 years in his red-brick house, which is fronted by a high brick fence and sprouts several video security cameras. Neighbours said he was occasionally seen walking a small white, fluffy dog.

Kinniburgh had many friends. One of them was the ill-fated Lewis Moran, whose sons Jason and Mark were also victims in the underworld war.

When evidence was led at one court hearing that Lewis had been caught on police telephone intercepts talking about crime, Kinniburgh just shook his head as if perplexed that his old friend could be so stupid.

Perhaps Graham Kinniburgh was killed because of his wide network of friends and it may have been his Godfather-like reputation that made him a target.

One theory was that members of the criminal New Boys saw the powerful gangster as a threat because they believed he was aligned with the Moran/Carlton Crew. Police say the New Boys may have simply feared that Kinniburgh could become involved and decided to move first. In an underworld war, perceptions can be deadly.

A MONTH before Kinniburgh's death the Purana task force arrested the New Boys' front man over making threats to kill a detective and the man's wife.

Two weeks before the Kew killing, the man was freed on bail.

So when Kinniburgh was murdered, the frontman's name was put on top of the suspect list. But the day after the killing he told one of the authors he was not violent and could not explain why so many of his associates had been killed over the past six years. He denied claims he was trying to take over the illicit drug market and said he was not systematically killing any opposition. He also said he did know 'The Munster'. 'I've never met him and I've never heard a bad thing said about him. I have nothing to profit from his death. It's a mystery to me.

'I haven't done anything. My conscience is clear.'

Seemingly relaxed, he and family members met one of the authors in a city coffee shop about 36 hours after Kinniburgh's murder. He said he did not carry a gun, had never owned one and did not employ any form of security.

But one of his best friends and seemingly constant companion was gunman Andrew Veniamin, a man with a growing reputation well known to police and of interest to the Purana task force. When the front man had his bail altered to allow him to fly to a luxury Queensland resort for his summer holidays, Veniamin went with him.

The frontman has had terrible luck with his friends. He admits that he knew many of the men who have lost their lives in the underworld war although he has few ideas why they have died. He says Nik 'The Bulgarian' Radev had been to his house to celebrate his daughter's birthday only weeks before he was murdered. 'I had no problems with Nik.' But someone obviously did.

Radev was murdered in Queen Street, Coburg, on April 15, 2003. Police want to speak to two men who they believe lured Radev to Coburg from Brighton on the pretext of a drug deal.

The front man says he knew dead gangsters Jason Moran, Mark Moran, Mark Mallia, Dino Dibra, Willie Thompson and Richard Mladenich. 'That doesn't mean I know what happened to them,' he says. 'People die ... that's life. I have known people who have died in car crashes and overdoses. I also know people who have been shot.'

According to police, he had a long-running feud with the Moran family, a well-known Melbourne crime dynasty. This began with a potentially fatal shooting in Broadmeadows in 1999. Police believe Jason Moran pulled the trigger. But the victim, who ended up with a scar, says he did not see his attacker. 'I have no idea who shot me and I've never asked. I don't know who did it. Police told me who they think did it but that's their business.'

Jason Moran and Pasquale Barbaro were murdered while watching an Essendon North junior football clinic on June 21,

2003. Jason's half-brother, Mark, was murdered outside his luxury Aberfeldie home on June 15, 2000.

Graham Kinniburgh was a close friend of Lewis Moran, the father of Jason Moran and stepfather of Mark.

Speculation that Lewis was on an underworld death list seemed to be conclusively confirmed when he, too, was shot dead. Police from the Purana task force gave evidence supporting a variation to Moran's bail reporting conditions because they said he was at risk.

The man suspected of wishing Moran harm says it's no big deal. 'I've only met Lewis once,' he said before the latter's death. 'I haven't got a problem with Lewis. If he thinks he has a problem with me I can say he can sleep peacefully.'

But a few months later Lewis was put to sleep – permanently. The frontman, who cannot be named, said he had been interviewed by police over the murders of all the Morans but had been unable to assist. He was a close friend of one of the men charged with the murder of former kick-boxer and hot-dog seller, Michael Marshall, who was shot dead outside his South Yarra home on October 25.

'[He] is a good friend but I don't ask him about his business. I'll stick by him now.'

He said he was between jobs although he dabbled in property development and was a lucky punter. 'I did well over the spring carnival.'

He says he does not know why Melbourne's gangsters are killing each other. 'I don't know how this started and I don't know where it will end. All I know is that I have had nothing to do with it. This should all stop. It is only hurting everybody else.'

He says public speculation was putting his life at risk. 'They can have a go if they like. They know I'm unarmed. If it happens I won't know about it.'

In the office of the Purana task force in St Kilda Road there is a short list of potential victims. The name of Graham Allan Kinniburgh was on that list. The name of Lewis Moran was also there. So was Andrew Veniamin's.

KINNIBURGH. — Graham.
Tragically taken
Graham, you were my loyal
friend for more than 40 years.
No words can explain the
way I feel.
Deepest sympathy to Sybil,
Darren, Brent, Suzie and
families.
Memories last forever
— Lewis Moran.

SEVENTEEN

BACKROOM BOYS

Here we go again,
fasten your seatbelts.

EVERYONE knew it was coming – the police, the gangsters, the media, and even the victim.

But while the event was never in doubt the date and the venue had to be decided.

It is unlikely that in the last seconds of his life, suspected gangland hitman Andrew Veniamin would have been able to appreciate the irony of where he was about to die.

For a man who wanted to be a heavyweight gangster it seemed fitting that he was to be shot in the back room of an Italian restaurant.

It could have been New York or Sicily, but it was Melbourne and Veniamin was just the latest in a long line of wannabe tough guys to die in a vicious underworld war.

The venue was out behind the kitchen in a corridor-storeroom of a restaurant in Carlton, the inner suburb that rates as Melbourne's 'little Italy'. The date was March 23, 2004, and the killer was Mick 'The Don' Gatto. These three facts are beyond dispute.

How and why remains less clear cut.

When Andrew Veniamin, known to all as 'Benji', was approached in 2003 by detectives and told that he was a likely gangland murder victim, he didn't miss a beat.

He told police that not only were they stating the obvious, but he had already made the appropriate contingency plans.

Veniamin told detectives he had instructed his parents not to cooperate with any murder investigation – even his own.

'So we can put it down as no offence detected?' one asked.

Veniamin responded that he didn't care whether police ever found the man who was to kill him.

But they did – in record time.

Mick Gatto was in custody within minutes of the long anticipated violent death of Benji. Gatto, a man with more than two decades' experience in the untimely demise of associates and colleagues, knew the routine.

He told the first police at the scene that Tuesday afternoon at La Porcella family restaurant that it was a clear-cut case of self-defence.

Veniamin was in no position to argue.

The story was that Gatto was sitting at his normal table, at the back of the restaurant at the corner of Faraday and Rathdowne Streets just after 2pm, when Veniamin pulled up outside and double-parked the borrowed silver Mercedes he was driving. Why Gatto and Veniamin, two men who were not seen to be close friends, would have a daylight meeting in a Carlton restaurant is open to speculation. But it was always likely to end badly.

What is known is the two men left the public area of the restaurant and walked to a small room at the back of the kitchen. There was a short discussion followed by several shots.

As ambulance officers fussed over a lost cause, Gatto told police that he and Veniamin had walked to the room, that Veniamin had pulled a gun and fired a shot before the much larger Gatto relieved him of the revolver and shot him three times.

Gatto said the shot fired by Veniamin had just missed his ear.

For a man who had just killed and was a few centimetres from his own death big Mick remained remarkably calm. The ever-polite regular at the restaurant was composed enough to apologise to the owner about all the fuss before he headed away to assist police with their inquiries.

Detectives listened patiently to Gatto's story. They already knew his background. Gatto, 48, had for many years been a well-known and respected figure in certain parts of Melbourne society.

He had a seemingly unique ability to solve problems. Many people over the years had travelled to La Porcella to share pasta or sample the excellent veal with big Mick and talk of their concerns. Sometimes Gatto couldn't help. Sometimes he could. Either way, it could be an expensive conversation. It was rumoured to cost $5,000 to sit with him and tell him what was on your mind. If he could fix it with a telephone call, that was it. Any more effort on his part would cost more. Many clients maintain it was money well spent, as such a service depends on a high success rate and word of mouth.

One businessman in Melbourne's east was a busy man who sometimes found himself distracted. A big-picture man, he had a habit of forgetting to pay bills, even large ones.

Gatto prided himself on his ability to help people remember. It was a natural gift honed over many years. He rang the forget-ful businessman on his mobile phone to remind him that he had an outstanding debt of $75,000 and was expected to pay within three days.

The businessman was indeed forgetful because he said he was in Queensland and would, in fact, be there for the next ten days but would be happy to discuss the matter on his return.

The man seemed to have forgotten that he was not in Queensland but actually standing in the lounge room of his well-appointed eastern suburban home.

Gatto, ever helpful, pointed this fact out – breaking the news that he was parked outside and could actually see the businessman on the telephone through the window. The man immediately lost any semblance of a Queensland tan. Eager to help and desperate to quash any suggestion he was tardy on payments, the man had the money in full to Gatto by the next day.

Veniamin, by contrast with the phlegmatic Gatto, was a relatively new player and considered dangerously erratic.

Police tried to interview four of Mick's friends who were at the restaurant. Their recollections appeared hazy and detectives were somewhat disappointed with their answers, though perhaps not surprised.

Gatto was charged with murder that night and remanded in custody.

So far, there appear to be no witnesses to the event and it has long been held in matters underworld that dead men tell no tales.

Which is unfortunate for the Purana gangland task force and the Australian Crime Commission because it put an ugly bullet hole in the plan to eventually grill Veniamin over four unsolved underworld murders.

Police say Veniamin was involved in the murders of market identity Frank Benvenuto, in Beaumaris in May 2000; of Dino Dibra, in his West Sunshine home in October 2000; of Paul Kallipolitis, shot two years later, and of Nik Radev in Coburg on April 15, 2003.

But you can't charge a corpse with murder so officially Veniamin died an innocent man.

Benji, who had a reputation as an irrational hothead, was the constant companion of another big player in the scene. When Benji's friend was allowed to vary his bail and spend Christmas at a resort in Queensland, the faithful Benji was with him. Even though he could hardly swim he dog paddled around in the surf with his mate.

In the last few months of his life, Veniamin lived in a city penthouse and drove a $200,000 car. Yet he was still registered to pick up the dole.

His friend, frontman for the New Boys opposed to the Carlton crew, had invited Radev home to celebrate his daughter's birthday. The frontman also knew Jason Moran, Mark Moran, Mark Mallia, Dino Dibra and Willie Thompson, all of whom have been shot dead as part of Melbourne's underworld feud. 'That doesn't mean I know what happened to them,' he says.

Police believe Radev was lured to a meeting on the pretence of a drug deal and that Veniamin was probably waiting for him. Police want to track down two men in a red Holden Vectra seen driving away at the time of the murder.

Veniamin took exception to a report in the *Age* on December 14, 2003, which identified him as a suspect in some of the underworld murders. 'I am offended by your article ... The suggestion that I have been involved in ... murder is slanders (sic) and wrongly could endanger my life,' he said.

Before they exchanged shots in the backroom, Gatto and Veniamin may not have exactly been friends, but they were at least known to be associates. In one incident Benji and his mates decided to take on security staff at a Melbourne strip club. Seen watching in the background was Gatto.

The two apparently went their separate ways after a suspected major drug importer was beaten severely in Lygon Street. After the bashing the importer is said to have persuaded Veniamin to join the New Boys against the old-school crims.

The journey that led Veniamin to the morgue began at least 12 years earlier when he was just 16. That's when he began to gather convictions that ended up ranging from assault to arson.

He was involved in two shootings, drug dealing and a series of violent crimes.

His first recorded offence, as with so many violent criminals, was relatively minor compared with his later 'form'. In 1992 he was fined $50 for theft of a motorcar. In 1993 he was convicted of intentionally or recklessly causing injury and sentenced to 200 hours of unpaid community work.

Over the next decade he was found guilty of theft, robbery, false imprisonment, assaulting police, arson, deception and threatening to cause serious injury.

In the last year of his life he seemed to think he was above the law. A suburban detective once drove past him in an unmarked car. Veniamin gave chase and confronted the policeman in a petrol station, demanding to know if he was being followed. Veniamin, well built but not much bigger than a jumps jockey, seemed comfortable trying to intimidate the detective. In just a few months he managed to acquire more than 40 speeding and parking fines. Even when he went to see Gatto he double-parked the Mercedes.

Gatto was 20 years older and in a different class. A former Australian heavyweight boxing contender, he didn't get the nickname The Don because of his ability with a cricket bat. Then again, maybe he did – but he didn't hit many boundaries. At the building industry royal commission in 2002 Gatto was rudely labelled as a standover man – although he always preferred the title 'industrial consultant'.

Police say Gatto has never been a believer in mindless violence and that if and when he spoke sternly to people they tended to listen. 'I treat people like they treat me ... the meek and the mild and the strong. I don't care. It makes no difference,' he told a respected court reporter from the *Age*, Steve Butcher. 'I'm not frightened of anyone. I'm frightened of the person I see in the mirror. I'm not frightened of anyone else.

'I'm a negotiator and mediator, and I do a good job at it.' Sadly, he failed to negotiate a peaceful outcome with Benji.

So why was there bad blood between Veniamin and Gatto even before blood was ultimately spilled?

One theory goes that someone was systematically picking off Melbourne's established crime figures.

The feud was supposed to go back to 1999 when the New Boys' frontman was hurt in a confrontation that might have left a lingering resentment. Although he showed a remarkable lack of curiosity about who hurt him, police believe it was Jason Moran.

In June 2000 Jason's half-brother, Mark, was shot dead outside his Aberfeldie home and three years later Jason and his friend Pasquale Barbaro were also murdered while watching a children's football clinic.

More than 12 murders could be linked to the underworld feud. They believe the spate began out of revenge but broadened as a group of criminals tried to eliminate potential competition and to deal with drug dealers who had not paid their debts.

The man allegedly at the centre of the controversy is large but not particularly threatening looking. He has a ready laugh and is often prepared to talk, although he rarely provides answers of substance. Like Gatto, he seemed remarkably calm after 'Benji' Veniamin's death.

Only hours after it, he remarked: 'Here we go again, fasten your seatbelts.' It was unlikely he was referring to road safety.

He said he believed Veniamin had been set up. 'Andrew wasn't frightened. He wasn't expecting this.' Although one of his friends had just been killed and another was facing murder charges, he said he saw no reason to believe he was at risk. 'I've got no problems. I'm sweet, mate.'

Police disagreed. They thought he was a target.

Many thought Jason's father Lewis Moran was the ultimate target, so much so that Purana investigators gave evidence to allow Moran senior to alter his bail conditions on serious drug charges so he would not be an easy execution target.

But in leafy Kew, Graham 'The Munster' Kinniburgh, the biggest name in Melbourne crime, was becoming apprehensive.

Closely aligned with the Morans, Kinniburgh feared he could be on the death list and began to carry a gun for the first time in years. He was right, but it didn't save him.

Mick Gatto treats death in the underworld as an occupational hazard. Police joke that it is not officially an underworld killing until Mick has placed a death notice in the *Herald Sun*. Some claim he has the newspaper's classified-advertisement number on speed dial.

But Kinniburgh's death is said to have hit 'The Don' hard. His death notice in the *Herald Sun* read: 'I love you "Pa" and I will never ever forget you.'

The man with a reputation for finding answers to difficult questions began to make active inquiries on who killed 'The Munster'. It was considered unlikely he would have shared his knowledge with investigating police.

Police suspect he blamed Veniamin. It is not known if he asked Benji of his alleged involvement before he shot him twice in the neck and once in the head.

After the shooting Gatto said: 'He said he'd killed Graham and he tried to kill me.'

The irony is that while police believe Veniamin was a killer they don't believe he was that killer. He had been a suspect for Kinniburgh's murder but had been eliminated because he had a rock-solid alibi. Police surveillance found he was on the other side of Melbourne, in Sydenham, not Kew, at the time of the shooting.

Police electronic surveillance showed that shortly before Veniamin was shot he and Gatto had chatted in a friendly manner on the telephone as they arranged to meet at the restaurant.

But then things went horribly wrong in the back room.

Gatto said very little to police about what happened, but he did volunteer: 'I've done nothing wrong and I've acted in complete self-defence.'

The only witness who could corroborate or dispute that version of events was lying dead on the restaurant floor.

Gatto didn't get a reputation as a man who could fix problems by being ill prepared. But even so, police were somewhat surprised when they opened the boot of his car to find a plastic body bag and eight rounds of .32 calibre ammunition.

About two blocks away from the Veniamin shooting a group of taxi drivers were having an early afternoon tea. When they heard police sirens heading their way many of them scattered – fearing that police and immigration officials were about to raid them to ask embarrassing questions pertaining to work visas. But police had more sinister characters to worry about, one of them very dead. The owner of La Porcella restaurant was shaken by the death and concerned that his family restaurant would lose business once it was identified as a 'mobsters' hangout.' He needn't have worried, at least in the short term.

Later in the week many of his tables were filled with magazine colour writers, comedians and food reviewers with expense accounts. But weeks later it all became too much and the owner closed the restaurant, relieved that he would no longer be connected with an underworld war not of his making.

Mick Gatto likes to help people – even when he is in jail.

He donated $5,000 to the Good Friday Royal Children's Hospital appeal while still behind bars. A hospital spokesman said: 'If he wishes to donate to the hospital, we appreciate that. We're certainly not here to judge people.'

People who wear horsehair wigs do that.

VENIAMIN. — Andrew.
To a friend I haven't known for
very long, you were a true
friend. My deepest sympathy to
all his family.
  — Antonios Mokbel
Will Be Sadly Missed

EIGHTEEN

A NICE DRINK

'I think we're off here.'

LEWIS Moran was a traditional criminal with traditional tastes. And that, in part, led to his violent demise in the front bar of the Brunswick Club on March 31, 2004.

For many years Lewis Moran's regular pub was the Laurel Hotel in Mount Alexander Road in the inner western suburb of Ascot Vale, strategically placed mid-way between Moonee Valley and Flemington racecourses.

The Laurel was a pub of choice for gangsters of discernment. Moran's son Jason once pulled a gun on another drinker there. Graham 'The Munster' Kinniburgh popped in for a drink in the bar there before he headed to a meeting with Alphonse Gangitano in January 1998 on the night Big Al was murdered.

But when the old style pub turned trendy and began to serve foreign Tooheys beer, that was enough for Lewis.

The Moran clan had drunk at the Laurel for years and while he was comfortable surrounded by friends and associates there, he decided that if the pub didn't have his favourite Carlton United product on tap it was time to move to the Brunswick Club in Sydney Road – just a few hundred metres from the local police station and near a proposed redevelopment said to have been funded be a man heavily involved in the drug world.

Melbourne is known for its exclusive establishment men's clubs but the Brunswick Club is not one of them. Despite his colourful background Moran the elder felt welcome there and became a fixture. Several times a week, he would turn to the left when he walked in and stand at the bar to sip seven-ounce glasses of beer.

All his friends knew they could find Lewis in the bar at his favourite spot, known in the trade as his 'lean'. The trouble was, so did his enemies.

Lewis Moran knew he was marked for death but, according to friends, he 'was too stubborn to take any notice'. When he was facing serious drug charges, police tried to keep the elder statesman of the crumbling Moran crime dynasty in jail for his own protection.

Police had varied his bail to make his movements harder to track for a hitman, but that hardly mattered because he could always be found at the Brunswick Club.

Lewis Moran may have wanted a quiet life, but, according to police, he was still active in the crime world. Detectives gave evidence in the Melbourne Magistrates' Court that he had been involved in drug deals worth $10million over four years.

Senior Detective Victor Anastasiadis told the court one informer gave Moran $5.5million in pseudoephedrine-based tablets, used to make amphetamines, and was to receive a share of the amphetamines in the deal with Moran. Moran, 57, was facing

17 charges, including trafficking commercial quantities of amphetamine, hashish, ecstasy and pseudoephedrine.

He was charged with his old mate, Bertie Wrout, a senior citizen who might have been well advised to stick to, the old age pension.

Senior Detective Anastasiadis said he feared for the informer's safety if the accused pair were released.

But on July 22, 2003 – after nine months on remand – Lewis Moran was granted bail despite police opposing it on the grounds he would seek retribution for his son's murder and pose a threat to a police informer. He was released on condition that he reported daily to police, obey a night curfew and not contact witnesses.

In his successful bail application, his lawyer argued Moran should be freed so he could act as a father figure for his murdered sons' children.

This was a reference to the obvious fact that the once entrenched Moran crime family had been virtually destroyed by underworld feuds.

Lewis Moran's son Jason and stepson Mark had already been murdered.

In October 1978 Leslie Herbert Kane was shot dead in his Wantirna unit. His body was never found. But one of his children, Trish, eventually moved in with her childhood sweetheart – Jason Moran – and the couple had children.

Les Kane's brother, Brian, was also shot dead in a Brunswick hotel in November 1982, apparently as revenge for the brazen shooting of Raymond Patrick 'Chuck' Bennett in Melbourne Magistrates' Court three years earlier.

Among the mourners for Brian Kane was a young Jason Moran.

In the same month, in an unrelated shooting, Mark Moran's natural father, Les 'Johnny' Cole, was shot dead in Sydney as part of a NSW underworld feud.

Exactly when the decision to kill Lewis was made has (at the time of writing) yet to be established, but police speculate it may have been at a reception centre near Keilor Cemetery the previous evening.

It was there that many of the western suburbs' most dangerous criminals gathered for a wake for Andrew 'Benji'Veniamin, who was shot dead in a Carlton restaurant on March 23, 2004.

Veniamin was at the forefront of the group of New Boys making their presence felt in crime circles. Police believe he was close to people who might directly or indirectly be involved in about 12 murders. Veniamin has been linked to at least four.

The day after the wake, Lewis Moran was murdered and his friend Bertie Wrout was shot. It was more than a coincidence. Some say revenge is a dish best eaten cold, while others claim there is no time like the present.

Moran saw the gunmen enter the club and said: 'I think we're off here.' 'Off' is an underworld expression for dead.

Lewis ran in an arc trying to escape. He didn't have a chance and was shot dead a few metres from where he had been enjoying a quiet beer just seconds earlier.

The moments leading up to the murder were caught on the Brunswick Club's security camera, but the killers were wearing balaclavas.

Staff at the club were deeply traumatised and were said to be worried when a wake was planned to be held at the bar where Lewis was murdered.

A few years earlier Lewis was still a powerful figure with powerful friends.

Some say that after the murder of his stepson Mark he was bent on revenge.

A secret police report, later to be leaked to the underworld with disastrous consequences, claimed that a police informer was offered $50,000 to kill the high-profile frontman for the New Boys, the group seen as challenging the established underworld order. The offer was said to have been made in May 2001 and in the name of Lewis Moran.

Moran had a big reputation in the underworld, but in his final year he was close to a spent force. His son, Jason, and stepson, Mark, were gone. His friend Graham Kinniburgh was murdered and his respected associate, Mick Gatto, was in jail over the Veniamin shooting.

Isolated and without a power base, Lewis, 58, let it be known he no longer wanted to fight back. Crippled with arthritis, he was no longer a threat. But his enemies were not sure and they wanted to be. Dead sure.

In the previous few weeks police had been hearing that some would-be gangsters were offering their services to kill the New Boys' frontman.

The frontman maintained he could not imagine why anyone would wish him harm, yet he made no effort to conceal his friendship with known gunmen suspected of, or charged with, 'hits' against the so-called Carlton Crew and its hangers-on.

There was a confrontation in a western suburbs Tabaret not long before Lewis Moran's death, when the old crook was called outside by the younger man. He declined the invitation.

Lewis was said to have lost his personal taste for violence, although he did not seem to mind when Mark and Jason Moran used guns, baseball bats, fists and feet to exact revenge against real and perceived enemies.

Lewis Moran was another of Melbourne's old-style crooks who seemed to sail through life with few financial concerns and no pressing need to work for a living.

His crime record charts post-war criminal history. He was said to be involved in protecting backyard abortionists, SP bookmaking and steal-to-order break-in rings before moving into modern crime and, inevitably, drug trafficking.

Police say there was no need to shoot Moran's friend, Wrout. At 62, small, thin and harmless, he could not have been seen as a threat by the two gunmen who walked into the Brunswick Club and opened fire.

It is believed the two men in balaclavas were armed with a handgun and shotgun, the same weapons used to kill Mark and Jason Moran.

In the hours following the shootings the name of a major suspect surfaced. He is a former armed robber and a veteran hitman who police say is one of the most dangerous men in Australia.

Police believe he had killed several times before the latest underworld war. He is said to have cut the throat of a couple at their outer Melbourne home during a drug rip-off and to have shot a man during a dispute at a northern suburbs party.

Once, when the elite Special Operations Group raided him, the suspect ran from the bedroom naked except for a gun he took from under his pillow. He aimed at one of the police and pulled the trigger, but the bullet did not discharge.

The SOG policeman later wanted the bullet for a good-luck necklace.

Although the hitman is not physically imposing, police say he will kill without conscience. He is also close to an influential amphetamines dealer said to be an enemy of the Morans. He once planned to kill a detective who had arrested him. During his sentence, he spent his quiet evenings drawing – not landscapes or still life, but figures of a man hanging from a gallows. It is believed the hanged man in the drawing represented the detective.

Less than an hour after Lewis Moran's murder the normally chatty suspect said: 'I've got no more to say.' When asked if he feared for his life he said: 'I'm all right.'

But his wife was more animated. 'My heart goes out to them

[the Morans],' she said. ' I don't know anything about it. This is insane. It just has to stop.'

But it was never going to stop without police action. The killings were always likely to continue.

On the night Veniamin was shot dead in a Carlton restaurant the frontman made it clear that the shooting was unlikely to be the final chapter.

Veniamin was shot by Mick 'The Don' Gatto. Gatto was charged with murder although he has claimed long and loudly that it was self-defence.

Gatto was a close friend of Kinniburgh and Lewis Moran. But after the Kinniburgh murder in December, 2003, the frontman said he was unaware of the suggestion that Lewis Moran was on a death list.

'I've only met Lewis once,' he said. 'I haven't got a problem with Lewis. If he thinks he has a problem with me I can say he can sleep peacefully.'

It has been suggested that Veniamin was a suspect for the murder of Graham Kinniburgh, but police had established he had a strong alibi. He had been eliminated as a suspect.

But the question is: did Kinniburgh's friends know the violent Veniamin was, for once, an innocent man?

While police and politicians expressed outrage over the Moran murder, Melbourne citizens seemed to have become accustomed to bloodshed on their doorsteps.

Upstairs at the Brunswick Club is a billiard room. Hours after the murder two snooker players tried to pass the police lines to head upstairs for a game.

Even though Moran's body was visible they twice argued with police that they should be allowed inside to play.

After all, life goes on.

From his prison cell, Gatto was able to organise a death notice for his mate. It read: 'Lewis you knew it was coming, you just didn't care ... Deepest condolences to Tuppence [Lewis's brother] and the Moran family. Rest in peace my Mate and a big hello to Pa. [Kinniburgh] – Mick Gatto.'

The funeral was not a lavish affair, but Judy Moran would not let the story die with her estranged second husband. She was signed by promoter and agent Harry M. Miller to tell all and write a book.

It is understood she has plans to help finance the redevelopment of a Melbourne hotel with an accent on fine dining. It is unlikely that patrons will be encouraged to complain about the food.

Just 12 days after the murder, Judy Moran was quoted as saying: 'I decided I wanted to write a book the moment I found out Lewis was dead. I have lost two sons, two husbands and two very dear friends and I am finding it very hard to cope with it all.

'My solicitor approached Mr Miller about signing a contract and I met him in Sydney on the weekend.

'It was a very harrowing 24 hours, but the contract was signed.

'Lewis and I were both worried about his safety but he didn't care; he was sick and tired of it all. I was horrified when I found out he'd been murdered about three minutes after it happened.

'But I am outraged that my family has been portrayed in the way they have. They were good people, not bad people, but they keep calling Lewis a drug baron – which is not true.

'I am doing this for my grandchildren as a legacy to their grandfather.'

One television current-affairs programme tested the water but found that Judy was more interested in money than in putting the record straight. Her 'tell-all' style was basically to deny loudly any knowledge of how her husband made his money.

Police telephone intercepts indicated she and Lewis were no longer close, but the fact that they had separated did not seem to worry Judy. She was always practical when it came to money, and known to put it ahead of sentiment.

It is well known in certain circles that when her estranged parents happened to die within a week of each other, she arranged a double funeral and had them buried together ... the first time the pair had been that close in years.

NINETEEN

A DEAD END

*'I thought he was trying
to lead a normal lifestyle.'*

LEWIS Caine was tough, confident and at the peak of his powers until he found too late that in the underworld tough guys often end up dead.

Good looking and with piercing eyes, Caine could have been mistaken as a former sportsman on a gradual decline – the type who is past his best but remains a formidable opponent.

But fellow crooks and police knew without asking that Lewis had done some serious jail time – the giveaway was the way he moved. He had a cocky, almost confrontational walk that some men pick up in prison. A cross between a boxer's strut and a street brawler's stride. It gave a message that he was always ready for action and was confident he could handle any challenge. He was wrong.

Caine, a self-proclaimed karate expert, kicked a man to death outside a Melbourne nightclub in 1988. He was convicted of murder and was considered dangerous enough to spend most of his ten years inside in maximum security.

Caine, 39, was a friend of Mick Gatto, the man charged with the murder of alleged hitman Andrew Veniamin. But Caine was also known to an alleged major player who was Veniamin's best friend – and by 2004 Gatto and the player didn't share too many friends. People in the underworld were expected to pick sides. It may be that Caine chose the wrong one.

The player's wife said she had seen Caine only days before his murder. Both the player and Caine had abandoned anonymous suburban life, choosing to live in central Melbourne high-rise apartments.

'He came over to say hi,' the player's wife said. 'We didn't know him well. He seemed like such a nice person,' she told one of the authors. She said Caine's killing was 'just another kick in the guts' and added: 'When is this all going to end?'

It was a rhetorical question.

Most criminals go bad by degrees. They start with minor property offences as kids, graduate to theft and then become violent. These are the building blocks of the gangster.

But Caine was not your average crim. He went from indecent language to carrying a gun to murder, with little in between.

The son of a Tasmanian police inspector, he loved the idea of being a hard man but lacked the discipline to prove himself in a legitimate way. According to a confidential police report he joined the army on May 11, 1982, but went AWOL five months later and was discharged.

He was born Adrian Bruce Bligh, in Devonport, Tasmania, on April 22, 1965. His parents divorced and his mother moved to Queensland. According to police he had 'an intense hatred of his father'. He claimed to be a martial-arts expert but police found it was a lie. 'He did some classes but was only a beginner,' one officer noted. But he knew enough to kick a harmless man to death.

It was obvious Caine was fascinated by death and destruction. When he was arrested for murder he was found to have books on terrorism, Special Forces tactics and weaponry. Earlier he had been found with a book on explosives.

He was a courier who once injured both wrists in a motorbike accident. According to a police report, at the time of his arrest 'Caine was under suspicion of being a large drug dealer, using his employment as a courier as a cover for his trafficking activities.' It was believed that Caine's position in the syndicate was one under the actual importer. He would not sell to street addicts, only to other heroin dealers.

In the early hours of September 18, 1988, two lives collided: one of the man who courted violence and the other of a bloke just out for a good time.

David Templeton was 34 years old when he crossed Caine. He lived with his parents in Williamstown until he married in 1978 and moved to Essendon. In 1984 he separated and later divorced. He then returned to live with parents until 1985 when he bought a house in Newport.

Templeton was always gainfully employed and regularly promoted. After leaving Williamstown Technical School he had worked for three years as a bank teller. He then moved to Medibank where he started as a clerk and was later promoted to branch manager.

After ten years with Medibank he decided he needed a change and became a sales representative.

His family described him as honest, hard-working and community minded. He was an active member of the North Melbourne and Point Gellibrand Rotary Clubs.

But on the night of Saturday 17, 1988, the likeable and responsible Templeton was a pain in the neck.

He had been admitted to the Melbourne nightclub, Lazar, and proceeded to make a scene.

At the same nightclub was Caine, who arrived at 10.30pm to see a friend who worked as a bouncer and to catch up with a woman he had met the previous day at a motorcycle store in Elizabeth Street.

As they stood at the bar Templeton and Caine were to have the briefest of conversations.

The salesman had grabbed a policewoman friend's badge and, without her knowledge, used it to pretend he was in the job. It is an offence to masquerade as a policeman but Templeton's antics were immature rather than malicious.

He was guilty of being a show-off, and probably a drunk one. He should have woken up the next morning with a sore head and an attack of guilt. But he was never to wake up.

Templeton and Caine appeared to show a sudden interest in one girl and an instant dislike for each other.

Caine was seen to be loud and aggressive and Templeton, still pretending to be a policeman, complained to a bouncer, who happened to be Caine's friend.

Caine was taken outside and told there had been a complaint and that he was no longer welcome inside. He took it badly, swearing and kicking a parked car.

He continued to yell and swear, claiming a policeman was trying to steal his girlfriend. Twenty minutes later Templeton came out and Caine attacked him. Templeton ran away but Caine jumped into a cab already occupied by four people and hunted him down in Spencer Street.

According to a witness: 'The victim was lying on the ground and Caine was punching and kicking him in the head and body.'

A police report said later: 'Caine pursued Templeton and subjected him to a savage and merciless beating and kicking, causing multiple abrasions, lacerations, contusions, and fracturing of skull.' He died on the footpath.

Caine went back to the nightclub and was seen with blood on his hands. According to police he was heard to say: 'That bloke copped it; I knew I'd get him. Don't fuck with the Wing Chun boys.' He was also heard boasting in triumph: 'I got the guy who got my girl.'

He was arrested around 3am. He showed no concern for his victim and no regard for his future, glaring and trying to intimidate the arresting police. When he was handed over to homicide detectives, one told him that staring might work in the schoolyard but not in the interview room.

Manslaughter and murder convictions are not easy to get in prosecuting alcohol-related fatal assaults. But in the Templeton case the jury was so horrified by the cold-blooded nature of the attack they were prepared to convict Caine of murder. Not once, but twice.

He was convicted in November 1989, appealed and was convicted again in August 1990.

During his appeal Caine managed to slip his handcuffs and escape from court. He was caught close by after falling over. Police who grabbed him saw him trying to get rid of a knife. 'How Caine came to arm himself with a knife and avoid detection of same is not known,' a policeman noted.

A police summary said, 'Caine is a loner with no strong family ties. He is a keen and regular exerciser who maintains an excellent standard of fitness. He is fit and healthy. He has an unpredictable nature and to this day has shown little or no remorse for his conduct.'

A detective who interviewed Caine had no doubt he was already a lost cause: 'In my opinion he is capable of killing again either whilst in custody or when released. Members should exercise extreme caution when dealing with him.'

Far from being mortified that he had killed a man, Caine, also known as Sean Vincent, became a hard man inside prison.

When moved to a less violent part of the prison system, he asked to move back. He loved the dog-eat-dog nature of the violent jail culture. In 1997 he was one of five prisoners subdued with tear gas after a three-day stand-off in the top-security unit in the Barwon Prison.

The inmates, led by Caine and double murderer and escapee John William Lindrea, were demanding contact visits, extra time in their cells, access to recreational equipment and a more 'relaxed regime' in the management unit.

On the first day of their protest in July 1997, an emergency response team went into the cells and forcibly carried the inmates out into the exercise yard. The following day the prisoners again refused to move and the head of the jail's emergency response team issued a series of progressive warnings telling the inmates they could be subjected to force unless they complied.

After two hours the inmates were told they would be given no more warnings. The emergency response team then moved in and ordered the inmates to lie on their cell floors with their hands behind their backs.

When the inmates refused the team used an aerosol tear gas spray, but the prisoners went to the air intake valves in their cells to breathe fresh air.

The team then dropped two tear gas grenades, each the size of an egg, through the door slots of Lindrea and Caine's cells.

The wing filled with tear gas and prison officers, wearing gas masks, stormed the area, grabbed the five inmates and forced them into the open air. They were stripped, showered and taken to an exercise yard. Prison sources said the inmates declared they would refuse to dress as a continued protest.

'After two hours in the nude in the cold they decided that discretion was the better part of valour and dressed,' a prison source said.

By the time he was released from prison, Caine had many criminal contacts and it was those links that would ultimately get him killed.

He made the fatal mistake of choosing sides. Police say he accepted a contract to kill Mario Condello, a close associate of Gatto.

But the story got out and someone decided to stop Caine before he could close the deal. He was shot and his body dumped in a dead-end street called Katawa Grove in Brunswick on Saturday May 8, 2004. Police believe he was killed elsewhere.

At first the investigation was run by the homicide squad, rather than going to the Purana task force. It was as if police did not want to accept that yet another Melbourne gangster had been hit. But within 48 hours the case was acknowledged to be part of the state's underworld war.

Caine was last seen after he left his city apartment about 8pm that night.

He was known to drink with a group of colourful racing identities and at least one convicted murderer in a Carlton hotel.

One man who knew him, Keith Faure, told the *Herald Sun* he had seen Caine since his release. 'I thought he was trying to lead a normal lifestyle. I don't think he was a gangster or a big-timer,' Faure said.

Certainly Faure's views on Caine were of interest to the Purana task force. Less than two weeks after the killing Faure was arrested by the Special Operations Group in Geelong and charged by the Purana detectives with Caine's murder.

Caine may well have been a nasty standover man with connections in the drug world, but away from business he had an attractive and devoted live-in lover from the other side of the legal tracks.

He was living in the city with a solicitor from a prominent Melbourne criminal law firm.

The solicitor, who lived with Caine for almost three years, was shattered by his death and made a request to the Coroner's Court to have sperm taken from his body and frozen. The request was made after Caine's body was released following the autopsy.

The sperm had to be taken from the body within four days of death to ensure it remained fertile. The Supreme Court would have to approve the release of the sperm before the woman could use it to become pregnant.

The solicitor had told friends before the murder she planned to marry Caine.

Underworld sources said the pair had only recently postponed plans for a lavish wedding with guests expected to fly in from around Australia and overseas.

The couple first met when the solicitor was assigned to represent Caine over a routine .05 charge. Love bloomed among the lawyer's briefs.

The irony is that like most crims Caine fought to stop police getting body samples from him that could be used to link him to unsolved crimes. But after his death, he had no say in the matter.

You may not be able to get blood from a stone, but you can get sperm from a dead gangster.

TWENTY

LAW OF THE JUNGLE

*With Hodson dead, charges
against one of the police were
dropped because of lack of evidence.*

TERENCE Hodson was not a big name in the crime world, but his murder – and that of his wife Christine – became a political smoking gun. The double execution of a couple in their own home was shocking, but it was also sinister because it was more than an example of criminal brutality spiralling out of control. It had a deeper significance – it linked allegedly corrupt cops with the underworld war.

The murders caused many, including the Liberal Opposition in Victoria, to call for a royal commission into the police. The Labor Government responded with a raft of reforms, including a revamped Ombudsman's office, coercive powers for the Chief Commissioner and new asset-seizure laws.

But as the crisis deepened and it was revealed that possible police involvement in the murders was being investigated, former Queensland Royal Commissioner Tony Fitzgerald was called in to inquire why confidential police documents about Hodson's role as a drug informer had been leaked to violent gangsters.

Terry Hodson was a drug dealer turned drug-squad informer who provided information on friends and competitors to a detective at the drug squad.

Hodson was charged in December 2003, with two detectives from the major drug investigation division, over an alleged conspiracy to steal drugs worth $1.3million from a house in East Oakleigh in September.

Police later raided the house as part of the biggest ecstasy bust in Victoria's history.

Hodson had been a drug-squad informer since August 2001, but after his arrest in 2003 he agreed to inform for the police anti-corruption task force, codenamed Ceja.

Christine Hodson had no convictions and had not been charged with any offences. She was an innocent victim of Melbourne's underworld war.

Her tragedy was that many in the criminal world knew her husband Terry was an informer. Their suspicions were confirmed when the leaked police documents began to circulate in the Melbourne underworld in early May 2004.

A month earlier lawyers for Hodson indicated in the Supreme Court that he would plead guilty. It became obvious he was prepared to give evidence against the two police charged with him. Police sources say he had originally agreed to be an informer to try to protect family members who were also facing drug charges.

He acted as the inside man for police on at least six drug-squad operations – specialising in helping police expose cocaine and ecstasy networks.

Charismatic and likeable, Hodson knew most of the major

crime figures in Melbourne. A carpenter by trade, he had built secret cupboards and storage areas for some of Melbourne's biggest drug dealers, according to police.

According to an old friend, the Hodsons arrived in Perth in 1974 from Britain. They had married in July 1967, in the city of Wolverhampton. Hodson used his carpentry skills to land a job as a maintenance officer looking after rental properties. He was said to have had a deal with an insurance assessor to rip off the company by submitting over-inflated bills for damaged kitchens.

He began his own building business and was successful enough to buy a luxury home.

The friend said the couple became obsessed with possessions. 'She [Christine] would vacuum three times a day.'

Hodson was a bookmaker's son but he struggled at school and was barely literate. When he made money in Perth, he hired a private tutor to help him with reading and writing. He didn't need any help with arithmetic, especially counting money.

He built a small business empire in Perth and became involved in a partnership dealing with prestige cars. The story goes that he believed his partner was ripping him off so he hired some oxy-acetylene blowtorch gear and found a safebreaker to get into his partner's safe. But a neighbour came by to feed the cat and the safebreaker left suddenly, leaving the gear behind.

Police were able to trace the fact that Hodson had hired the gear and he was convicted, only to later escape amidst claims he paid officials to turn a blind eye.

He later moved to Melbourne. The old friend recalls: 'I lost track of him until I got a call from his wife asking for $50,000 for bail. I said no.'

Hodson loved the idea of being a gangster, he says. 'He wanted to be a flamboyant type; I guess he didn't make it. Every time there was a murder of a crook in Melbourne I thought it would be Terry. In the end it was.'

The Hodsons' bodies were found by their son in the lounge room of their home in East Kew on Sunday May 16, 2004.

Hodson almost certainly knew the gunman. Like most drug dealers he was security conscious and no one entered his home without an invitation.

He also had two large and loud German shepherd dogs to deter intruders.

One theory is that Hodson knew the killer, let him into the heavily fortified house, and was ambushed in the lounge room: his wife was then killed because she could identify the gunman, probably a business associate or 'friend' of her husband.

It is believed Hodson was smoking a roll-your-own cigarette when his guest produced a handgun and ordered the couple to kneel on the floor, where they were executed.

The couple were killed some time after Saturday evening. Their guard dogs were locked in the garage, either by the killer or by the couple when they welcomed their guest.

One neighbour said: 'I didn't hear the German shepherds, so I wondered what had happened. I heard what sounded like a shot about 6.15pm, but didn't pay any attention.'

Hodson had been offered protection but had declined it. Being in protection would have meant he couldn't keep seeing his grandchildren. Although he knew his life was in danger, he decided to carry on as normal.

But the police information report, written in May 2002, mysteriously began to circulate.

It contained many allegations. Amongst them was the claim Hodson had been offered $50,000 to kill a man who was seen as an enemy of Lewis Moran.

By the time the information became public Moran was already dead, but it could be interpreted as placing Hodson on one side of the fence in the underworld war.

On May 14, 2004, a story in the *Herald Sun* newspaper repeated some of the information from the leaked report, including the contract offer.

The following day Hodson and his wife were murdered. Some might draw conclusions about cause and effect.

The leaking of the confidential police document was a massive breach of security – but homicide-squad detectives had to investigate not only whether the leak caused the murders but if that was the intention of the leak.

Certainly members of the underworld had seen the police report before the newspaper story was published. The father of the man who had been named as the victim of the proposed $50,000 hit confirmed he had seen the police report in the previous few weeks.

Both police who had been charged with Hodson over the East Oakleigh drug rip-off were interviewed by homicide-squad detectives and provided alibis.

But with Hodson dead, charges against one of the police were dropped because of lack of evidence.

It is not the first time a selective leak might have contributed to murder.

Isabel and Douglas Wilson were drug couriers for the notorious Mr Asia heroin syndicate in the 1970s. When they decided to talk to police about their activities that fact soon appeared in the Brisbane *Sun* newspaper.

The Wilsons' bodies were later found in Rye, Victoria, on May 18, 1979. They had been shot on the orders of the syndicate boss, Terry Clark, because they had been talking.

TWENTY-ONE

SNAKES AND LADDERS

For the Carlton Crew, George Defteros
has long been the lawyer of choice.

PUB bouncer turned criminal lawyer George Defteros always prided himself on being able to avoid a king-hit. But the solicitor with a survivor's instinct was visibly shaken when he was arrested near his city office on June 17, 2004, in connection with Melbourne's gangland war.

For more than ten years Defteros has been the lawyer of choice for many colourful identities when they face serious criminal charges, although his client list has been shortened because of the underworld trend of gangsters killing each other.

Defteros helped finance his Monash University law studies in the 1970s by working part time as a bouncer at the Croxton Park Hotel in Preston, the heart of Melbourne's tough northern suburbs. There he learned that the gift of the gab, backed by the subtle threat of violence, helps win most arguments.

More than once in his early days of practising criminal law, an offender would pull him up and ask if he was the bouncer who once threw him out of the 'Croc'. Diplomatically, he would always plead not guilty – a tactic he recommends for most of his clients.

But since Defteros's arrest some of those clients have had to find a new mouthpiece because the day after his arrest he voluntarily handed back his practising certificate until the court process was completed.

This saddened his long-time confidant, Mick Gatto, who was in jail charged with the murder of Andrew Veniamin – who, as *Leadbelly* readers will already know, was a suspected underworld hitman shot dead in a Carlton restaurant on March 23, 2004.

Defteros was served with the police brief on Gatto in early June and was busy building a case for his client – who had pleaded self-defence – when he ran into his own problems.

Gatto was planning to apply for bail in the Supreme Court, but that application had to be delayed due to his lawyer's pressing matters.

Police say two warring sides are central to many of Melbourne's gangland murders. The battle is between an established criminal network, known as the Carlton Crew, and a group of so-called up-and-comers, the New Boys.

For the Carlton Crew, George Defteros has long been the lawyer of choice.

He represented not just Gatto, but the late Alphonse Gangitano, Perth criminal identity John Kizon, security expert and kick-boxing referee Dave Hedgcock and fugitive Mexican banker Carlos Cabal Peniche, who was wanted over a misunderstanding involving an alleged fraud of $1.12billion.

Another prominent Defteros client was St Kilda footballer Stephen Milne, who was investigated and cleared of rape allegations earlier in 2004.

He also represented former lawyer turned 'businessman' Mario

Condello – a man known to be close to Gatto and who from appearances could have had a regular role in the cult US crime series *The Sopranos*, which he appears to have been watching closely.

If clothes make the man then Condello was serious trouble. Around 194cm, in his early 50s and heavy-set, his dress sense could be described as 'mafia chic', although it is no crime to dress like a mobster – only to act like one.

On June 9, a week before Defteros's arrest, police arrested four men over an alleged plot to kill Condello. One of those arrested was a man said to be a key figure for the New Boys.

But on June 17 police charged Condello and Defteros with conspiracy to murder that man, his father and an unidentified minder for the father–son team.

Police from the Purana task force would allege in court that they had uncovered two simultaneous murder plots. That while members of the Carlton Crew were planning murder, the New Boys were doing the same. It would be a matter of time who would get there first. As it turned out, the police did.

Police ran the two investigations at the same time, allowing the plot against Condello to run in a bid to grab the alleged offenders at the last minute.

Then they would move on the Carlton Crew.

On June 9, police arrested two men outside the Brighton Cemetery. Police would allege they were waiting to murder Condello as he followed the daily routine of walking his two dogs from his nearby double-storey, heavily fortified home. Later that day they grabbed two other men and all four were charged with conspiracy to murder.

The arrests were seen as a big breakthrough for the Purana task force, but the following day the accused men seemed anything but broken-hearted.

They laughed, smiled, joked and swore as if the hearing was being held in the back bar of city hotel rather that in a secure court in the magistrates complex. At least they were playing to a full house.

The court was packed with police from Purana, reporters, family and friends of the accused men, and a group of year ten schoolgirls on an excursion.

A man who cannot be named was charged with one count of conspiracy to murder and incitement to commit murder. Michael Thorneycroft, 27, and Gregg Hilderbrandt, 34, were each charged with conspiracy to murder. Sean Sonnet, 35, was charged with conspiracy to murder and incitement as well as seven other charges including car theft, possession of a firearm and drug trafficking.

During the first hearing the unnamed man was flanked by armed guards wearing flak jackets while a police helicopter hovered overhead.

Sonnet, no stranger to court proceedings, ranted from behind security glass on matters ranging from legal procedures to the role of the media in a free society. 'I'm representing myself and I want a suppression order … Don't write anything, you fucking dogs.'

He told Deputy Chief Magistrate Jelena Popovic he wanted a suppression order because he felt he could not get a fair trial and he also feared for his family.

One of his fellow-accused, Thorneycroft, added somewhat unhelpfully: 'I want the same fucking thing.'

Thorneycroft claimed he was thrown in a cell and left naked with no blankets.

He then asked: 'Why can't my mates be naked with me?' Sonnet responded: 'I don't want to be naked with you.' They were close, but not that close.

When the magistrate refused the suppression order Sonnet tried a more direct appeal.

'They're already writing. I don't give a fuck, I'll see you when I get out,' he said in what was interpreted as a threat.

But then Sonnet suggested the media should tell the police that he has everything he needs in jail except the kitchen sink, but added: 'I want the sink.'

As he was led from court Sonnet had a parting shot at reporters: 'I'll read your paper. Any of you fucking dogs who write it down, I'll see you when I get out.'

IN the life of George Defteros, the line between client, associate and friend had become blurred over the years.

He considered Graham 'The Munster' Kinniburgh a friend and would sometimes dine with the suspected organised-crime figure.

Defteros also enjoyed the company of Gangitano, so much so that he agreed to provide the criminal identity with something most lawyers hate – a discount on his bill. He dropped his fee from $100,000 to $70,000 as part of an informal customer loyalty programme.

He described Gangitano as a respected businessman, devoted family man and loyal friend. Police found the description overly generous.

Their relationship was long and mutually beneficial. Defteros stepped in when Gangitano was charged with the 1995 murder of standover man Greg Workman, who was shot outside an underworld party in St Kilda in February 1995.

Gangitano was in serious trouble because the police had two witnesses – sisters who were put under protection to testify against the accused.

But when the women became disenchanted with police protection and rang Gangitano's then right-hand man, Jason Moran, Defteros knew what to do.

According to a confidential police report: 'Both witnesses were then debriefed by Defteros and a staged audiotape made of both women recanting their statements.'

The witnesses were then sent overseas – Gangitano paid the bills – and the murder prosecution collapsed.

Police investigated whether they could charge Defteros with conspiracy to pervert the course of justice, but were told they didn't have a case. To make matters worse Defteros sent police a legal bill for $69,975.35 for Gangitano's defence fee.

As his clients began to take on higher profiles during the underworld war so did their lawyer, and Defteros found himself the victim of regular threats.

Police have been concerned for some time that a small number of criminal lawyers have, in their view, crossed the line and become players rather than neutral advocates.

High-profile lawyer Andrew Fraser was seen as one who ran with his clients. He was eventually sentenced to a minimum of five years for cocaine trafficking.

Some police suspect that a high-profile defence barrister of the 1970s and 1980s, the late Robert Vernon, used his considerable skills to advise criminals on how to avoid detection.

In more recent times, another lawyer was alleged to have used court documents to identify an informer in major drug cases and it is speculated that such potentially deadly information was passed on to clients willing to kill or intimidate potential witnesses.

But Defteros wanted it known that he wasn't a player in the action, just a man doing a difficult job to the best of his ability. He told the *Herald Sun*: 'I think people should calm down and people should appreciate that we, as lawyers, act in the criminal-law area for the best interests of the client ... I am concerned, however, to portray myself first and foremost as a criminal lawyer, and nothing else.'

But legal and ethical dilemmas were no longer the concern of Mario Condello. He was once a practising solicitor, but lost his ticket after he became the subject of police interest in the 1980s.

Top left: Last drinks (2) … the Brunswick Club where Lewis Moran was shot dead.

Top right: Judy Moran – lost two husbands and two sons to murder

Bottom left: Forensic experts check the Brunswick Club where Moran was gunned down.

Bottom right: Graeme Jensen – shot dead in his car by police in Narre Warren, October 11, 1998.

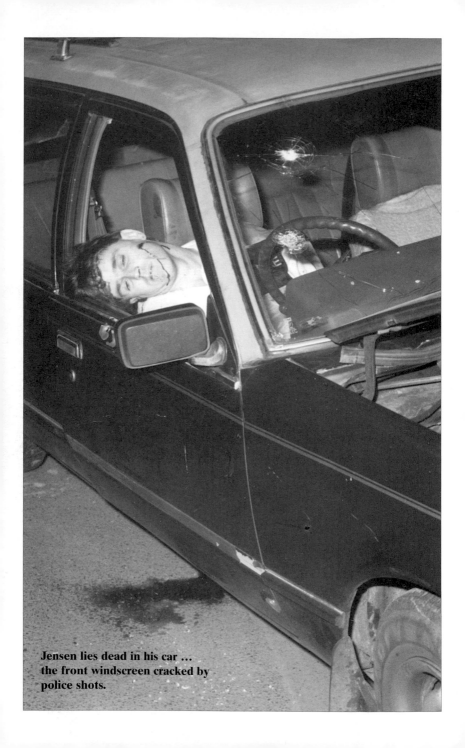

Jensen lies dead in his car …
the front windscreen cracked by
police shots.

The Peirce-Jensen crew at work.

Jensen threatens a man and child.

A prosecution reconstruction of police shots fired at Jensen.

Senior Detective Cliff Lockwood reconstructs the last moments
for Gary Abdallah.

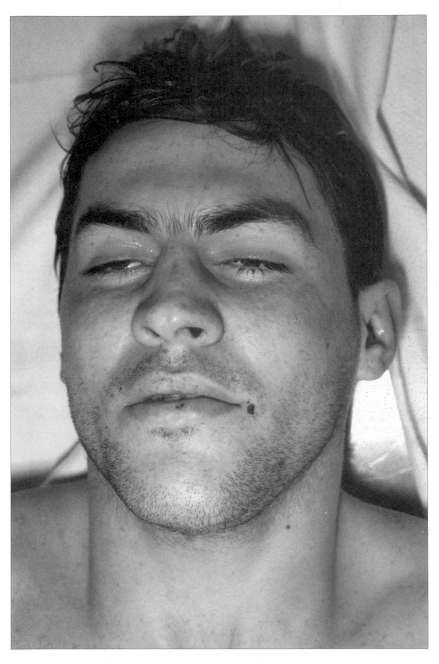

Jedd Houghton – shot dead by police in a Bendigo caravan park.
He had five guns – it wasn't enough.

Jockey Smith falls at the last.

Days after four men were arrested for allegedly plotting to kill him, Condello went public in an interview for the *Bulletin* magazine. He was photographed in the laneway near his office and about 50 metres from Defteros's city office.

Condello no longer speaks like a lawyer, but prefers the language of the colourful Carlton identity he has become.

Once criminals liked to conduct business in the shadows. Today's underworld figures agree to photoshoots and compete to produce media one-liners. The only time it seems they make no comment is when police are asking the questions.

In his interview Condello showed himself to be somewhat of a crime snob, claiming moral superiority over the New Boys. 'We really didn't have a problem with them because we are not in the line of business they are in. We don't have anything to do with their line of business and, quite frankly, we despise anyone who has anything to do with that line of business.'

'No one wants any further destruction of life. No one wants any further traumas, stress or anything of the like least of all taking a life. It's absolutely absurd.'

He said he had been involved in peace meetings with members of the up-and-comers just days before the arrests related to the alleged plot to kill him.

Rather than showing any concern for his safety, or that of his terrified wife and children, Condello continued to talk tough about his alleged would-be killers.

'Once they reached the other side of the road where my place was, they would not have been able to walk back to the car, I can assure you they would not have been able to return. Now you make your own assessment of what I'm saying and thank God it turned out the way it did. Thank God for them and thank God for me.'

But the truth was that Condello, aware of threats against him, had moved from the house much earlier. And it wasn't God he had to thank for intervening. It was the police Special Operations Group – known as the Sons of God – who made the arrests.

But while Condello talked the talk, he also was prepared to show his softer, more forgiving side. 'I didn't like what happened. I hope it just doesn't continue to happen to others or to myself for that matter because ... I am prepared to forgive once and that's as far as it goes. No more.'

Detectives had a different story to tell, but decided to tell theirs in court rather than to a respected national magazine.

Police believe that another man, lately known as Lewis Caine, first took the contract to kill Condello, but the Carlton Crew learned of the plot and Caine was murdered first. He was found dead in a dead-end Brunswick street on May 8, 2004.

Caine's lawyer girlfriend successfully asked for sperm to be taken from Caine's body so she can make a court application in a bid to have his baby. In a bizarre twist, the girlfriend worked for Defteros.

It must a sobering thought for the would-be mum to ponder that her lover might well have been killed by hitmen hired by associates of her boss. Life can be cruel like that. You don't know who you can trust when you associate with gangsters.

Condello said after the alleged plot against his life was foiled: 'My message is stay away from me. I'm bad luck for you people. Stay away, don't come near me, please.'

The Purana task force chose to ignore that advice when they came knocking.

In a bail application for Condello, just hours after his arrest, Purana investigator Detective Sergeant Martin Robertson gave evidence that a police informer had been offered a contract to kill three members of the New Boys.

It was claimed that Condello and the informer discussed payment of $150,000 per hit, the use of getaway vehicles and the need to obtain false passports. Detective Sergeant Robertson said the pair allegedly also talked about the use of disguises for the killings. He described Condello as a man with 'no legitimate source of income' who 'displayed an extraordinary amount of wealth'.

Police gave evidence that they found a loaded .32 pistol at Condello's city apartment. The gun's serial numbers had been removed and it had been modified to take a silencer.

TWENTY-TWO

THE SILENT WAR

*We lost something and I don't
think we will ever go back.*

FOR 20 years the Victoria Police Force was the most popular and respected force in the country. It was also the most deadly.

The state's peacekeepers killed its citizens at a rate unprecedented in more than 100 years. In the six years from 1980 to 1986, police shot five people dead in Victoria. But in the ten years after 1986 they killed thirty, compared with ten fatal shootings by NSW police in the same period.

The killings sent shockwaves through police, legal and political circles, attracted huge media attention and fuelled bitter controversy among rival interest groups. They also resulted in eleven police being charged with murder-related offences over two of the killings, the suicide of one of them, and the dropping of charges against eight of the men before trial. And they resulted in the Government admitting the police had got the use of deadly force terribly wrong, prompting a massive re-education programme to teach every operational police officer how not to kill.

The shootings also contributed to the professional demise of the coroner who heard the cases, the Director of Public Prosecutions who laid the charges against police, and the virtual sacking of a prominent QC who prosecuted one controversial case.

The events were clouded on one hand by lurid allegations of political interference, of police corruption, of investigators concealing evidence, and the existence of a police 'death squad'.

On the other hand there were allegations that detectives were cynically put in the dock to provide a show trial to appease a vocal minority pressure group; and there was the suggestion that a respected detective was persecuted until he took his own life.

One thing is certain. It was a shameful episode for the criminal justice system, which took almost seven years to examine the controversial events. World War II was fought and won in less time than it took the coroner to return a finding on the death in 1988 of armed robber Graeme Jensen.

The shootings were dragged from the Coroner's Court to the Supreme Court and the High Court. And yet, for all the time, words and money spent, no one was convicted of any criminal charges relating to any of the shootings.

Courts around the nation and experts from the Canadian Royal Mounted Police and the United States FBI, criminologists and serving police all questioned why Victorian police killed citizens at the rate of one every six weeks by 1994. Buried underneath the avalanche of expert attention in the 1990s was a simple fact: the rising tide of deaths had its origins much earlier.

IF one moment marks the beginning of the police shootings it was a winter night in 1985. Following a report of a suspected burglary, two policemen on patrol pulled over a yellow Cortina in a Cheltenham street in Melbourne's quiet southern bayside area.

It was routine, something both had done many times before. But this time it was different. How could they know that the driver was a psychopathic Bulgarian Army deserter who'd turned himself into a deadly marksman, a suburban guerrilla with a secret pistol range under his house and a collection of lethal weapons? A Jekyll & Hyde character who prowled the suburbs by night, breaking into houses and factories, and waiting for the inevitable confrontation with malice in his heart and a heavy-calibre pistol in his hand.

How could they guess that the driver of the Cortina was better armed and probably a better shot than any uniformed police officer in Australia? And that he was willing to shoot on sight, even at two blokes just trying to earn a living?

They found out the hardest way. Pavel Vasilof Marinoff waited until the pair came close enough that he couldn't miss. Then he started firing. Seconds later Senior Constable Peter Steele, 26, was bleeding from a wounded hand. He was lucky. His partner, Sergeant Brian Stooke, 40, was left a paraplegic. Stooke had been hit by four bullets. One severed his spinal cord.

It was a big night for Pavel Marinoff. Within hours 200 angry and frightened police were hunting a terrifying new public enemy number one.

Unfortunately for two of them, they found him – briefly – in Noble Park. He shot them both. Sergeant Ray Kirkwood was wounded and Constable Graeme Sayce was trapped in their police car, miraculously escaping serious injury when Marinoff repeatedly shot at it, shattering the headrest of Sayce's seat and grazing his head with a bullet.

Soon afterwards a police dog handler, Senior Constable Gary Morrell, also got too close to Marinoff. He, too, was shot – but saved from serious injury by his ballistic vest.

It was June 18, 1985. Policing in Victoria was never quite the same after that night.

PAVEL Marinoff, dubbed 'Mad Max' by the media, was to shoot two more police, eight months later, on February 25, 1986. But this time his luck ran out; they shot back.

It happened on the Hume Highway in the country slightly north of Melbourne.

Sergeant John Kapetanovski and Senior Constable Rod MacDonald, acting on crime intelligence, followed a panel van driven by the man they believed was Marinoff. Before they could move they had to wait for him to drive outside Wallan, the town where he was hiding in a heavily fortified house owned by a motorcycle gang member.

The policemen decided to move quickly, and stop the van on the highway before the driver got back into the town, where any gunfire could harm passers-by. They pulled the van over and approached it cautiously, armed with shotguns. They ordered the driver to place his hands outside the car, where they could see them. For a second, it looked as if he might obey – but then he drew a pistol and, lightning fast, squeezed off several shots before trying to speed away.

Marinoff hit Kapetanovski in the shoulder and hand and MacDonald in the chest. Despite his wounds, MacDonald fired two shots from his police-issue shotgun through the rear window of the escaping van. His shotgun was loaded with buckshot, a heavy load with the hitting power to drop a wild pig. The slugs went through the glass, then the driver's seat, then the driver. The van slewed off the road, through a fence and into a paddock. 'Mad Max' was dead at the wheel. But no one knew that until some time after the bleeding, dazed policemen drove to a nearby farmhouse to raise the alarm.

IN a literal sense, Marinoff's death was the end of one of the police force's most gruelling experiences. But, in reality, it was the first milestone on a grim journey into hostile territory where almost every police officer felt threatened by unknown assailants who could be lurking in any car, any doorway, any hotel.

If the Bulgarian had fancied himself as an urban terrorist, he succeeded: he robbed police of peace of mind, waging a one-man war that meant for the first time that Victorian police sensed they could be injured or killed at random for no reason other than the uniform they wore.

Once, police didn't need ballistic vests; their uniforms made them 'bulletproof'. Criminals, even dangerous gunmen, knew it was crazy to shoot police. The consequences, both professionally and physically, were dire. Before capital punishment was abolished, to kill a policeman was virtually to sign your own death sentence. And even after hanging ended, the prospect of tough treatment by police followed by a life sentence was daunting.

Of course, some police met violence. But only those who sought the dangerous jobs in specialist 'heavy' squads were perceived as the ones at risk. Few of the force's then 9,000 members were in the front line against known vicious criminals.

But Marinoff changed that. It was the random nature of the attack on any police who crossed his path that wormed into the collective psyche of the force. Suddenly, the uniform that had been a blue shield had turned into a gunman's target, and it wasn't a comfortable feeling.

IT got worse. One month and two days after Marinoff died by the side of the highway, lightning struck again.

A stolen Commodore filled with gelignite was parked outside the Russell Street police complex, then the force's communications and crime centre. The car bomb was designed to explode just after 1pm, when police would be in the street, going to lunch. As a segue to this display of cold-blooded evil, the bombers set a second bomb to explode a short time later to kill rescuers. Miraculously it didn't go off.

The bomb killed policewoman Angela Taylor, who died in hospital days later, and injured 22 people. In the circumstances, it was amazing that dozens of others weren't killed and maimed. And had the bombers been able to carry out their original plan to park the car in a courtyard inside the complex, it would have brought down the building, killing hundreds of people. Just as, nine years later, the Oklahoma car bomb did with a US federal government building.

The most frightening thing was, again, the randomness of the attack. Everyone liked Angela Taylor, a happy 21-year-old without an enemy in the world. It was the uniform she wore that got her killed. And every other police officer in Australia knew it could have been him or her.

Not just a city, but a nation, had lost its innocence. 'The implications of an outrage like this sort are so extreme,' the then Chief Commissioner of Police, Mick Miller, said. The State Premier, John Cain, echoed this view. 'I think this incident does add a terrifying dimension of violence new to Melbourne.'

Police fears that any member, on any shift, anywhere, could be a victim were heightened when Senior Constable Maurice Moore was shot five times with his own pistol in the quiet country town of Maryborough on September 27, 1986. Moore had left the station to get some milk from home for the night shift when he stumbled on two men stealing a car. One of them, a one-legged petty thief called Robert Nowell, snatched Moore's pistol and emptied it into the well-liked country cop as he was writing down details of the offence.

RISING random violence sucked police into more and more violent confrontations with armed offenders willing to kill for no apparent reason.

In August 1987, a failed Army officer recruit, Julian Knight, decided to make a name for himself by taking out his frustrations with a gun. He walked into Hoddle Street, Clifton Hill, armed with a high-powered rifle, and killed seven unarmed civilians and injured 19 more before meekly surrendering to armed police, whimpering 'don't shoot'. In December the same year, Frank Vitkovic killed eight people in the Australia Post building in Queen Street, before throwing himself through a window and falling to his death.

In October 1988, two constables, Steven Tynan and Damian Eyre, answered a routine call about a suspicious car parked in Walsh Street, South Yarra. It was an ambush. Both were murdered.

Years later, Deputy Commissioner (Operations) Bob Falconer, said he believed the series of incidents in a short time permanently altered the police culture in Victoria: 'It created an enormous change. Police found there were people out there who were prepared to kill them even if they did not know them personally. We lost something and I don't think we will ever go back.'

AFTER Walsh Street, senior police looked to the United States for a role model. The result was state-of-the-art 'firearms and operational survival training' for all Victorian police. Even the quasi-military name smacked of urban warfare.

Police were taught how to draw their firearms faster, to shoot more accurately and more rapidly. It was going to be seven years before the force was to acknowledge that the training was unbalanced, inadequate, and too reliant on using deadly force.

The random nature of attacks forced police to become more gun-conscious. It became an arms race. Criminals began to carry better and heavier firearms, and police were quicker to draw theirs. And to use them. But while police on the beat were coming to terms with a perceived rise in violence, there was one group in the force that was determined to meet criminals head-on.

This was the armed-robbery squad, which comprised the hard men of the force. They were the unsubtle using the unedifying against the unlawful. And, to quote the sort of bumper sticker slogan that might have appealed to many in the squad, in the 1970s and 1980s it was a case of 'when the going gets tough, the tough get going'.

For cops who liked getting results, the going was getting tougher. At least ten years before Marinoff, Russell Street and Hoddle Street there had been a subtle shift in the balance of power between police and the underworld which, ultimately, contributed to the spate of police killings.

The seeds of change were sown by a quiet Queens Counsel, Barry Beach, in 1975 when he was appointed to run an inquiry into 119 allegations of police corruption. It resulted in 32 police being charged. None were convicted, but the inquiry shone a strong light in dark places – particularly into consistent allegations of the police practice of 'verballing'. This referred to police making up written confessions and admitting into evidence the unsigned statements and swearing in court that they were true. The inquiry largely concentrated on the armed-robbery squad. Following the Beach Report, uncorroborated evidence was not deemed sufficient to convict in the criminal courts. Without the threat of the 'verbal' several major criminal groups grew powerful. Two of the 'heavy' squads – the 'consorters' and the major-crime squad – were disbanded. From the mid-1970s until intercepts on criminals' telephones were made legal in 1988, police felt they had been robbed of the tools they needed to catch and convict hardened armed robbers who would refuse to confess and were too cunning to be tricked into damaging admissions.

The criminal gangs, which began to invest armed-robbery money in drugs, became wealthy enough to retain expensive lawyers who remained on call 24 hours a day for their new class of client.

The armed-robbery squad raised the stakes. Some detectives began to use intimidation to try to gather evidence and to cultivate informers from the periphery of the criminal gangs. The squad's stock-in-trade was the early-morning armed raid. The door would be smashed in with a sledge hammer (known as 'the 12-pound key'), suspects thrown to the ground and handcuffed at the point of a shotgun.

In Victoria, armed-robbery detectives and a renegade element of the underworld were more than just professional rivals: they hated each other's guts.

SMART crooks don't kill cops. It's bad for business because it buys trouble. For police, a job becomes a crusade. The best crooks go about their business quietly and acquire wealth discreetly. But in the 1980s and early 1990s, at least two groups of criminals were driven by more than mere greed: they had a pathological aversion to police. The Russell Street bombers and the Walsh Street killers committed crimes motivated by this blind hatred, and it drove them to do things against their interests.

It was not in their interests to blow up Russell Street. It was not in their interests to shoot two innocent young policemen. 'Good crooks', as police call them, commit crimes to make money without working or going to jail. But these were criminal renegades, even by the standards of the underworld. Driven by hate and a lust for power, they enjoyed terrifying people in armed robberies as much as they enjoyed the spoils. They spoke of the 'rush' of violence, of being in control, of using weapons. They craved notoriety ... even though public attention brought police attention and a greater risk of apprehension. They may have been ultra-violent, but underneath they were neither good businessmen nor good criminals. A gun doesn't make you smart. It makes you a potential target.

THE violent deaths of armed robbers Mark Militano in 1986 and Frank Valastro in 1987 fuelled the underworld conviction that detectives, particularly the armed-robbery squad, were out of control and killing criminals rather than taking them to court. Even though the Special Operations Group (SOG) fired the shots that killed Valastro, the armed-robbery squad was involved in the investigation leading to the raid.

The underworld's accusation was stark. Criminals claimed that 'the robbers', tired of not getting convictions in court, had become a secret hit squad.

Police exploited the underworld's fear as a further tool of intimidation. They did nothing to dispel the rumours – and some actively promoted them to perpetuate the 'hit squad' myth. In one case an armed robber and murderer was under investigation by both the homicide and armed-robbery squads. A homicide detective passed a message to the wanted man: 'Come in and see us and be charged – or you could run the risk of being knocked by the robbers.' The wanted man reported to the homicide squad office next morning.

But playing on the fears of violent men courted risks. The first sign of a new level of hostilities came when word filtered back from informers that a group of criminals was planning to assassinate armed-robbery squad detectives as a payback. On one side were criminals driven by hate and its close relation, fear. On the other were detectives who epitomised a culture of bravery whose central tenet was that no good copper ever takes a backward step. They were headed for war. A silent war.

Police were told that one of the detectives was going to be hit in the driveway of his home. The killer or killers would lie in wait and kill the man as he stepped from his car – in fact, in precisely the way Federal Assistant Police Commissioner Colin Winchester was murdered in January 1989, outside his Canberra home.

But the police had a problem. They didn't know who the would-be killers were – or who the target was.

The fire was set. All it needed was a spark. When Graeme Jensen was shot dead by armed robbery detectives on October 11, 1988, the match was struck.

TWENTY-THREE

THREE SECONDS LATE

If things go wrong, you are stupid.
If nothing happens, you are courageous.

GRAEME Russell Jensen was well-known in police and underworld circles but his name meant nothing to the public until the day he went to buy a spark plug for his motor mower. What was to happen would spark death, revenge and betrayal – and would ultimately make every police force in Australia rethink the way it dealt with dangerous suspects.

At the time of his death Jensen was unemployed, single and 33 years old. He should have been in the prime of his life but his use-by date had been reached.

Born in Carlton on May 7, 1955, the youngest of five children, Jensen lived with his parents until they separated when he was seven. In the next four years he moved around Victoria and tried living with his father, mother and his sister.

After two years in the country town of Tongala he moved to

inner suburban Collingwood, where he finished his primary school education. But his real tuition was outside school hours.

He was just 11 when he was arrested for stealing money from taxis. He was also charged with eight counts of gross indecency, but was more a victim than an offender – the other person was an 18-year-old male friend of the family.

A policeman at the time wrote: 'He is inclined to be smart and is apparently a show-off.' At his Children's Court hearing a welfare officer gave evidence that Jensen was an outstanding athlete and a good scholar. He was given two years' probation.

Jensen moved from house to house. He went to Prahran High School, South Melbourne Technical School and Tally Ho Boys School until he was 14. He was made a Ward of the State in April 1969.

He left school in third form. His first job was at the Excelsior broom factory. He lasted just two weeks. At 14, he and four others used wire to pull six fur coats, valued at the then considerable sum of $2,468, through a letter opening in the door of a Melbourne shop. The arresting officer noted with cynical accuracy: 'Offender is a Ward of the State and at this early age shows every indication of becoming a hardened criminal.'

At the age of 15 Jensen became one of Australia's youngest bank robbers. Armed with a rifle, he raided the National Bank in Queens Parade, Fitzroy, and took $1,363. The arresting officer wrote: 'This lad, in my opinion, will in the future become a very active criminal.' In what was an obvious message to police who would have to deal with Jensen in the years ahead, the detective added: 'He requires firm handling.'

After Jensen was arrested for a burglary a policeman wrote: 'Will always be in trouble and will never tell the truth. Will become a very dangerous criminal. Has priors for bank hold-ups and at the moment he is only 16 years.'

At the age of 18, Jensen was involved in a brawl in a Carlton hotel. Whatever happened inside the hotel left the teenager with a sense of unfinished business. He and a friend returned and threw a hand grenade at the hotel door, injuring three men. Police claim the three survived only because the explosive power of the grenade had deteriorated with age.

He was charged and convicted over the incident, but the conviction was quashed on appeal.

It was a story to be repeated through Jensen's short life – violence, robbery, arrest and then jail. At 19 he was drinking in a Fitzroy hotel with a group of mates. At closing time the group spilled out on to the road, stopping a car.

What started as a light-hearted dispute ended when the passenger was hit with a full beer bottle, splitting open his face. He was taken to hospital and had to take eight weeks off work. Jensen pleaded guilty to assault and was sentenced to two weeks' jail.

The arresting officer made a scathing and accurate prophecy. 'He has nothing in the world in the way of assets. Is a complete violent no-hoper who does as he likes, whenever he likes. If a prediction has to be made about him, then one day he will kill someone or finish up being killed. He will always be in trouble for violence and he is an arrogant bash merchant after a bout of drinking. Will always come under notice.'

In 1977 Jensen was arrested in Canberra over three armed robberies totalling $70,000. The arresting officer, one of Australia's best investigators, Senior Detective John Weel, observed: 'Offender is a very dangerous type of person who according to his girlfriends and other persons always slept with his shotgun loaded under his bed. When arrested also had the weapon fully loaded in his possession. WARNING: WILL FINISH SHOOTING A POLICEMAN OR SOME OTHER PERSON HE HAS A DISLIKE TO IF GIVEN AN OPPOR-TUNITY. TREAT WITH CAUTION.'

It was hardly surprising police believed that the violent young criminal organised the armed robberies. He was eventually sentenced to ten years six months with a minimum of eight years and six months, but not before he and another career criminal, Lance Chee, assaulted a man with a cricket bat. Jensen was sentenced to 18 months over the attack.

When interviewed by Weel, Jensen remained calm and told the detective he planned to behave in jail … not because he planned to reform, but so he would be transferred to a low-security jail from which he could escape.

So confident was Jensen that he told the amused investigator he would drop him a card when he was free. He escaped from the Geelong Prison in 1981, went straight back to armed robberies – and, true to his word, he sent a card to Weel. It read: 'I told you so – Graeme.'

Rather than hiding, Jensen went back to stick-ups, robbing the Essendon branch of the National Bank with two other criminals, escaping with $9,000. When caught, he was sentenced to nine years with no minimum. He was released on May 26, 1987.

When he was freed on parole he gave a fake address – his old family home at 7 Charles Street, Carlton, where none of the family had lived since the mid-1970s.

He had no skills beyond stealing, no prospects and few, if any, friends outside the criminal world. He was badly injured in a car crash three months later, suffering a broken pelvis and a broken arm.

He had to walk with a stick for some time but, according to police, he recovered well enough to get back into armed hold-ups in a big way.

Jensen was popular in the underworld. Among his network of criminal mates was Frankie Valastro, an armed robber and drug dealer.

Within four weeks of Jensen's release in 1987, Valastro was shot dead in a police raid. Police said that when they entered Valastro's

Bentleigh house he reached down the front of his jeans and grabbed a gun, which was later proved to be faulty.

A member of the Special Operations Group fired a blast with a shotgun, which hit Valastro in the shoulder, severing an artery.

Jensen was soon regularly seeing three of his closest criminal associates – Victor Peirce, Jedd Houghton and Peter McEvoy. Like him, they were violent men who hated police.

This small sub-culture in the underworld did not see themselves as parasites living off the lawful community, but rather as a group engaged in a battle against the police.

They felt that police, or more particularly, members of the armed-robbery squad, were engaging in a strategy of picking them off, one by one. They believed that if the police lacked the evidence to put before the courts they were happy to act as judge, jury and executioner.

An associate of the loose collection of gunmen, Lindsay Rountree, would later tell police that about two months after Valastro's killing, Peirce approached him to join an underworld pact to murder two police for every criminal killed by police. Rountree said that in February 1988 he was again approached about the plan, this time by Jensen with Jedd Houghton.

Rountree told police that while many crooks talk tough about revenge and then do nothing, he had no doubt this mob was murderously serious.

According to Victor's wife, Wendy Peirce, the gang, known as the Flemington Crew, was involved in many armed robberies on banks and security vans.

Jensen and Houghton were later identified as among the bandits who robbed the Oak Park branch of the State Bank in March 1988. A shotgun was used in a failed bid to open a security door. Forensic tests later identified the weapon, a Japanese KTG model, as the gun used to kill Constables Tynan and Eyre at Walsh Street seven months later.

In 1987 there was a series of burglaries, which police believed were conducted by one gang of criminals. A police investigation, codenamed *Nightburg*, failed to crack the group.

In 1988 the tactical investigation group started a new inquiry, codenamed *Hawk*. Members of the armed-robbery squad helped in the investigation, doing surveillance and searches. Several known criminals were identified as suspects. They included Houghton, McEvoy, Peirce and Jensen.

Jensen was not a prime target of *Hawk* but was swept up in the investigation. He was charged with receiving a stolen jacket.

On January 18, 1988, four bandits robbed the ANZ Ringwood branch. As with all bank robberies, the armed-robbery squad headed the investigation.

The underworld is full of fickle friendships, shifting alliances, divided loyalties, greed and treachery. Today's best friends are tomorrow's sworn enemies. Today's lovers are tomorrow's police informers.

Detectives' greatest assets are informers prepared to betray confidences and contacts – often for a price.

Soon after the Ringwood robbery, a woman rang the anonymous Crime Stoppers number, and said two of the men involved in the armed robbery were Bruce Farrell and Victor George Peirce.

The source was impeccable. The woman was closely connected to the gang. Police were so impressed with the quality of the information they paid her $6,000 for the tip that she knew would almost certainly put her lover in jail.

Three detectives from the armed-robbery squad – Paul Mullett, Robert Hill and William Coburn – visited the woman at her Elwood flat on May 3, 1988. She agreed to become their secret informer.

On the basis of their insider the armed,robbery squad began an operation codenamed *No-Name* to investigate the raid. Farrell was given the target number 58/88. Two weeks later the Bureau of Criminal Intelligence put Farrell under continuous surveillance as part of *No-Name*.

On May 19, police suspected Farrell was planning to rob a bank but when they followed him they found him at a funeral at St Joseph's Church, Malvern. The wait went on. On June 2 the woman told detectives that Farrell and Peirce were planning another job. Police followed Farrell to the ANZ branch in Bell Street, Preston. Farrell left his car and stood staring at the bank. He went to a nearby bus shelter where he sat watching the bank. He didn't board any buses that stopped. He didn't need to. He had a car to drive home. To police it was obvious he was observing a potential target, committing to memory movements of staff at the bank.

In August, police received further information that the gang had changed targets and was planning to rob a bank in Boronia.

On August 30 police followed Farrell to the complex, where he met Jedd Houghton, who had arrived on a green trailbike with altered number plates. The two men appeared to 'case' the National Bank branch. Next day the two men again met and checked the National Bank and the Commonwealth Bank branches.

Houghton and Farrell walked back to Houghton's motorbike on the top floor of the car park to find his helmet had been stolen. They pushed the bike out of sight and Farrell drove Houghton to Balmain Street, Richmond.

About a week later, police followed Farrell back to the shopping centre.

They saw him meet Jensen, who arrived in a blue Commodore station wagon registered to Joan Hegarty, mother of his new de facto, Sandra Faure, former wife of the notorious Keith Faure, one of the most dangerous criminals in Australia.

It was not a lucky car. The station wagon, registered ATO 098, had been used in a fatal armed robbery, but not by Jensen. On December 29, 1987, Keith Faure had gone to rob a

Thornbury jewellery shop. He shot dead Mario Sassano in front of his wife and child. The Commodore was the getaway car. Sandra was the driver.

Faure was later sentenced to a further 11 years over the robbery. The couple decided to end their marriage early in 1988. Within months Jensen had moved in with Keith's wife.

On September 7 the woman informer told police that Farrell was to meet Jensen and Peirce in South Yarra to plan the robbery. Police photographed the meeting. On September 12, Jensen and Farrell were seen at Boronia looking at the ANZ bank, following Armaguard guards and generally studying the area. On September 19, Farrell met Jensen, Peirce and Houghton outside the ANZ bank. It looked as if the job would be on within days.

But on September 25 the team changed plans again. The Boronia raid was off; the new target was to be a gem dealer in Montrose. The next day Farrell was seen casing the area, driving down the dealer's street, but not stopping.

On October 5, Farrell and Jensen met in York Street, South Melbourne, and police followed the Commodore back to Moray Court, Narre Warren.

It was only then that they were able to confirm where Jensen was living.

Police had plenty of pictures, lots of suspicions and intelligence that the gang was about to pull a job, but no date and no evidence. Police surveillance is costly and never open-ended. It was decided it was time to move on what they had. On October 6, police arrested Lindsay Rountree in Euroa over the Ringwood armed robbery.

Rountree admitted his role and said the other three were Peirce, Farrell and Paul Prideaux. Rountree was later convicted of the offence but Peirce, Farrell and Prideaux were not.

Rountree claimed that during the arrest detectives told him they were planning to kill Peirce. Rountree passed this on to his wife when she visited him in Pentridge. On October 10, Mrs Rountree met Victor Peirce in a car at the Mountain Gate Shopping Centre and warned him that police were out to kill him. That evening, Wendy Peirce rang Jensen to tell him of the alleged threats. Jensen and Wendy Peirce were also lovers. Police put Victor Peirce under surveillance but, as often happened, he slipped the net.

Meanwhile, another armed-robbery squad crew, led by Detective Sergeant Peter Butts, was investigating the murder of a security guard, Dominic Hefti, in a Brunswick supermarket robbery on July 11, 1988.

Butts went on leave on September 26, but kept in contact with the office to receive regular briefings on *Operation No-Name*, because he strongly suspected Peirce and Jensen of the Hefti killing.

Butts and his team had been told by several informers that Peirce and Jensen had pulled the job as Hefti, a Swiss migrant, and another security guard were about to pick up $33,000 takings from the supermarket. A lone bandit jumped Hefti – they struggled and each fired two shots. Hefti was fatally wounded and the robber was also shot, leaving bloodstains at the scene. Detectives suspected Jensen was the injured bandit.

Police were confident that DNA testing of the blood would eventually identify the killer.

After the arrest of Rountree and Farrell, and the planned arrest of Peirce on the Ringwood job, it was clear that it was time to move on the Hefti shooting.

Police were confident they were on the point of crushing one of Australia's most prolific, and violent, armed-robbery gangs.

Butts cancelled his leave and was in his office at 7am on October 10 so Mullett could brief him on latest developments. After the briefing Butts decided it was time to act.

His plan was to arrest Jensen the next day and charge him with murder. He intended to question Jensen over the murder but he knew the professional criminal would refuse to answer questions.

He had several informers, inside and outside jail, who had identified Jensen and Peirce as the robbers. He had a photofit, which looked like Jensen. He knew the target had been seen the previous month casing banks and following an Armaguard van.

Butts decided it was enough to go on. But he knew that ultimately his case would live or die on the results of the DNA tests and was confident that the blood results would prove that Jensen was the mystery bandit who'd killed Hefti. On his first day back at work he told seven other members of the squad that it was time to grab Jensen for the Hefti job.

The eight-man arrest team comprised:

- Peter Leslie Butts, who joined the force in February 1972 and graduated in May 1974. He worked general duties, traffic, CIB and community policing before going to the armed-robbery squad as a supervisor in January 1988.
- Senior Detective Robert John Hill, who joined the force in January 1978 and served in a variety of positions before joining the squad in March 1988.
- Glen Robert Saunders, who joined in February 1976 and was appointed to the squad in May 1988 as a senior detective.
- Senior Detective Donald William Nash Smith joined the force in May 1978 and joined the squad from Frankston CIB in April 1988.
- William John Coburn, a policeman for nine years and a senior detective in the armed-robbery squad for six months.
- Jeff Forti joined in April 1978 and moved to the armed-robbery squad as a senior detective in March 1988.
- Rodney Thomas Grimshaw joined the force in 1978 and was appointed to the armed-robbery squad soon after.
- Christopher Ferguson joined the force in April 1974 and worked in several areas before becoming a police law instructor as a sergeant. He transferred to the armed-

robbery squad on the day of the briefing and the day before the Jensen arrest. He was to spend the next seven years dwelling over the events of those two days.

WHEN Sandra Faure woke at 7.30am and began to get her two children ready for school, the eight detectives had already been at work for an hour. Butts had ordered them to meet at Dandenong police station at 6.30am.

By 7.30am the detectives had parked their three unmarked police cars next to the weatherboard Mechanics Institute Hall in Webb Street, Narre Warren, just over two kilometres from Jensen's house in Moray Court. The detectives moved to the spot so they could keep in radio communication with the surveillance police who were tailing Jensen.

They were in position behind the hall in a car park, but it was unsatisfactory because it offered a poor view of Webb Street and they could be seen from the road. The team decided to move to a spot further away from the Princes Highway corner, between two sheds at a local transport depot. It offered a better view of the street but the tin sheds were set about 100 metres from the road along a bumpy dirt track at least 500 metres north of the highway. At this point, police had no set plan on where to arrest Jensen. First, Butts wanted confirmation that Jensen was at Moray Court.

Meanwhile, Sandra Faure was going through the same mundane domestic routine as thousands of other parents. She got the children breakfast, put them into the blue Commodore station wagon and took them to school, leaving at 8.35am.

What she didn't know was that several carloads of surveillance police, known as the 'dogs', were following. Jensen, never an early riser, stayed in bed. He had moved in with Faure in June that year, after beginning a serious relationship the previous month.

When Sandra returned home she did housework until about

10am, then got breakfast for her sleeping de facto. He ate, read a newspaper and got up about midday to watch *The Postman Always Rings Twice* on television. Faure continued doing chores, including cleaning the car and hosing the driveway, with hidden surveillance police watching every move.

It is possible that Jensen had known for several days he was under surveillance.

Much later, investigators would be told that a surveillance policeman having a relationship with a woman told her they were working on Jensen. She said she had passed this information on to a friend of Jensen's. It is impossible to know if this were true but, at least four days before the shooting, Jensen told Faure he had been warned he was being followed.

The stakeout meant hours of boredom for the watchers. The detectives could do little until they received confirmation Jensen was in the house. After a long discussion, they decided that if they could isolate him they would attempt a textbook 'mobile intercept' of his car.

In theory, the plan was to perform a simple 'box' intercept: when Jensen pulled up at the lights or a shop, two police cars would move in on either side of his car and, using a pincer movement, sweep in front and slightly across his path, blocking forward movement.

Butts's car would then move in behind, blocking any attempt to reverse.

They were relying on the 'five Ss' to conduct the operation – surveillance, speed, surprise, superiority of numbers and safety. Well, that was the theory.

The police sat around, some smoking, others chatting while they waited. Some took their bulletproof vests out of the cars but because the vests are hot and uncomfortable to wear none actually put them on.

Which is why the vests were back in the car boots when Butts got the message from the 'dogs' that the man they believed was Jensen was on the move.

It was 3.20pm.

It took Jensen just three minutes to drive the 2.4 kilometres to a nearby mower shop in a small shopping strip off the Princes Highway. The armed-robbery squad detectives saw the car go past but did not immediately make their move.

Butts called them together and they waited for confirmation that Jensen was in the car. Jensen parked his car near a tree in the gravel car park outside a row of shops. He got out and walked about ten metres into the Mower City store to get the spark plug he needed. It was 3.23pm.

But the surveillance police had a problem. They weren't positive it was the right man. Two of the eight surveillance police, Senior Detective Ashley Perry and Senior Detective Ross Coles, went separately into the shop. Both identified Jensen.

It was 3.25pm.

The police cars were parked in a line in readiness. Forti was driving the first car, with Smith in the passenger seat with a shotgun and Saunders in the rear. The other car was driven by Coburn with Hill, also with a shotgun, in the front seat and Grimshaw in the rear. The driver of the third car was Butts, with Ferguson as the passenger.

The original plan, to grab Jensen before he could get out of the car, was scrapped because the positive identification came too late. Butts gave last-minute instructions to the men in the first two cars. If the man in the blue Commodore was Jensen, they would grab him when he got back into his car and before he drove off, he said.

The new plan was hatched in the two minutes that Jensen was in the shop. The logic was that they should grab him in case he was heading off to pick up Faure's two children from school; they did not want to endanger children in a potentially dangerous arrest.

Smith's car was to go to the right, Coburn's to the left and Butts to the rear to block Jensen's Commodore. The detectives figured they had about a two-second margin of error to surprise Jensen before he could start shooting.

If everything went to plan the first two police cars would stop close enough to the target's car that he would be caught inside the vehicle's cabin and arrested on the spot.

But it didn't go to plan.

Butts was still giving last-second instructions when the first two police cars began to move. By the time he was behind the wheel the first two cars were already heading down the bumpy lane. He was at least five seconds behind. A passing car stretched the delay and by the time they turned right on to the bitumen Butts was 30 to 50 metres behind.

It was to prove a crucial gap.

Meanwhile, Jensen was in no hurry. He wandered back to his car, opened the driver's door and sat behind the wheel. Police estimated that for the next 20 seconds, he looked down and was doing something with his hands. He was probably checking that the spark plug he had just bought was the one he needed for the mower.

It was 3.27.

Jensen started the motor and slipped the automatic gearshift into reverse.

Surveillance police, seeing the reverse lights go on, and believing the armed-robbery squad was late, got ready to continue tailing their target.

Just then the cars driven by Forti and Coburn pulled into the 40-metre gravel car park and headed straight for the station wagon. Forti looked in his mirror and saw Coburn was just behind him. He saw that Jensen's car could not go forward because a tree blocked it in.

He slammed to a halt on the right, parallel to the rear wheel.

A second later Coburn's car pulled up on the left-hand side of the station wagon.

But after eight hours of waiting to move, the third car was three seconds late.

It wasn't his fault, but at the business end of the operation Butts was 50 metres behind, just entering the car park, as his partners stopped either side of the station wagon.

If Jensen had not had the car running and in gear then it might not have mattered, but that – and the gap left directly behind him – gave him a chance of escape.

A fatal opportunity.

It might have been a textbook manoeuvre, but Jensen wasn't following the textbook. He gunned the motor. Wheels spinning, he sped off in reverse.

The arrest, planned for more than a day, collapsed in seconds. Saunders and Forti jumped out of their car and drew their service revolvers. Hill, holding a shotgun, and Grimshaw, with a revolver, jumped from the second car.

The detectives were yelling: 'Police. Stop. Police!' As Coburn pulled up, he realised Jensen was reversing. He swung the wheel to the right to try and block him, but it was already too late.

As Smith was getting out of the first car, he testified later, he heard Saunders yell: 'Police. Stop. Police,' and 'He's got a gun.'

Smith later told the inquest he had to grab the passenger door of his car and hold it in as Jensen reversed towards it for fear it would be ripped from the hinges.

Smith claimed that Jensen was holding a gun in his right hand although the driver's side window was still wound up. Smith said he'd taken aim with his shotgun when he'd seen Jensen's gun, but hadn't fired because Saunders ran into the line of fire, chasing the station wagon on foot. Grimshaw had to jump out of the Commodore's way as it reversed.

He said later he'd heard the warning that Jensen had a gun but did not see the weapon. He said Jensen was driving with only his left hand on the wheel.

Grimshaw took aim and had a clear shot at Jensen until Hill, running after the target, veered into the line of fire. Grimshaw did not pull the trigger.

Coburn, realising Jensen might get away from the car park, started doing a U-turn to give chase. Grimshaw jumped in the passenger side with him.

Coburn said he saw the gun in Jensen's right hand. He said it was being carried, rather than pointed at any police officer. As he was doing a U-turn two shots were fired by Saunders with his police issue .38 calibre Smith & Wesson five-shot, snub-nose revolver, serial number 208.

One bullet hit the driver's door, piercing the outer skin of the vehicle but not entering the cabin.

It might have looked like a scene in a B-grade action movie, but there were no cameras and no one was firing blanks. These were real cops, a real robber and real bullets in a shopping area where ordinary people were going about their daily business.

Margaret Gordon and her husband Roger owned and operated the Narre Warren Produce Store, next to Mower City. Mrs Gordon arrived at the store with her two-year-old daughter, Kate, about 3.30pm that day. She parked her red and silver Ford to the right of the windmill in the car park close to the Webb Street exit. Having to take packages into the shop, she left her daughter secure in her car seat. She dropped the packages, greeted her husband, and then started back to the car to collect her daughter.

It was then, through the window, she saw unmarked police cars hurtling into the car park, men with guns jump out and Jensen's Commodore screaming in reverse. She heard shouting but could not make out the words over the noise of the cars and the flying gravel.

Then she heard a shot, and was filled with dread. 'I shouted to my husband that Kate was still in the car,' she later told investigators.

Roger Gordon ran from the shop towards his daughter – into the middle of a gunfight. Desperate to protect his daughter, he jumped straight in front of one of the police cars, forcing it to stop.

'Roger yelled out something along the lines, "What do you think you're doing?" The driver slowed, wound his window right down. I heard him yell the word "Police",' Mrs Gordon was to recall.

'The cars kept going and Roger collected Kate.'

Coburn later confirmed the incident, saying he saw a man run from a shop waving his arms and yelling frantically, then stepping into the path of the police car. The police and Jensen all passed within metres of the toddler, who was oblivious to the events surrounding her.

Forti later told the coroner that what happens in such a situation can rarely be accurately predicted – and while theoretical police training assisted, it was different on the street. He said the police courses 'are well and good when you're sitting in the theatre watching them, but when it really happens you don't know why you do things. You just do it.'

The plan had already begun to unravel when Butts's car reached the car park a fraction late. He saw the reversing Commodore and detectives on foot chasing it. Ferguson yelled from the passenger seat: 'Ram him! Ram him!' Butts wrenched the wheel, planning to hit the station wagon square in the tail. Jensen instantly moved to pass Butts's car on the inside. The policeman swung the wheel hard left to try to hit the station wagon but because he was on gravel his car went straight on.

Jensen's car clipped a parked Holden Kingswood, which helped straighten his course towards the Webb Street exit, and he kept going.

If he hadn't hit the Kingswood he probably would have careered into the nearby shop window.

As Jensen's car passed the passenger side of the police car Ferguson said he saw that Jensen had a sawn-off weapon 'sort of resting on the side of the door'.

He yelled to Butts: 'Look out, he's got a gun.' Ferguson jumped out and joined the chase. 'If things go wrong, you are stupid. If nothing happens, you are courageous,' he later told the inquest.

Butts did a U-turn and fell in behind Coburn's car to give chase. The five other detectives, two with shotguns and three with handguns, were on foot. It might have looked like an episode of *Keystone Cops* but it was to end in one man's death that day, and several more later.

Butts's and Coburn's police vehicles nearly collided as they tried to enter Webb Street, chasing Jensen. Their quarry reversed out of the car park just as the detectives reached the roadside. He slammed the car into forward gear, but his position meant he had to pass the police again to get away. Saunders said he believed Jensen was still pointing the gun in his direction and so fired another shot, his third. As the car sped away he fired two more. It was later established that of Saunders' five shots, one struck the vehicle, lodging in the front door.

As Saunders fired his third shot, Hill pulled the trigger on his shotgun, shattering the driver's side window. He was directly opposite Jensen at a distance of a few metres.

Jensen flung his right arm up and across his forehead in a protective motion, the police said later. Two of the nine solid slugs contained in the SG cartridge hit Jensen's right forearm, breaking the bone in the arm. He also had a bullet nick on the left arm, which the coroner believed meant he was driving with his left hand and shielding his head with the right when he was struck by the first shotgun blast. But the injuries were not enough to stop Jensen, who planted his foot to the floor.

Hill pumped the shotgun and fired a second shot from the edge of the gravel car park through the back windscreen of the car.

Forensic evidence at the inquest indicated the second shotgun shot was fired when Jensen's car was at least ten metres away, but no one accurately established the distance beyond doubt.

The rapidly accelerating car suddenly slowed before crashing into a street sign and an electricity pole.

Forti told the inquest that during the chase Jensen held a sawn-off firearm in his right hand, 'making it obvious to everyone chasing him that he had a gun'. The time between the two shotgun blasts was a matter of controversy for seven years after the incident.

Forti later said the shots followed immediately one after the other: 'As quick as you could click your fingers; it was just bang, bang.'

Police argued they were trained to fire the shotgun in multiples of two rounds in quick succession.

As police ran to Jensen's crashed car, Forti yelled: 'Be careful. He's got a gun,' he said later.

Saunders was the first to the car, and trained his gun on Jensen. The other members were there within a split second. Coburn could see Jensen bleeding profusely from a head wound. He felt for a pulse in his neck and found none.

Grimshaw opened the passenger door and got in.

Grimshaw didn't see the fatal shot. He had been leaning back in the car driven by Coburn looking for a portable blue flashing light to stick on top of the car because he expected Jensen would get away and there would be a high-speed chase.

Grimshaw said that when he got in Jensen's car he kept his gun pointed at the fatally wounded man. He said he leaned over and saw a sawn-off, bolt-action firearm on the floor near the driver's legs.

Of the nine balls fired in the second shotgun blast the fatal one lodged in Jensen's head, three were found in the car boot, two in the driver's headrest and three in the windscreen. He had died instantly.

A ballistics expert, Senior Constable Alan Pringle, later found that the gun police said they found in Jensen's car was not cocked for firing. It was not loaded and the magazine in the weapon was upside down, meaning the bolt action could not load bullets into the breech to be fired. Two .22 bullets were found in the car. The serial number of the weapon had been removed.

Forti gave evidence that he opened the boot of one of the police cars, removed a towel, walked back to the Commodore and handed it to Grimshaw, who used it to cover Jensen's head. There were repeated allegations that police had the sawn-off weapon hidden in the towel and planted it in the car.

No civilian witness saw Jensen with the gun – but no one said they saw the gun planted, either. The towel was later destroyed without being tested for gun residue. Ultimately the coroner dismissed the gun 'plant' theory, saying: 'There is no evidence to support this suggestion.'

A local doctor, Jari Hryckow, was called to examine the body. He declared life extinct. It was 3.40pm.

The arrest gone wrong would dog police for years. There were many questions that would be raised, from the sensible to the stupid, but the most important was, why would an experienced criminal like Jensen wave a non-operational firearm at armed police when he must have known his actions could result in them shooting to kill?

But the only man who could have answered that question was already dead.

Dead men tell no tales.

WHEN Jensen left to get the spark plug, Sandra Faure was preparing vegetables for dinner.

At 3.45pm her son arrived home from school and said: 'Mum, there's been a shooting.' She asked where, and the boy replied: 'Down in Webb Street.'

'I said, "That's where Graeme went." He said, "Don't worry, Graeme will be all right." I thought that something was wrong, as Graeme should have only been ten minutes.'

About ten minutes later four detectives arrived at the house with a search warrant. She asked one of the police: 'Graeme's dead, isn't he?'

He replied that uniformed police would be there shortly. A police inspector arrived and told her Jensen was dead. Faure was driven to the scene by a neighbour. She said later that a policewoman asked her: 'Are you Wendy?' Faure believed this meant that police thought she was Wendy Peirce and that detectives actually intended to arrest Victor Peirce, not Jensen.

The policewoman, Debra Keogh, said when Faure had given her name and address, Keogh had mistakenly thought she knew someone who lived in the same street and had said: 'You'd know Wendy then, would you?' But Keogh had the wrong street; she was referring to Wendy Ionescu of Murrell Court, not Moray Court. Faure became hysterical and yelled: 'Why, you coppers shot the wrong person, didn't you? You thought Graeme was someone else, didn't you?'

GRAEME Jensen died an innocent man. Though guilty of many violent crimes, Dominic Hefti's murder was not one of them.

But even after his death – or perhaps especially after his death – police wanted to prove Jensen was Hefti's killer. They had a mortician dress Jensen with a wig as worn by one of the bandits, and had a witness attempt to identify him as the robber. It was a waste of time; the blood tests proved it couldn't have been him. The killer's blood, found at the scene, was type AO. Jensen's was not.

Ironically, if Jensen hadn't run he wouldn't have had much to fear.

According to the evidence, he would have been charged with having a gun and nothing else.

Then why did he flee – and supposedly wave an ineffective weapon at police?

The possession of the weapon may have been enough to put him in jail.

He may have feared, wrongly, that police had enough evidence to charge him with some of the armed robberies he had committed. Or was it simply that he was a victim of the campaign of whispered threats between armed robbers and the armed-robbery squad, and feared he was to be murdered in the car park that afternoon?

After all, he had been 'warned' only the previous night that police intended to kill his mate and fellow armed robber, Victor Peirce. Police had also killed Frankie Valastro, another good friend, the previous year.

Rightly or wrongly, Jensen's gang believed that police, particularly some armed robbery detectives, were out of control and on a killing spree.

If Rountree is to be believed, Jensen was so concerned and angry he was prepared to form a pact to kill two police for every criminal killed.

So when he saw armed police leaping from cars to surround him it is possible he instinctively tried to escape in a blind panic. Police argued it was conceivable, even likely, he could have waved a firearm at police as a warning to keep away, to buy himself a few precious seconds. The fact the rifle magazine was jammed in upside down, as if by a man in panic driving one-handed, bears this out.

Other options were also canvassed.

Did police, lacking evidence to convict Jensen, decide to murder the suspect? It is a theory that does not stand up. Why would eight detectives, including one who joined the squad only days before, conspire to murder a man in front of witnesses in a suburban shopping strip?

Another theory was that when he went to escape, police believed Jensen was armed and fired in self-defence, only to find they were mistaken. Then a gun was planted to make sure there would be no later arguments. The coroner later dismissed this option.

Why Jensen did what he did that day will never be known.

AT 3pm that day, a daily ritual was being carried out on the ninth floor St Kilda Road office of the homicide squad. It was the passing of the beeper. Each homicide crew was kept busy with ongoing investigations and court commitments but each had to take its turn as the on-call crew, which carried that beeper.

From 3pm until the next morning a crew had to deal with any murders in Victoria. Most days the beeper remained silent, but that day it started a chain of events that would last seven years and change lives forever.

In charge of Crew One was Detective Senior Sergeant John Noonan, a tough, no-nonsense man who makes up for his lack of subtlety with a strong sense of dedication. Things are either black or white with Noonan. He was pursuing inquiries east of the city that day when he was told that police had killed a man in Narre Warren, and that he was in charge of the investigation. He arrived at the scene at 4.30pm.

Noonan's number two was Detective Sergeant John Hill, a quiet veteran of the squad who was well-respected by his peers as a thorough investigator. He left St Kilda Road with Senior Detectives Jim Conomy and Kevin Casey. They arrived at the scene at 4.56pm.

Homicide detectives dread some deaths more than others. The death of a child, multiple murders, and serial killers all place different pressures on investigators. But a killing where police are involved is seen as a potential minefield.

The detectives have sympathy for the shooter, who is often

dazed and distressed, wanting assurances that he or she has done the right thing and that the taking of the life was justified. Senior police are there, demanding answers so that they can brief the media, who usually arrive at the scene before the body is cold.

Investigators also know that some time in the future they will have to give evidence before the coroner, and that one slip can be viewed as an attempt to cover up for fellow police.

The eight armed-robbery squad members stood around Jensen's car but eventually moved into a nearby antique shop for about 30 minutes to discuss what had happened. Detective Inspector John Sharp, head of the armed-robbery squad, also wanted a briefing.

Noonan walked into the antique shop and directed the eight men to drive to the Berwick police station for questioning.

When Noonan left to take statements from the police, Hill took control of the crime scene, gathered evidence and took statements from eye witnesses.

The two shooters, Hill and Saunders, were kept in separate rooms so they could not be accused of concocting a story together. But the remaining six members were able to sit and discuss their recollections in a mess room at the Berwick station.

Homicide-squad members took Hill and Saunders back to the St Kilda Road police complex. They were interviewed separately.

The six other members returned to their St Kilda Road office and began to compile their written statements. This was later to be criticised time and again because it gave them the chance to coordinate their stories. If there were disparities, kinks could be ironed out before they committed their versions to paper.

One of the last things Noonan told the armed-robbery squad detectives before they were allowed to leave was that they had to be back at the scene early the next morning for a full video re-enactment.

At the beginning Hill was not in charge of the investigation but events 13 hours later were to change that.

Even though Crew One members obviously had their hands full with the Jensen shooting, they were still on call. (This system has since been changed: when a crew gets a job now another homicide group moves up to be on call, but in 1988 the first crew had to plough on.)

Noonan had been in bed only about three hours when his phone woke him. It was 5.27am. Two police had been murdered in Walsh Street and he was in charge of the investigation.

Noonan did not contact his second-in-command that morning to attend the scene; he knew that Hill was required in the Supreme Court that day to give evidence in another case.

It was obvious Noonan could not oversee both the Jensen and Walsh Street shootings. That morning Hill rang Noonan, who was still at Walsh Street, and offered to help. Noonan said he would handle the murders of the two police while Hill would prepare the brief on the Jensen killing.

The decision cost Noonan the next two and a half years. It cost Hill his life.

Graeme Jensen's criminal record

November 9, 1966
Larceny from motor cars (three counts).
Larceny of bicycles.
Gross indecency with male person (eight counts).
Two years' probation.
September 3, 1967
Illegal use of a motor car.
October 14, 1968
Illegal use of a motor car.
Two years' probation.

May 20, 1969
Unlicensed driving, illegal use of a motor car, receiving.
February 2, 1969
Larceny.
May 5, 1970
Larceny from a shop.
52 weeks' probation.
July 3, 1970
Armed robbery.
Two years, youth training centre.
Illegal use of a motor car.
One year, youth training centre.
May 18, 1971
Illegal use of motor cars (two counts).
Attempted illegal use of a motor car.
Escaped youth training centre.
Larceny in a dwelling.
15 months, youth training centre.

March 3, 1972
Housebreaking and stealing (two counts).
Escape from youth training centre.
Six months, youth training centre.
February 26, 1973
Exceeding .05 blood alcohol.
Banned from obtaining licence for two years, fined $50.
Unlicensed driving.
One month's jail.
Failing to exchange name and address after an accident.
$50 fine.

February 1, 1974
Larceny, housebreaking and stealing, possession of
housebreaking implements.
Three years' jail.
May 20, 1974
Assault with a weapon.
14 days' jail.
October 2, 1978
Robbery in company (three counts).
10 years six months' jail.
September 3, 1979
Wounding with intent to do grievous bodily harm.
Three years' jail.
October 1, 1981
Escape from jail.
Six months' jail.
Theft of motor car (two counts).
12 months' jail on each count.
Armed robbery.
Nine years' jail.

TWENTY-FOUR

THIRTEEN HOURS LATER

'… for God's sake get an ambulance.'

PETER Ellis was an early riser. As manager of a South Yarra newsagency, he had no choice. On Wednesday October 12, 1988, he was up before dawn, as usual, when he glanced out the bedroom window of his flat at 222 Walsh Street, South Yarra.

He saw a white Holden Commodore in the street with its bonnet up, the driver's side door open and the rear passenger side vent window smashed.

He also saw a person with his head under the bonnet, possibly wearing blue clothes. It was 4.15am. Ellis made a mental note of the registration number because he believed joy riders had dumped the car.

He then wheeled his bicycle out and headed for work.

Around 4.30, Mr Ellis rang the Prahran police station to report the car, giving the registration number as BDQ 988. The watch-house keeper contacted the police communications centre, D24, with the report. It was 4.34am.

Three minutes later a D24 operator contacted a divisional van in the area to deal with the routine call. 'Prahran 311, if you could slip down to Walsh Street in South Yarra, Mr Ellis, of 222 Walsh Street, states there's a white Holden sedan, not known what the rego is, got the lights on and the smashed windows in the middle of the road. Comes from Prahran at 4.38am.'

Constable Damian Eyre, the observer in the van, grabbed the microphone and replied: 'Yeah, Prahran 311, received that,' then gave his police number, 26483.

The call would normally have gone to the South Melbourne van, which that night was staffed by a policeman and police-woman, but it was tied up with a suicide in St Kilda. Prahran 311 was clear, so it got the job.

For the two young men in the police car, it was a routine call. Steven Tynan had been a policeman for two years and nine months. He had already shot a man in the line of duty ten days before. He had been so upset by the incident he had taken time off, and had returned to duty just three days earlier.

Damian Eyre, 20, was from a police family. He had been in the job for six months after graduating from the police academy in April 1988. He had failed in his first bid to join but had passed the admission test on the second attempt. His father, Frank, was a police reservist in Shepparton and his brother a Melbourne detective.

It took about seven minutes for the pair to reach the suspect sedan.

Tynan parked the divisional van behind the Holden. Both vehicles were facing north.

Eyre got out of the passenger side of the van and walked to the car.

He glanced at the registration sticker on the front window and jotted down the number and expiry date on a sheet of paper on his clipboard.

At the same time his partner went to the open driver's door and slipped behind the wheel.

Eyre then walked around the car and squatted next to Tynan, who was still in the car. They would have seen that the ignition lock was broken so that the car could be started without a key.

Tynan had started to get out of the car when the shotgun blast hit him. The deadly force threw him back into the car, where he collapsed, with his head between the front bucket seats. It was 4.48am.

Eyre began to rise from the squatting position when he was shot across his back in the upper left shoulder, also with a shotgun. It should have been enough to stop anyone dead, but Eyre somehow rose and turned to face his attacker. He grabbed the gunman and fought. Police believe the shotgun discharged twice more, one blast hitting the wall of a Walsh Street house.

Even though he was seriously, but not fatally, wounded, Eyre continued to fight until a second man slipped up next to him and grabbed the policeman's service .38 revolver from its holster, put it to the policeman's head and fired.

Eyre collapsed and was shot again in the back as he lay next to the rear driver's side wheel of the stolen car. He was already dying when the second revolver bullet hit him.

It all took about one minute. At 4.49, police started to get the first calls from residents with reports of gunfire. Within two minutes, Sergeant Ron Beaton began calling Prahran 311 for a response.

There was silence.

After a few calls, Beaton called for other units to respond.

The duty inspector, who was listening from South Melbourne police station, asked for an update and was told there were several reports of shots fired but no word from Prahran 311.

It didn't sound good. Within moments several units were heading to Walsh Street. Nothing gets a response from police as quickly as the suggestion that fellow police are in trouble.

The first car into the street was a South Melbourne unit.

South Melbourne: 'South 250, urgent, South 250, urgent.'

D24: 'Unit calling?'

South Melbourne: 'South Melbourne 250. Two members down, urgent.'

D24: 'Roger, need an ambulance?'

South Melbourne: '250, urgent. Yes, an ambulance please. Two members down.'

Police unit: 'City West 250, do you need assistance?'

D24: 'City West 250, affirmative.'

South Melbourne: 'South Melbourne 250, for God's sake get an ambulance.'

D24: 'Yeah, we're getting one now.'

South Melbourne: 'South Melbourne 250. We need an ambulance. We've got two members down with gunshot wounds outside 222 Walsh Street, 222 Walsh Street.'

D24: 'All members take care.'

Steven Tynan and Damian Eyre were fit and strong but their wounds were massive. A nursing sister, Jillian Ball, came from a nearby flat to offer help. Surprisingly, both victims were still clinging to life when the ambulances arrived, but nothing could undo the gunmen's terrible handiwork.

Eyre was rushed to the Alfred Hospital, Tynan to Prince Henry's. They were dead an arrival.

A MURDER, any murder, is handled by the on-call homicide-squad crew, headed by a Detective Senior Sergeant. On this occasion the officer in charge was John Noonan, who had just returned home from the Jensen shooting scene at Narre Warren.

Homicide detectives hate a cold trail; the first 48 hours in a murder investigation are vital.

It didn't take investigators long to get an idea of who or what they were looking for. From the moment they arrived at the scene they were faced with two possible scenarios: either the constables were killed by car thieves who were surprised by the police patrol ... or they were lured into a cold-blooded ambush.

Two things indicated the killers weren't car thieves. The car had been abandoned in the street for a long time – and the killers had come up from behind the police as they examined the vehicle. Any 'thieves' could have easily escaped without shooting police.

There was no reasonable doubt that the two young policemen were victims of a terrorist-type trap. It was obvious the gunmen planned to kill police at random, because there was no way they would have known who might have got the fatal call to go to Walsh Street that morning.

The gunmen wanted to kill police. Any police.

The Commodore had been in Walsh Street for at least 40 minutes before the divisional van arrived. Most car thieves can break in and start a vehicle in about 30 seconds.

At 3.50am a taxi driver had taken a call from his base to go to 212 Walsh Street, Prahran. He knew there was no Walsh Street in Prahran and so went straight to the South Yarra address.

The driver saw the Commodore at 3.55am. Police believe one of the gunmen called the taxi so the driver would see the sedan in the middle of the road and call the police.

As it happened, the driver saw the car, walked up to it to see if it had broken down and the motorist wanted a lift, then jumped into his cab and drove off. He did not report it to police.

The owner of the car, David Wilkinson, had parked the Commodore outside his Walsh Street flat. Two men were seen looking into the car about 12.45am. The killers broke into the car, broke the ignition lock and started the car within seconds, then did a U-turn and moved it only ten metres before stopping it in the middle of the road.

Police soon learned that two cars in adjoining Acland Street had been broken into and a brown, cotton *Country Road* jumper taken from the rear seat of a Honda Civic.

The jumper was recovered a few hours after the shooting in the front yard of 252 Walsh Street. The sleeves had been cut from the jumper before it was thrown over the high front wall. Police believed one of the killers used the sleeves as a balaclava, or to hide the weapons, or possibly to cover his own sleeves.

Detectives drew up a list of criminals they believed had a sufficient hatred of police to launch a premeditated, random attack. The list was surprisingly short.

But experienced investigators did not discount the possibility of a wild card, a group of criminals who had evaded detection.

In the case of the Russell Street car bombing, the offenders were a group of armed robbers no one knew anything about.

In the Walsh Street case the field narrowed quickly. The most logical view, favoured by most investigators, was that the double murder was a direct payback for Jensen's killing just 13 hours earlier.

A huge investigation began within hours. Emotions ran high. Some police virtually declared war on the underworld. They wanted to mount raid after raid on known criminals and their relatives and associates.

Many in the force saw this reaction as justified. Others saw it as blind rage, which would do nothing to gain evidence admitted in court. The more clear-thinking members of the force knew that the day in court mattered far more than letting off steam by kicking down doors.

In the first few days senior police refused to establish a task force. Some were concerned at a potential public backlash if the murders of police were treated differently to the murders of other citizens.

But they had misread the depth of anger and the sense of outrage the community felt for two innocent young men gunned down while doing their jobs.

Eventually, a task force was set up to investigate the killings. But meanwhile, other sections of the force were conducting raids in the hope of 'cracking' the underworld.

It was an emotional time.

Some senior police were not prepared to delegate the responsibility for running the show to the men they had chosen to do the job. Others were so desperate to 'get a result' they wanted to use illegal tactics to get evidence before a court.

As pressure mounted, the inevitable happened: internal divisions split the task force.

THE police had several leads by the dawn of October 12, 1988. But even then, friends of Jensen were the most obvious suspects.

Part of police stock-in-trade is to say of any crime under investigation that they will 'keep an open mind' about who might be involved.

This calculated 'copspeak' ensures that a defence lawyer cannot pull out old quotes during a court case to embarrass investigators over something said in the heat of the moment months, or even years, before.

But this time, behind the routine charade of 'open mind' and 'several lines of inquiry being checked' the dogs were barking – loudly. Certain members of the underworld were quick to point the finger at a Melbourne crime family with enemies on both side of the law.

It was also obvious to the suspects that they were in the frame. So began a war of attrition that was to last more than four years.

The criminal clan rumoured to be behind the ambush was the Pettingills.

Within hours of the killing, the matriarch of the clan, Kath Pettingill, told one of the authors: 'It wasn't us.'

'I hate coppers but those boys didn't do anything. Our family wouldn't do that. We were not involved,' she said. 'You don't kill two innocent coppers. If you want to get back you would kill the copper who killed Graeme.'

It was the beginning of a very public battle between the police and the suspects. Newspaper reports appeared containing information that pointed towards the Pettingill family as being heavily involved.

On the other side, the Pettingills and their allies were quick to push their line to eager reporters.

So many stories appeared that it moved the then Deputy Commissioner, John Frame, to claim there was a conspiracy among sections of the underworld to try to damage the credibility of the task force investigating the Walsh Street murders.

Frame said the media was 'simply peddling and regurgitating the assertions made by some of these people who, for their own self-interest, I am sure are trying to denigrate the members of the task force.'

In fact, some police believed a few journalists lost their objectivity and were too close to the Pettingills. They claim recorded telephone intercepts showed conversations between reporters and criminals that indicated some reporters were 'taking sides'.

The Pettingills, on the other hand, believed they were portrayed unfairly in the press and claimed sections of the media were too close to the police. One member of the clan referred to a newspaper as 'Police Life', expressing the view that nothing was published in the paper that was not approved by the police.

FIVE men were charged over the Walsh Street shootings. Two others, Jedd Houghton and Gary Abdallah, also alleged to have been involved, had already been shot dead by police.

Four of those charged stood trial in the Supreme Court – Victor Peirce, his half-brother Trevor Pettingill, Peter McEvoy and Anthony Farrell. The fifth, Jason Ryan, had been indemnified to give evidence against his former friends.

The first charged was Anthony Farrell. Police thought he might have been the weak link in the gang and so would be prepared to give up his alleged co-offenders.

Farrell and his co-accused belonged to the underworld, that loose collection of individuals who live outside the law and associate with fellow criminals both in and out of prison. Myths have been built up about this antisocial sub-class, mainly because there is a perceived glamour about being on the wrong side of the law. Some people think gangsters are masterminds with the brains and the nerve to beat the system, 'anti-heroes' and 'rebels' who snub conformity to 'live their own lives'.

The truth is most are too stupid, too lazy and too immoral to make a mark in the mainstream community. They don't decide to opt out of orthodox, law-abiding society so much as drift into crime because it seems easy and smart compared with working for a living. Others, of course, are born into criminal families, condemned by breeding and circumstances to a lifetime cycle of crime and punishment.

Many criminals are 'stupid' by conventional standards – in reading, writing and comprehension, for instance – but some survive and prosper, at least until the law or even more predatory criminals catch up with them. Some develop a rat cunning, which trumps 'normal' intelligence in their bleak and brutal world. They can't read, yet can spy a police surveillance car a kilometre away. Others can barely count, yet can organise a bank robbery with split-second, military precision.

There are always clever lawyers and accountants to help them invest the money if they get lucky.

THE Pettingills were a typical criminal clan, only more so. Made out by some to be a brilliant crime cell in the Australian underworld, they are (or were) in reality not that smart – just white trash with a taste for violence, drugs, easy money and chunky gold jewellery. Many of the family members have spent most of their adult lives in jail. They are inarticulate and socially inept, but have a sharp knowledge of the criminal law and their rights.

One member of the family, Dennis Bruce Allen, was a prime example of how cunning can, for a while, outstrip conventional intelligence and formal education. Allen built a drug empire in the inner Melbourne suburb of Richmond. From 1982 to 1987 he was charged with more than 60 offences, but always managed to get bail. The sureties amounted to almost $225,000. He was able to run free because he was a big police informer who would give up other crims and help police solve crimes.

At one stage he was supplying 100 people a day with heroin from his massage parlour. The syndicate had a turnover of between $70,000 and $100,000 a week. He was able to bank $7,000 a week, and bought several houses in Richmond with drug money.

Allen, known as 'Mr Death', was involved in several murders before he died in 1987 from heart disease, aged 35.

LIKE Dennis Allen, the men who ended up standing trial over the Walsh Street double murders were not particularly clever by normal standards.

One of them was Peter David McEvoy, convicted armed robber and career criminal, and an aggressive, swaggering bully, but not respected by the hard men of the crime world.

In the mid-1970s McEvoy came to public and police notice for alleged involvement in a series of rapes in the Heidelberg area. Police alleged that McEvoy, then aged about 20, was one of two gang leaders responsible for the abduction, torture and sexual abuse of up to 24 girls. According to police who worked on the case, the abuse was probably the worst of its type in Victoria.

It was alleged at the time that for about two years a group of girls, mostly aged between 13 and 16, were forced to submit to gang rape by a group that threatened them with further physical violence if they complained to parents or police.

The girls were often forced to introduce further victims to the gang.

A policewoman who investigated the case said: 'Sometimes a victim would be told to submit or their mother or little sister would be next.'

It was alleged at the time that one victim was repeatedly bashed before collapsing on a bean bag. Another almost drowned in a swimming pool. Some of the girls were allegedly put on a 'roster' to submit to sexual abuse.

The gang of rapists was smashed when one girl eventually told her parents. McEvoy was found guilty of two counts of rape, acquitted of several more counts and three more were withdrawn.

Parents at some of the court cases were shocked at how their daughters were cross-examined by a battery of barristers working for the accused men. One policeman who interviewed McEvoy at the time said: 'He was an arrogant smart alec then who showed no remorse or normal human compassion.'

A policewoman went further: 'He was a truly evil man who frightened even some of the other people in his group.'

McEvoy has also been tried and acquitted of abduction, rape, and indecent assault on a girl under 16, aggravated burglary, and armed-robbery. In fact, in five criminal trials, McEvoy has been found not guilty. On another occasion, in 1979, the Crown withdrew three rape charges against him.

When convicted of the two counts of rape, he was sentenced

to a minimum of three years. Police say that while inside jail he made friends with a group of serious criminals and graduated from pervert to gunman.

His introduction usually came through Dennis Allen's half-brother Victor Peirce, who was a feared and, in some circles, respected criminal.

Among professional criminals, McEvoy, who is also known as 'Bubble Brain' and 'Pink Panther', was thought of as a joke.

When he went to Sydney in the early 1980s, he hit a hurdle – being sentenced to seven years with a minimum of four years' hard labour for two counts of drug trafficking.

According to police, when McEvoy returned to Melbourne after his release he teamed up with one of the better groups of armed robbers, headed by Graeme Jensen. Jensen's group would alternate with a second armed-robbery gang called the 'Sunshine Crew' to confuse investigating detectives. After a few months the second group would start pulling jobs, taking pressure off Jensen's team.

Detectives believe McEvoy was not part of the brains trust. He was never used to case banks because 'he was a bit of a dill'. But if the gang leaders thought there was a need to terrorise bank staff or customers, McEvoy was their man. 'He always liked to frighten people. He would get his rocks off doing it,' a detective said.

Police are convinced that the gang robbed the State Bank in Newmarket in November 1987. Detectives believe two members of the gang jumped into the tellers' area while McEvoy stood guard over the staff and customers before escaping with about $46,000. He was charged and convicted in 1992 of the armed-robbery of the National Australia Bank in East Bentleigh in August 1988. He was sentenced to seven years with a minimum of five and released in 1995.

While he may not have been a master planner, in jail McEvoy

learned several anti-surveillance techniques, which made him difficult to follow. He also checked any house he stayed in for police listening devices.

After Walsh Street he knew, in the jargon of the underworld, that he was 'hot'. He knew he had to be careful about what he said in case the police were listening. But he made a slip when he decided to confide in a woman during a conversation bugged by police early in 1989. Any pretence that he had nothing to do with armed robberies was dropped when he described what doing a bank job was like during late-night 'pillow talk'.

This tape was admitted as evidence at his committal but was not used in the County Court armed-robbery trial.

According to the tape, McEvoy says: 'At the time, dead set, your life is on the ... line, you know what I mean? At the wrong time during that five minutes you run into a couple of ... bank guards, you know what I mean? The wrong place at the wrong time and you're ... dead.

'They're gunna shoot ya, you know what I mean? You're gonna have to get out with your gun in the middle of a ... street shoppin' centre and have a ... gun battle with the Jacks [police] in there.'

When McEvoy became a suspect for killing Constables Tynan and Eyre, he loved to bait police. When followed by police he would drive up Walsh Street, past the scene of the crime.

THE murder trial lasted seven weeks. The accused men chose to give unsworn evidence, which was their right at the time. This meant the prosecution could not cross-examine them on their stories. Each said he was in no way involved in the murders.

The law in Victoria was later changed to ban unsworn statements.

But the police case suffered badly when their key witness,

Victor Peirce's wife Wendy, changed sides. She had made a series of statements implicating her husband and others in the murders and was put in witness protection. But by the time of the trial she had changed her mind and refused to give evidence supporting her statements.

The trial was complex. Witnesses were examined and cross-examined. But in the end, the entire police case rested on one vital question.

Would a jury – could a jury – believe the word of Jason Ryan?

Ryan, a grandson of Kath Pettingill, had changed his story many times. He stood in the box and told the court that while he had lied before, he was telling the truth this time.

It took the 12 men on the jury six days to make a decision. They took their duty seriously. Many times they returned to check evidence with the trial judge, Justice Frank Vincent.

On March 26, 1991, the jury filed back into the packed Supreme Court room. The foreman announced four verdicts of not guilty.

Some police in the court could barely control their anger. The four accused were jubilant. One cried. McEvoy yelled that he wanted an inquiry. The four men embraced, and looked as though their trauma would bond them together for life. It wasn't to be. Within months of the trial they had a falling out and two of the four were hardly speaking.

In the court, McEvoy baited police. He turned to a group behind him after the verdict and said: 'What do you think about that? … "I'll fix you, I'll fix you." Is that what you said? I'll be waiting. I'm not afraid to die.'

Outside the court, McEvoy spat at police as he was loaded into a prison van to be taken back to Pentridge, where he was still awaiting trial on armed-robbery charges. He repeated his call for an inquiry.

A grim-faced Inspector Noonan, of the Ty-Eyre task force, said that as far as he was concerned the case was closed. 'The jury has found them not guilty. They didn't find them innocent,' he said.

TWO mothers in the court had waited tensely for the verdict. Kath Pettingill sat upright and clapped when she heard the last verdict of not guilty.

'I knew they were innocent,' she crowed. 'I didn't hear the press say "hip hip hooray" for the boys. You're very biased, you're very biased.'

Later she repeated that her family had not been involved. 'We are not as bad as that. We would not do something as bad as that [Walsh Street]. One day they will find who did it. I hate coppers, but those boys [Constables Tynan and Eyre] didn't do anything.'

She said she felt for the family and friends of the two murdered police. 'My heart goes out to them. I'm a mother, too.'

Tynan's mother, Wendy Tynan, walked out after the verdict and spoke briefly to reporters on the step of the court. She paid tribute to the task force and thanked the members for their efforts. At the end, she referred to the killers of her son.

'We think that in a higher justice they will get what they deserve. They will do it again. Policemen are not safe.'

• *Three of the four men charged didn't have the brains to grab their second chance. Anthony Farrell became a hopeless junkie, Trevor Pettingill was in and out of prisons for the next 15 years and Victor Peirce was shot dead in Port Melbourne in 2002. Ironically, the man with the biggest mouth, Peter McEvoy, slipped away to country Victoria and so far has managed to keep a low profile.*

TWENTY-FIVE

SHOOT OR BE SHOT

*Jedd Houghton wouldn't be taken
by the police without a fight.*

THE tin cans and milk cartons were hardly touched by the fusillade of shots whistling through the sharp winter air. Three gunmen had fired some 60 rounds from their handguns, but few hit the targets.

Graeme Jensen, armed robber, decided it was time to get serious. He picked up one of Paul Widdicombe's two shotguns, then went to grab an SG cartridge from the gunbelt of Widdicombe, who stopped him.

'I said, "Do you know what you're putting in that?"' Widdicombe later recalled. Jensen admitted he didn't. 'I said, "Do you know what they do?"' Jensen didn't.

Widdicombe thought the easiest way to explain would be to show him. He set up an old steel barbecue plate six millimetres thick that he had found lying around the Wedderburn property where they were shooting. As Widdicombe prepared to demonstrate the potency of SG shot, Jensen's good mate and fellow armed robber, Jedd Malcolm Houghton, rode up on his trailbike. Houghton, 22, watched as Widdicombe, a Bendigo mechanic and panel-beater, loaded his gun with two standard number four shotgun shells.

He fired twice at the plate, causing a number of little dents over a 30 to 40cm diameter, before showing the plate to the onlookers, among them two other friends, Robert and Steve Baxter. Widdicombe then loaded two SG shells. An SG cartridge contains nine lead balls packed in with a polystyrene type filler. Each ball is only slightly smaller than a .38 revolver slug. In other words, firing an SG is virtually the same as firing nine .38 revolvers simultaneously, producing awesome firepower. The effect was not lost on those watching Widdicombe's impromptu demonstration.

The shotgun roared twice. The result was startling. The SG had punched four or five large holes through the steel; another ten slugs had almost penetrated. Widdicombe's display left a lasting impression on one of the men.

Two months later, Jedd Houghton rang Widdicombe from Melbourne. Could he buy some SG shells for him?

AT this stage of his short and violent life, Houghton was regarded as little more than a small-time criminal. He had, in police vernacular, not much serious 'form'.

Born in Melbourne on September 10, 1965, the third of four children, Houghton spent his adolescence in the inner -western suburbs of Flemington and Kensington, which had a reputation as a tough area. Houghton soon came to the notice of police. In September 1982, just 11 days after his 17th birthday, he was placed on probation for car theft and unlicensed driving.

Similar offences followed, although charges were adjourned without conviction. Between 1983 and November 1988, his name appeared six times in the charge book at Flemington watch-house. He was also interviewed five times at the station by uniformed police and detectives.

On May 5, 1987, Houghton was convicted of hindering police and resisting arrest, being fined $100 on each charge. On May 11 he was convicted of unlawful possession and failing to appear and was fined a total of $900. Two days later, he was fined another $450 when convicted of theft and being unlawfully on premises.

On June 12 he was arrested by police investigating the theft of a motorcycle.

Houghton was interviewed at the station and later charged with assaulting police, although he in turn complained to the police Internal Investigations Department that he had been bashed.

The incident rankled Houghton, fuelling a long-standing hatred and mistrust of police. More than a year later he would tell a friend: 'You don't understand what it's like – they don't give you a chance.'

A former girlfriend, Dawn Campone, was to tell police of driving with Houghton and being passed by a police car. 'He would make a gun with his hand and fingers and point it at them and call them "pigs".'

In April 1988, Houghton failed to answer bail. In effect, for the rest of his life, he was on the run.

Graeme Jensen also frequented the Flemington area and, although he was ten years older, it was inevitable their paths would cross. Unlike Houghton, Jensen was 'big time' from the time he was big enough to reach the pedals of a car.

In mid-1987, after more than five years in jail for armed robbery and escape, Jensen was released. He soon met up with the young, impressionable Houghton, who idolised the older criminal and was delighted when Jensen invited him to become part of a robbery 'crew'.

Jensen had spent the last part of his jail term in Bendigo Prison, where he shared a cell for more than a year with one Joe De Clementi, and a Bendigo man, Robert Baxter. After their release, the three rented a home in Moreland Road, where they were sometimes visited by Baxter's Bendigo mate, Paul Widdicombe.

Widdicombe's visits were reciprocated, with Jensen travelling several times to the house in Sparrowhawk Road, Long Gully – an inner Bendigo suburb notorious for a large Housing Ministry estate well known to police – where Widdicombe lived with his wife Donna and young son.

In December 1987, Jensen brought a new visitor – Jedd Houghton.

Five months later, in April 1988, Widdicombe, then celebrating the birth of his second son, was surprised to receive a phone call from Houghton, whom he had met briefly during that December visit.

Houghton was in Ballarat visiting his mother and asked if he could 'pop in for a while' to Widdicombe's. Three hours later, he arrived on a trailbike with a man introduced to Widdicombe only as 'Hash'. To Widdicombe's surprise, Houghton announced he was 'hot' in Melbourne and asked if he could stay a while. So, for two days, while Donna Widdicombe was still in hospital after the birth, Houghton and 'Hash' stayed at Sparrowhawk Road.

On the second day, Widdicombe was working in his shed when Houghton walked in. 'While we were talking, he pulled out a small handgun from the front of his tracksuit pants and showed it to me.'

Widdicombe later told police: 'I was quite shocked when Jedd showed me this gun because it was the last thing I expected to see. I had only seen handguns on one occasion previously and that was earlier on in the year when Graeme Jensen came up to visit and had two in his possession, a .25 Beretta and a .38 snubnose Smith & Wesson revolver.'

Houghton's gun was a Colt .25, a weapon he frequently referred to as his 'toy'.

He asked Widdicombe, himself a shooter, if he could buy bullets for him from a Bendigo gunshop as 'gunshops in Melbourne won't sell them to anyone who walks in off the street'.

'While you're at it,' Houghton said, 'can you buy some shells for a .38 police special I've got back in Melbourne?' Widdicombe agreed and on Thursday, while Houghton and 'Hash' were visiting Houghton's father at Korong Vale, 60km north of Bendigo, he bought the shells at H.E. Allen Guns & Ammo in View Street.

Houghton paid and thanked him, before asking another favour: could Widdicombe sell his trailbike for him? Widdicombe agreed and Houghton arranged for Jensen to drive from Melbourne to collect 'Hash' and himself early Friday.

On the following Monday, Houghton and 'Hash' arrived back in Bendigo, staying with Widdicombe until Thursday.

Houghton's next trip to Bendigo was a few weeks later, in June, when he and Jensen arranged a shooting trip with Widdicombe. Again they asked him to buy bullets for their handguns. At 6am on a Saturday, they drove 20km south to the rolling hills of Sedgwick, where the sheep are outnumbered by granite boulders and the rabbits that burrow beneath them.

Houghton and Jensen both had their .25 pistols; Widdicombe the snub-nose .38. 'Jedd and Graeme were like little kids with new toys,' Widdicombe recalled later. 'They were both very excited and just started blazing away at rabbits, but didn't hit any. They seemed very childish about handling firearms and had no idea about safety.' As Widdicombe found out, almost to his cost. It was not the ideal spot for indiscriminate shooting.

As the men fanned out across the paddock, bullets suddenly started ricocheting off the granite boulders close to where Widdicombe stood.

Rabbit shooting with the city boys, he decided, was out. After he had fired once, and Jensen and Houghton perhaps 40 times each, Widdicombe set up some milk cartons as targets.

The experienced shooter's concern about his visitors' accuracy was vindicated: both fired eight times from ten metres, with Jensen hitting the target just once and Houghton twice.

Next time the pair wanted to go shooting, in July, Widdicombe decided against Sedgwick. He opted instead for Wedderburn, where he was to conduct the SG demonstration.

In late September, Houghton rang Widdicombe and asked him to buy SG shells and bullets for him. These he collected on October 1, when he and his new girlfriend, 20-year-old disco queen Kim Cameron, went to Bendigo for Donna Widdicombe's birthday party.

As he had been on other occasions, Houghton seemed relaxed and happy during the couple of days before they returned to Melbourne.

But when he rang Widdicombe on Tuesday October 11, it was a very different Jedd Houghton – an aggrieved and agitated young man.

The call came at 4.30pm. Graeme Jensen was dead, Houghton told Widdicombe. Shot by police. 'Jedd was very upset and agitated about the way Graeme had died. He said that Graeme didn't even have a gun on him when he was shot.'

Houghton asked Widdicombe to tell his father in Korong Vale the news. Widdicombe rang him next day.

'Jedd's father told me that it was the second or third close mate that Jedd had lost recently. He said something similar to, "Jedd's likely to do anything; stay out of his way. He's uncontrollable once he blows his top."

'I told his father I would try to get Jedd up in Bendigo and calm him down. Jedd's father said something similar to, "Jedd wouldn't be taken by the police without a fight." I don't know why he said this, but I can only assume he knew what Jedd was up to.'

BILL Cameron had never seen his daughter Kim so infatuated with a man as she was with the rough but good-looking Jedd Houghton. It seemed an unusually intense relationship from the start. Within a few days of meeting him in September 1988, she had brought him home to Colby Grove, Bundoora, and he soon moved in with Kim, her parents and her 16-year-old sister.

The Camerons did their best to be friendly. Houghton seemingly had nowhere else to stay and little money. 'He was a likeable type of bloke,' Bill Cameron would later tell police: 'happy go lucky ... what I would call a knockabout bloke – a person who, maybe I'm being kind to him, maybe got money without working.'

But Cameron made a few inquiries about his new boarder. Jedd Houghton, he decided, was a 'bit of a scallywag' and he quietly advised Kim to keep away from him. Kim was having none of it: she was in love with a man whose surname remained a mystery to her until the day he died. Houghton settled in to life with the Camerons, even inviting his mates to call around.

One of those friends was Gary Abdallah, a ladies' man and car thief, who visited Colby Grove four times. Bill Cameron was also introduced to others among Houghton's associates, including a tough-looking, bald man who went by the nickname 'Macca'.

The name on his police docket was Peter McEvoy.

WHEN Graeme Jensen was shot dead by police at Narre Warren about 3.20pm on Tuesday October 11, McEvoy was one of the first to hear the news, picked up from a news flash on his car radio. Wrongly, he believed it was another mate, armed robber Victor Peirce, and drove to Peirce's sister Vicki Brooks's flat in Brunswick. Within fifteen minutes, Peirce, who had also heard the news, called Vicki, confirming it was Jensen who was dead.

McEvoy went berserk, banging the sink with his fist and making noises like an animal. Soon Brooks's son Jason Ryan and his mates Anthony Farrell, Emmanuel Alexandridis and Brydon Shabo arrived. Ryan went white with shock; Farrell began crying. It was into this scene that the hot-headed Jedd Houghton walked minutes later. McEvoy broke the news. Houghton put his head in his hands and wept.

BILL Cameron had gone to bed about 10.30 that night. Woken by the sound of his daughter Kim talking with his wife, Lynette, he wasn't sure what time it was, but thought it was probably around midnight.

Kim needed to borrow Lynette's Commodore. She had to drop Jedd off in Carlton to meet two men called Macca and Gary.

A few hours later, two young policemen were dead.

Whoever killed Constables Steven Tynan and Damien Eyre in Walsh Street, South Yarra, that morning used SG shot, the same ammunition that had punctured the steel barbecue plate and so impressed Graeme Jensen and Jedd Houghton. What's more, the cartridges were the same unusual brand Paul Widdicombe had bought in Bendigo a month earlier. Only four Victorian shops stocked them. To police, it would be an obvious and important lead.

DONNA Widdicombe picked up her phone in Bendigo later that morning. It was Kim Cameron: she hadn't seen Jedd since she dropped him off in Carlton. 'If the police call,' she told Donna, 'tell them Jedd spent the night with me.'

Houghton finally arrived at Kim's work about 2.30 that afternoon. Although Kim Cameron was to give police various versions of what transpired that day, it seems Houghton picked her up from work and abruptly told her they were moving from her parents' house to a flat in Clarke Street, Northcote, which Houghton had rented for his sister. The couple spent that night in a flat with no furniture or electricity.

A couple of days later they were on the move again, this time to the Lower Plenty home of Cameron's old school chum Katrina Rankin and her husband Darren. On or about October 18, a week after Jensen's death, Houghton rang the Widdicombes and asked if he and Kim Cameron could move in, which they did on Saturday November 2, three days before the Melbourne Cup.

Houghton might have been on the run, but he didn't let it interfere with business. On October 21, a bandit ambushed a Brambles security van as it delivered money to a Target store in Reservoir. Although the man escaped without any cash, he did manage to grab one of the security guard's .38 revolvers, registration number D543462.

When police were to find the pistol a month later, it was in Houghton's possession.

According to police intelligence, the Reservoir robbery was not Houghton's first. He had been part of Jensen's crew since at least March, when the pair stormed into a State Bank in the Melbourne suburb of Oak Park, and terrorised staff. Unfortunately for them, the banking chamber was secured, prompting Houghton to fire his sawn-off shotgun at the lock after Jensen had failed to burst it open with a sledgehammer. The lock held and the pair fled. Houghton's shotgun, a Japanese made KTG model, was used again seven months later. It was the gun used by the Walsh Street killers.

Although at least three callers to police in the days after Walsh Street named Houghton as one of the killers, detectives in the task force investigating the murders doubted his involvement. Nothing in his criminal history suggested a propensity for such violence.

Then the armed-robbery squad passed on surveillance photographs taken at a Boronia shopping centre between August 13 and September 19. They depicted four men allegedly casing banks. Victor Peirce was there, so was Graeme Jensen and a tallish, good-looking young man – Houghton. The word went out: find Houghton.

Friends told police Houghton had cut his hair short after the shootings to change his appearance. A tip-off from an informer led police to bug certain telephones in Melbourne.

It paid off.

Houghton was tapped and traced to Bendigo.

On November 8, a Flemington detective who knew Houghton was driven to Bendigo and joined a surveillance crew following a man on a blue Honda 750 motorcycle. The bike turned in at 36 Sparrowhawk Road – Widdicombe's house.

Police had their man. Houghton was put under 24-hour surveillance.

However, despite police views that Houghton was part of the Walsh Street crew, there was still not enough evidence to charge him with the double murder.

In a bid to gather such evidence, police planted a listening device at Widdicombe's house on November 12. Although it was to provide little of use to the investigators, the tiny bug was to play a critical part in the drama about to unfold in the sleepy provincial city.

The bug might have failed to record the incriminating admissions police hoped for, but elsewhere Houghton was not so careful. A friend of Widdicombe, Shane Gray, later told police of an incident on November 9 when the two men went with Houghton to sit off a house in Acacia Street, Bendigo, to check up on a mate's girlfriend who was supposedly playing up on him.

Talk turned to police and Houghton suddenly stunned the pair by saying: 'There might be 200,000 reasons why they want to see me.'Widdicombe said nothing, but put two and two together: there was a $200,000 reward out for the Walsh Street killers.

By November 12, police had three bugs planted: at Widdicombes', Rankins' and the Camerons' Bundoora home. During this period, Houghton was flitting backwards and forwards between Bendigo and Melbourne on his motorcycle. On Tuesday November 15, he arrived at Bill Cameron's house and asked if Bill could drive him to Strathmore.

It was raining lightly about 9pm as Cameron's Commodore cruised around the area while Houghton searched for a particular location. At last they pulled into Wheeler Parade and Houghton spotted the vacant lot he had been searching for.

Cameron dropped him off, drove into Mitchell Parade and waited for up to 90 minutes before Houghton reappeared, clutching what looked to be a heavy parcel under his jacket.

It could have been a cache of firearms, Cameron later told detectives. When they got back to Bundoora, Houghton seemed depressed and reluctant to go inside. Instead, he and Bill Cameron leaned on the bonnet of the Commodore in the misty rain and talked.

'He spoke about his friend Graeme Jensen first,' Cameron recalled.

'He said when Graeme Jensen died – he said he cried because he loved him. That's the exact words that, the exact words he said to me. He said he loved Graeme Jensen and he was sort of crying to me while he was saying it … Physically crying, like a man who had had enough … And he was putting his arm around me – apparently from all reports he loved me; you know what I mean, had respected me. He must have thought I helped him out in things and I tried to look after him, you know, because his mother and father split up and he never sees – and he couldn't see his mother and he couldn't see his father because he is on the move a fair bit, and, um, he told me he was involved in Walsh Street.

'He said he was involved in the shooting and the main reason being if his friend hadn't have been shot – Graeme Jensen. He said, you know, that – the love for him. He said ... that was one of the reasons that triggered him off. He said he'd had trouble with police before. He said he got a bit of a bad hiding when he was young in a police station and things just went on from there and he said – he told me that he was the one that did the shooting at Walsh Street.'

Cameron told police he had been reluctant to question Houghton further, and the pair had gone inside.

Meanwhile, in Bendigo, tension was mounting at the Widdicombes' house. Kim Cameron and Donna Widdicombe never really got along. Paul Widdicombe thought Kim had a big mouth.

And, once, the Widdicombes' two-year-old son Dallas had wandered into the lounge room brandishing Houghton's silver .25 pistol.

By Wednesday November 16, Kim Cameron had had enough. With Houghton's consent, she set off in a taxi to find somewhere else to stay. One caravan park was full, so the driver took her to the Ascot Lodge caravan park in Heinze Street, White Hills, on the other side of town from Widdicombes'.

Using the name Kim Cadmen, she paid the proprietor Richard Naudi a $100 bond and $30 short of two weeks rent on an on-site cabin, number four. She said she would be back with her things and left to return to Long Gully.

Detectives from the Bureau of Criminal Intelligence (BCI) immediately moved in, obtaining keys from Naudi and conducting a ten-minute reconnaissance of the cabin, drawing a floor plan and checking out possible sites for a listening device.

Before moving their gear from Widdicombes' that night, Houghton arranged with Paul Widdicombe to go shooting early next morning.

That night found Houghton and Cameron asleep at Ascot Lodge in their cabin, the last of a row of four along a tree-lined central strip in the park.

There were some other new arrivals in the caravan park. In cabin one, near the gate, Detective Sergeant John Proudlock and Senior Detective Edward Starr, from BCI, were also settling down for the night.

The whole time he was on the run, Houghton was rarely without his police scanner, a hand-held radio device about the size and shape of a walkie-talkie programmed to eavesdrop on police radio broadcasts.

About six o'clock next morning, Thursday November 17, Houghton was at Widdicombe's house preparing to go shooting. The scanner was on. Outside, birds sang and a dog barked. Houghton heard the bark come through loud and clear on the scanner.

Alarmed, Houghton had Widdicombe go outside and speak. As he moved around towards the lounge room window, Widdicombe's voice came across the scanner loud and clear.

Houghton found the bug near the lounge room window. 'I've got you, you fucking mongrels,' he yelled. Police at the listening post knew instantly that any chance of gathering more evidence was gone. Their cover was blown.

Houghton was in a frenzy. 'They're not going to do what they did to Graeme to me without me putting up a fight,' he said, heading out to Widdicombe's shed.

Houghton loaded his arsenal of handguns, placing the Colt .25 in his pocket, holstering the .38 snub-nose and ramming the .38 police special and .357 Magnum down the front of his trousers.

He was ready. Or so he thought.

Houghton and Widdicombe set off for Sedgwick as arranged, Widdicombe driving his green Holden and Houghton follow-ing on his Honda motorbike. But Houghton's mind was wandering. He signalled Widdicombe to pull over to a wayside stop, where the two talked.

The scanner was quiet – too quiet for Houghton, who was by now convinced police would have raided Widdicombe's house and the Ascot Lodge cabin.

Widdicombe suggested they travel to a friend's house at the farming hamlet of Goornong, east of Bendigo, and ring Donna. Houghton agreed. The call woke Donna Widdicombe. This proved to Houghton that police hadn't made an early-morning raid. The two arrived at Ascot Lodge about 10am – Widdicombe continued home while Houghton rolled his bike past Naudi's office and parked it outside cabin four.

Naudi wandered down and had a brief conversation with Houghton, who did not seem perturbed at the proprietor noting the registration number of his bike. When Kim Cameron awoke at 10.30, Jedd was sitting on the end of their double bed watching television. She made eggs and hot chocolate for breakfast before they smoked a couple of 'bongs' of marijuana and Houghton fell asleep lying diagonally across the bed.

Cameron began to clear away the table. It was just after midday.

THE discovery of the listening device at Sparrowhawk Road presented the joint head of the Walsh Street murder investigation, John Noonan, with a dilemma: there was not enough evidence to charge Houghton and little chance of getting any more without speaking to him.

Noonan, a man who always chose action over inaction, decided to move. He ordered Houghton's arrest.

Circumstances dictated that the arrest would be a rushed job.

Detective Inspector David Sprague of the Ty-Eyre task force requested the police force's highly trained Special Operations Group (SOG) at 8.40am on November 17 on the grounds that

Houghton was a Walsh Street suspect and was likely to leave the caravan park that day.

While Kim Cameron and Jedd Houghton enjoyed their breakfast, a light plane was heading to Bendigo airfield from Melbourne.

Aboard were several armed members of the SOG. Others were coming by road in two specially equipped vehicles. The plane landed at 10am; those on board met BCI and task-force detectives at Strathdale Community Centre, set in parkland a few minutes drive from White Hills. Police were later to tell a court hearing that several plans were formulated and quickly dismissed.

Noonan told the raiding party that Houghton was armed and dangerous, was believed to have been involved in the Walsh Street killings, had been seen by Jason Ryan with a gun on the night of the murders, was a close associate of Jensen, had found a listening device at the house where he'd been hiding, and was likely to 'take off'.

He had shown he was prepared to kill police – and he was armed.

The SOG members were shown diagrams of the caravan park and the internal layout of cabin four, including details of doors and windows. They held their own briefing at 11.10am. Each member was allocated a role and told what weapons to carry.

At 11.45am the vehicles from Melbourne arrived and the drivers were instructed to act as cut-offs on either side of the cabin if Houghton managed to escape the raid.

The idea of surrounding the cabin and calling on Houghton to surrender was considered but quickly discarded.

The police tactician and SOG expert, Senior Sergeant Bruce Knight, said it was impractical for several reasons: police would lose the element of surprise; intelligence indicated that Houghton was unlikely to come out peacefully; large numbers of police would be needed; the number and potency of Houghton's weapons were unknown; and the caravan park would have to be evacuated.

Police later told the coroner that a tear gas attack was considered too dangerous as 'its effects are not instantaneous, it has little effect on some people and forcing Houghton out of the cabin would still result in problems of confrontation'.

Knight said Houghton was considered too cunning to be tricked into leaving the cabin, as he knew he was under police surveillance. A stun grenade attack was rejected because they did not always work and could be fatal in a small space.

It was considered that calling Houghton out might have prompted a siege with Cameron as hostage; intercepting Houghton on his motorcycle would be virtually impossible. Knight decided police had only one option: force their way into the cabin and arrest Houghton at gunpoint. It meant smashing the glass sliding door quickly enough to take Houghton by surprise. 'Speed was essential,' Coroner Hal Hallenstein was told much later.

The SOG prefer to conduct their own surveillance before a raid, but in this case, there wasn't time. It was a job on the run.

The group's truck set off for Ascot Lodge. It arrived at 12.08.

KIM Cameron recalls that she was standing at the table in the centre of the cabin and admiring the sleeping Houghton – 'you know, how beautiful he was' – when her world caved in. Suddenly, there was a tremendous crash and glass sprayed into the cabin. Men started yelling.

Cameron threw herself on to a bunk opposite the table.

As the glass in the cabin door gave way, Knight dropped his sledge hammer through the hole and on to the floor inside. According to Knight, he and the four officers with him – all dressed in SOG 'blacks' and wearing black baseball-style caps with Victoria Police insignia – began yelling: 'Police, don't move!'

At the same instant, Sergeant Paul Carr put his shoulder to the aluminium sash, which ran across the centre of the door, expecting it to give way easily. It didn't, and Carr was forced to duck under it to enter the cabin. The manoeuvre might have cost an extra second.

However, police evidence suggested that in the brief time it took them to smash in the door and enter the cabin, Houghton reacted quickly.

According to their evidence, by the time Carr and Constable Anthony Currie confronted Houghton, he was definitely not asleep.

Carr told detectives: 'As I moved through the curtains and burst into the cabin, I saw a male moving on the bed to my immediate left … As I was coming to the standing position, I became aware of a handgun in this male's right hand.'

By this time, he said, Houghton was lying across the bed facing the door, rather than the other way as Kim Cameron had last seen him.

As Carr and Currie took up position at the foot of the bed, Houghton was rolling to face them, a handgun in his right hand.

Carr continued: 'I then saw this male bring the gun into what I would describe as a "locked on" position to me. By "locked on", I mean the gun was pointed directly at me, his right arm was rigid with the elbow locked and he was in a position to fire at will.'

Houghton never got the chance. Carr leaned towards him and squeezed the trigger of his shotgun. Almost at the same instant, Currie fired too.

'The only reason I was confident that it wasn't the male on the bed who fired was because I knew I wasn't hit,' Carr said later. 'If he had fired, it would have been an absolute certainty that I would have been shot.' Houghton slumped forward, his head on the floor, his torso hanging out of the bed and his legs on the bed.

Knight entered the van and felt his pulse. There wasn't any.

The call to the ambulance was a mere formality. Jedd Malcolm Houghton was dead where he lay.

Carr and Currie walked outside.

They were met by SOG Chief Inspector Alan Johnson, who asked them to unload their weapons and hand them over. To Carr's surprise, he said later, he found one shell in the chamber and another two in the magazine. This meant he must have fired twice, yet he couldn't recall doing so. In fact, all three shots – two from Carr and one from Currie – had struck Houghton. The fatal wound in the centre of his chest would have caused almost instant death. Two blasts ripped into his left bicep, causing a large, open wound which tore away much of the muscle.

Inflicted by shotguns at point-blank range, Houghton's wounds were catastrophic. The SOG men use heavy shot. At that range it would have killed a draught horse.

WHILE Carr and Currie had been confronting Houghton, a lesser drama was being played out on the other side of the cabin, where Constables Michael McNamara and Craig Harwood's job was to secure the section to the right of the doorway. There they found Kim Cameron face down on the bunk. She was pulled to the floor and held down while Harwood tied her hands and covered her head with a hood – standard SOG practice in this situation.

After the shooting scene was secured, Cameron was carried bodily from the cabin and placed face down on a gravel driveway.

There is conflicting evidence as to how long she was left there, trussed, helpless and distressed. Police claim it was only a short time before she was taken to a billiard room in the park and unhooded. Lex Lasry, assisting the coroner, however, later suggested she might have been left in the gravel for up to 30 minutes. Cameron herself alleged she had a policeman's foot on her back and a gun at her head.

Wherever the truth lies, the rough treatment of Kim Cameron, who posed no threat to police at that stage, was criticised at the subsequent inquest by Lasry.

He said she should have been released immediately it was apparent she had not contributed to the incident and posed no threat.

CARR and Currie, the policemen who shot Houghton, refused to give evidence to the coroner on the grounds of self-incrimination.

There were three others in the cabin at the time of the shooting — McNamara, Harwood and Cameron — yet all claim to have seen nothing. The coroner was left then, with the brief statements given by Carr and Currie after the incident, and a wad of conflicting evidence and interpretation presented by Lasry, Boris Kayser for Houghton's family, Geoff Horgan QC for the Attorney-General, and Robert Kent QC for the police officers.

Ballistics evidence indicated the shot that entered Houghton's chest was fired with the muzzle of Carr's gun just five centimetres away. Carr's shotgun was modified; its barrel had been shortened and the stock reduced to a pistol grip.

Slung underneath the barrel was a rubber torch protruding further than the barrel. So, according to the Houghton family's barrister, Kayser, when Carr pulled the trigger, the torch must have been touching Houghton's body. Yet, continued Kayser: 'Mr Carr says that at that time Jedd Houghton has got a gun in his hand, his right hand, his arm is outstretched, the elbow is locked and the gun is pointing ... at Mr Carr's stomach. So that's what we've got is virtually that they've got to be touching each other ... What we say at the end of the day is that the accounts given by Messrs Carr and Currie just can't be right.'

Horgan, for the Attorney-General, agreed there was cause for concern about apparent contradictions between the statements of Carr and Currie and other evidence.

Medical evidence, for example, indicated that the two arm wounds were caused by pellets travelling from left to right across Houghton's body – in other words, from a position about where both policemen said Currie fired. Yet Currie fired just once.

Also, human tissue was found to the right hand side of the bed, indicating a shot across the bed from the left, rather than from its foot where the policemen said they were positioned.

'It might not be possible,' Horgan said, 'to come to a confident conclusion about what took place, the more so in view of Carr and Currie not giving evidence to explain apparent inconsistencies.'

He suggested that Coroner Hallenstein might recommend legislation compelling officers to give evidence in such cases, 'albeit with the possible qualification that evidence given not be used against them in subsequent proceedings'.

Those inconsistencies might well have been clarified by forensic examination of the scene – except that Houghton's body was moved by ambulance officers called to the cabin.

The body was dragged from the bed and into the middle of the floor. This left the coroner with the dilemma of weighing evidence suggesting that two shots were fired not from where police said they were, but from the left side of the bed.

Perhaps the greatest mystery in the whole episode is Houghton's failure to fire a shot. According to Knight, Carr yelled to Houghton three times to 'drop the gun'.

This evidence was corroborated to a degree by the caravan park owners, Richard and Glenda Naudi, who, while not certain of the words used, recall the police shouting to Houghton in a warning tone. So, on the evidence of police and independent witnesses, the SOG men had time to yell several warnings to Houghton, who, according to police inquiries, had proven capable of cold-blooded murder of two policemen.

Yet, when confronted by shotgun-wielding police, Houghton allegedly trains his gun on a policeman at point-blank range but doesn't shoot.

Kayser said it was incongruous to suggest that Houghton and Carr were at touching distance, yet Carr was calling on him to drop the gun. 'In my submission, that just can't be accepted. One of them would have shot; Houghton had the opportunity to shoot,' he said.

Much attention at the inquest focused on events immediately before the raid on cabin four. Particularly on the presence, three cabins away in cabin one, of the two BCI detectives, Proudlock and Starr. What were they doing?

Lasry told the coroner the two men had rented the cabin ostensibly as a 'static surveillance post'. They had been given the choice of three sites, yet had chosen cabin one, hardly an ideal position from which to watch cabin four in the same row. However, noted Lasry, it was an ideal position for a listening post if a device had been planted inside Houghton and Cameron's cabin on the previous night.

The BCI men had said their reconnaissance of the cabin on the Wednesday evening was to determine the best place to put a bug once they obtained a warrant to do so.

But, Lasry suggested, with no way of knowing whether they would get another chance it was clear that their reconnaissance offered the ideal opportunity to instal a bug. Proudlock and Starr, he noted, had been the officers in charge of monitoring the bug placed at Paul Widdicombe's house.

'The other matter that tends to suggest there was such a device is the way in which members of the Special Operations Group conducted themselves on November 17 as they approached the cabin for the raid. They approached that cabin, particularly when crossing (ten metres of) open ground, as though they knew

Houghton would be taken by surprise, despite the fact that the raid occurred in the middle of the day with all the curtains drawn.' Further, Lasry continued: 'worth noting the Special Operations Group do not ... as a matter of policy, enter premises unless they have positive confirmation that the person concerned is on those premises.'

Kayser, for the family, took the matter further. Proudlock and Starr, he said, claimed to be keeping a close look out from 10 o'clock on the morning of the shooting, yet inexplicably failed to see the SOG team arrive.

They sat in cabin one with the curtains drawn, 'precisely what they would have done had they been a listening post'.

Given that Proudlock and Starr were in no position to confirm Houghton's whereabouts by sight, it seemed likely the only way police could be sure Houghton was inside his cabin was if he was being bugged.

Kayser noted other circumstantial evidence supporting the listening post theory. The request for SOG assistance, he said, was made at 8.40am, at which time police had no idea of Houghton's whereabouts.

Further, the SOG arrived at Bendigo airfield at 10.30am, but waited there for half an hour before being picked up by task-force members.

'In my submission, unless Mr Noonan was confident that he had time up his sleeve – that is, that Houghton was not going to immediately depart from the caravan park – in my submission there is no way that a man of Mr Noonan's personality would have allowed a valuable half-hour to slip by.

'In my submission, that could only be because of what was being heard from inside cabin four. There was confidence that that half-hour was not being – would not be used by Houghton to escape.'

Lasry made a telling point: if cabin one were a listening post, and if there were a recording of the shooting which confirmed the police version of events, then surely it would have been presented to Hallenstein, its illegality by then being irrelevant. No such recording was put forward.

LASRY put to the coroner that it was imperative in any homicide investigation to conduct a rigorous examination of the crime scene, to obtain objective evidence against which verbal accounts of the incident could be tested.

The forensic examination of Houghton's cabin was, at best, perfunctory, he claimed. Little attention, he said, was paid to the blood patterns. The bedding was not taken away for examination, nor was the mattress.

There was no note of the presence of human tissue deposits, nor of deposits of cartridge filler. 'Your Worship,' Lasry concluded, 'this forensic examination is not of very much use to you, and in my submission that was because of the assumption made by Mr Thompson [Forensic Science Laboratory Sergeant Brian Thompson]. He didn't really need to bother. After all, the SOG had shot Jedd Houghton; Jedd Houghton was wanted for Walsh Street – couldn't be any real question about that; so it was, with respect, probably the sloppiest piece of forensic work that you'll ever see.'

Lasry said the coroner might consider whether it was time for Victoria to set up a forensic science laboratory that operated independently of police, as in South Australia.

Lasry alleged other shortcomings in the investigation. Although the scene was videotaped and photographed, the officers involved in the raid were never requested to make a video re-enactment. When asked at the inquest why this elementary and useful tool was not used, the homicide squad's Detective Sergeant Peter O'Connor claimed such a procedure would be unwieldy and he did not think it could be done. Nor were Carr and Currie questioned immediately after the shooting – when, police wisdom has it, events are freshest in the mind and evidence thus gathered is best.

In fact, O'Connor did speak to them – he drove to the airfield and conducted a brief conversation, as they were about to board the plane back to Melbourne. Later, the sergeant said he assumed they would be interviewed once they returned to Melbourne.

They weren't: their statements were taken next day by Senior Sergeant Danny Walsh, then of the homicide squad, who was not briefed on evidence found at the cabin and who did not question Carr and Currie but merely took their statements.

In Lasry's view, these problems arose because police were asked to investigate fellow officers and because they began with the assumption that the shooting of Jedd Houghton was justified: '... the dangers of using this sort of approach when a member of the public is shot by a member of the police force is obvious.

'When a decision as to whether to investigate properly or not is made on the basis of who the shooter is and who the dead person is, and on that basis alone, in my submission that opens the whole of society to corruption.'

WHETHER or not Jedd Houghton was the Walsh Street trigger-man, his reputation as such certainly played some part in his death.

Noonan's briefing to the SOG members left them in no doubt that the man they were to arrest posed a dire threat.

They were told Houghton was involved in Walsh Street, was an armed robber, associated with known criminals, that he hated police and was violent towards them, that he would probably shoot any policeman and that he was about to abscond.

Faced with that knowledge, police officers were then sent into a confined cabin to arrest a man known to be in possession of several handguns. Little wonder, concluded Lasry, that the raid finished in a shooting: '... it was extremely likely that a confrontation would occur, that firearms would be produced and either police or Houghton shot.'

Evidence pointing to Houghton's involvement in Walsh Street boils down to several damning facts: his recorded possession and use in an earlier bank raid of the KTG shotgun used at Walsh Street , his confession to Bill Cameron (and his '200,000 reasons' comment to Paul Widdicombe), and the SG shotgun cartridges bought for him by Widdicombe that matched the shot used at Walsh Street.

But in the final analysis of what happened that day, whether or not Houghton was the Walsh Street killer becomes irrelevant.

According to Robert Kent, for Carr and Currie, the only question to be asked was whether the policemen were justified in shooting Houghton because of the way he acted that day. Kent's view, naturally, was that they clearly were.

A loaded Colt .25 pistol was found under Houghton's pillow, a loaded .357 Magnum was found on the floor beside the bed, and three more loaded guns were wrapped in a towel nearby.

At what stage, asked Kent rhetorically, is a policeman justified in shooting to protect himself? Does he have to wait until a gunman trains a gun on him?

'It is our submission that even if the gun was not being pointed directly at either of the police, they would have been acting in lawful self-defence to shoot upon their demands to Houghton to drop the gun not being acted upon. It would probably not even be necessary to demand that the gun be dropped.'

The question of Houghton's involvement at Walsh Street will probably never be answered. What is incontrovertible, however, is that from the October morning that the two young policemen were murdered until Houghton's death on November 17, he chose to be on the run. 'From the evidence of Bill Cameron,' Kent concluded, 'it is submitted Houghton was, because of his involvement with Walsh Street, likely to engage in a desperate stand with police when they eventually came to arrest him, as they inevitably must.'

There was a macabre irony about the way Jedd Houghton died. He was killed by three rounds of nine-ball SG shot ... the same deadly ammunition used to shoot Damian Eyre and Steven Tynan at Walsh Street five weeks earlier.

IN his 265-page inquest finding on Houghton's death, Hallenstein was not greatly critical of any individual police action. He echoed his conclusion on many of the police shootings findings: the Victoria Police did not value human life highly enough – neither their own, nor the suspects they hunted.

In the coroner's view police were too quick to resort to smashing in a door and trying to overwhelm offenders they believed were armed.

'Forced entry is last option rather than first option when dealing with a dangerous person with a gun who may shoot police and others,' he wrote.

'This alternative to forced entry involves containment, police remaining behind ballistic cover, police surrounding with overwhelming force and negotiation ... The presence of a potential hostage within the subject's place of containment does not render forced entry anything other than last resort and by way of exceptional circumstances.'

Police too often chose forced-entry raids when other methods could be used, he said. Evidence by police at the inquest said that: 'Houghton himself created the circumstances in which he was shot by obtaining and attempting to use a firearm against police who were lawfully seeking his arrest. This is obviously so and Houghton has obviously contributed to his own cause of death.'

But, the coroner said, police always knew that in a forced-entry raid it was possible Houghton would react in a manner which would make it likely they would have to shoot him.

He said the basic problem lay not in the circumstances of the Houghton killing but with the police culture.

The Special Operations Group had a philosophy in which members' public duty and worth requires courage and personal risk of their lives by exposure to a man with a gun who is expected will or will try to shoot them.

'In these circumstances it is concluded that not only did Houghton contribute to his own cause of death but also there was contribution by the Victoria Police Force by the agency, tactics, planning and policy of its Special Operations Group, its raid members, its shooters and its personnel in command.'

A forced-entry raid should only be used as the option 'of last resort and only in exceptional circumstances', the coroner concluded.

– Owen Davies

Footnote: Some police can be traumatised by taking a life. Others remain unfazed. Some of the police involved in the attempted arrest of Jedd Houghton gather annually for a barbecue reunion. They always have a toast with a fine West Australian wine ... Houghton's White Burgundy.

TWENTY-SIX

SEVEN SHOTS

*Gary Abdallah himself believed he
was in the frame as a cop killer.*

THE life of Gary John Abdallah was – like the man himself – nasty, brutish and short.

Abdallah was an habitual criminal at an early age, a violent man who associated with other violent men who shared his disregard for the life and property of others.

Regardless of questions about how and why he died, there is no doubt this propensity for violence led directly to him being shot on April 9, 1989, and his death in hospital 40 days later, aged 24.

But Abdallah's brutal end was no ordinary example of one who lived by the sword – or, in his case, the sawn-off – dying by it. Controversial circumstances surrounding the case made it inevitable that his death caused a cloud of notoriety, which despite two detectives being acquitted of his murder, still looms over it years later. Rightly or wrongly, it is the police shooting everyone remembers.

MANY Australian police have been murdered while on duty – about 170 at the time of writing. But hardly any had been charged with murder in the performance of their duty in almost two centuries before 1989. (In 1891, an Alice Springs mounted constable, William Henry Willshire, was charged and acquitted of committing murder while on duty.)

So when two Melbourne detectives, Clifton Robert Lockwood and Dermot Patrick Avon, were charged with Gary Abdallah's murder it was bound to attract public attention and to polarise opinion about the sharp end of law enforcement.

There was more to the charges against Lockwood and Avon than historic rarity.

Because of the dead man's identity the shooting instantly became part of the biggest Australian police story since the Kelly Outbreak of the 1870s.

Abdallah was not just another crook who got in the way of a lawman's bullet: he was alleged to be a member of the gang that committed the Walsh Street murders, the cold-blooded, random execution of two young constables as a 'payback' for the death of Graeme Jensen, shot by armed-robbery squad detectives the day before.

Abdallah, raised in the same inner suburb as Jensen, associated with the same people and so was suspected of being part of the Walsh Street plot.

Although the task-force police assigned to the case had publicly stated Abdallah was not necessarily connected with the murders, there is ample evidence he believed he was in the frame as a cop killer.

All of which meant that when he was shot seven times by detectives, without any witnesses, it reeked of an act of revenge in a vicious vendetta between police and underworld.

To some, the theory that Abdallah's death was a police payback killing was not just conceivable; it was irresistible.

But a jury decided that appearances can be deceptive, and there was no evidence that he was murdered.

GARY Abdallah made a lot of mistakes in his short life. The biggest was to be closely associated with other criminals whose activities made them prime suspects for the Walsh Street killings and, therefore, on one reading of events, to be drawn into a vortex of violence and death.

Another serious lapse of judgement was to deliberately run over a man on a footpath in Collins Street, Melbourne.

If, as Abdallah claimed, he feared he was being blamed for Walsh Street, this was not the way to keep the heat off himself.

The events that led directly to Abdallah's death began on Friday night, March 3, 1989, when a storeman called Darren Hyde, then 24, and one of his workmates, Malcolm Pinney, ran a fund-raising disco at the Spencer Street premises of the office supply company they worked for.

The aim of the night was to raise money for a sick workmate.

Darren Hyde is the son of a senior police officer. According to the statement Darren Hyde gave police, the function ended about 1.30am, then he, Pinney and some other friends moved on to the X Club disco in the King Street nightclub strip.

Like many others who go to King Street between midnight and dawn, they might not have been looking for trouble, but it found them.

About two hours later, between 3.30am and 4am, Hyde and Pinney left the club and walked down King Street to a hot-dog stand.

There, Hyde stated, he was approached by two girls. 'The blonde girl appeared drunk and she asked me to buy her a hot dog. I had never met these girls before and I said "no". The girl got very upset and began to swear at me. She said things like "you lousy c…" and "buy me a fucking hot dog".'

Hyde was not impressed. 'I told her to piss off and leave me alone. I then began to walk along King Street towards Collins Street with Mal. These girls followed us and the blonde continued to abuse and swear at me.'

There was, Hyde stated later, a light-coloured car parked in Collins Street near the King Street intersection. The two girls went to the car: 'then the blonde walked back to me and called me a smart c… and spat in my face. She then went to the car and got in the back seat.

'I was very upset and walked up to the car. Before I could say anything the passenger leaned out of the window … [and] grabbed hold of my arm, and as he did the driver began to drive off.

'I struggled to get free but was unable to, and I had to run to keep up with the car. After a short time he let go and I fell to the road. I got to my feet and ran to the footpath. The next thing I knew the car had hit me and I was being rolled around under the car … I believed I was badly injured and could not move. The next moment I heard the gears changing on the car and I was horrified, as I realised it was reversing over me again. I felt both wheels run over me and I thought I was being killed. I thought I was going to die.'

That was Darren Hyde's last memory of his big night out. He regained consciousness in the Royal Melbourne Hospital.

He was treated for injuries to his face, arms, hands, legs and back. He was lucky to be alive.

It was a clear case of attempted murder – and there were plenty of witnesses, including two policemen who knew Gary Abdallah by sight.

JOHN Bell and Marino Ditullio were crane operators on a building site at 530 Collins Street. They didn't usually start work at 4am, but on Saturday morning, March 4, 1989, they were both rostered on for a special job at the site, which meant their working day began before hardened nightclubbers started heading home.

Although Bell and Ditullio knew rowdy scenes were not unusual in King Street before dawn, the scene that greeted them as they arrived that Saturday morning shocked them.

As Bell parked his car in King Street just before 4am he saw a light-coloured car reversing near the corner in Collins Street, with the man in the passenger seat gripping another man's wrist 'causing him to run very fast to keep up with the car'.

He then saw the car drive the wrong way in Collins Street and the man fall down, then run for his life, only to be chased and cold-bloodedly run down on the forecourt of the Rialto building.

The car zig-zagged as it chased the man across the forecourt, struck him head on, and reversed over the prone body and drove off, driving through a red light as it turned right into King Street and headed north, Bell stated later.

'The car drove straight past where I was standing, and I took down its registration number, which was BCX 831.

'At the time of this incident there were at least 12 other people watching and after this incident a larger crowd gathered,' he told police.

Bell handed the piece of paper with the car's registration number on it to the injured man's friend, then gave the details to another workmate, who rang police and an ambulance.

Marino Ditullio verified his workmate's version of events, but noticed there were four people in the car – two young men in front and two young women in the back.

He also saw the injured man's companion (Malcolm Pinney)

throw some punches at the head of the driver through the car window before the car sped off.

Ditullio made his statement to police three days later, at the building site. The last paragraph reads in part: 'I then went across the road and I had a look at the bloke … who at this time was lying on the ground.

'He was breathing and his eyes were closed. He didn't look too good; there was a lot of blood on his face.' The policeman who took the statement was Senior Detective Cliff Lockwood, of City West CIB.

DARREN Hyde and Malcolm Pinney weren't the only people buying hot dogs in King Street in the early hours of that morning.

About an hour earlier, an off-duty police constable, Daniel Johnson, wandered up from the Underground nightclub to the X Club, buying a hot dog along the way. After 20 minutes at the club, Johnson decided to go home.

As he left the club he saw two sisters he recognised from his three years stationed at Flemington Police Station, where they were well known.

Johnson had parked his car in Collins Street near the Menzies at Rialto hotel.

As he got in it he noticed a cream Sigma drive past very slowly, then accelerate away. The male passenger in the front seat was holding his hand over his face, and he could not see the driver clearly, but could tell he was a man with black hair.

The policeman was suspicious. As the Sigma drove off he tried to get the registration number, but could see only the first three letters: BCX.

He sat in his car for about a minute when the Sigma slowly drove past again.

The passenger still covered his face with his hand, and the driver leaned over to look at the policeman as he went past.

Johnson was getting worried. This time he saw the Sigma's number plate completely and wrote the full number, BCX 831, in the dust on the dash of his car, and memorised it.

The Sigma did a U-turn in Collins Street and drove past on the other side of the street. A street light lit the driver's face. This time the policeman recognised him.

It was Gary Abdallah.

Johnson had dealt with him many times in Flemington. This fact did nothing to reassure him.

Johnson started off, turned right into King Street and headed for his home in North Melbourne.

But after going two blocks he thought the Sigma was trying to follow him, so he took several turns to lose the other car.

'As I drove home I kept checking in my mirror to make sure no car was following me,' he said in the last line of his statement, made at Flemington Police Station 17 days later, on March 20, 1989. The same day Darren Hyde, the injured man, made his statement to a detective at Footscray Police Station.

A POLICEMAN'S work is never done. Inspector William Murphy, stationed at Broadmeadows in 1989, also had reasons to go to King Street that Saturday morning. According to the statement he made to a chief inspector at Broadmeadows three days later, he had gone to a nightclub about 2.30am to meet somebody he wanted to speak to.

He came out on to the street about 3.45am – just in time to recognise Gary Abdallah at the wheel of the Sigma at the traffic lights in Collins Street minutes before he ran over Darren Hyde.

Knowing Abdallah's reputation, Inspector Murphy took note of the car's registration number, reciting it to himself 'to write down when I got into my car'. As he drove off, the inspector saw the Sigma reverse over Darren Hyde, then speed up King Street. He did a U-turn and tried to catch the Sigma, but lost it.

Gary Abdallah could run. And for a few more weeks, he could hide. He was already suspected of serious offences, but now he had done something so brazen that the police had a watertight reason to arrest him.

It was only a matter of time before they found him.

THERE is a saying about giving a dog a bad name, and another that if enough mud is thrown some will stick. Gary Abdallah's name had been thrown up as a suspect for the Walsh Street murders almost from the start and rumours about him and his associates hummed through the underworld and the police force and, inevitably, found their way into the media.

This was hardly surprising. Walsh Street and the subsequent investigation by the Ty-Eyre Task Force was the biggest crime story in years; human nature did the rest.

The man in charge of the operational side of the Ty-Eyre task force, Detective Inspector John Noonan, could hardly be expected to control the rampant rumour mill – although he did appear to try, where Abdallah was concerned.

In a long and detailed statement made for the coroner's inquest into Abdallah's death, Noonan painstakingly outlines the task-force version of events.

He begins this by conceding, in the stiff and precise language police affect in court evidence, that Abdallah was one of 'a number of persons that we believed would be able to assist us in our inquiries.' The task force's interest in Abdallah stemmed from his well-known association with Graeme Jensen and Jedd Houghton, both shot dead by police.

The interest in Abdallah was sharpened by the fact that he was extremely wary of police in the months after the Walsh Street shootings.

The only address they could get for Abdallah was his mother's home, then in Anketell Street, Coburg. But Abdallah could never be found at that address and, despite what Noonan calls 'numerous inquiries', police could not find him at all in the period from November 1988 to February 1989. This fuelled speculation about him among police, the public and the underworld.

Abdallah's family and friends were not saying where he was hiding – but his brother Dale told police what they were already hearing from several underworld sources: that Gary believed he was in danger, had a firearm and was prepared to use it to prevent arrest.

Noonan stated he was so concerned by this that 'task force members personally visited Gary Abdallah's closest friends and family to guarantee there was no substance in these rumours [that police would harm Abdallah] and that they were obviously being spread by a criminal element intent on causing an unnecessary confrontation between the police and certain persons of interest to the task force.'

Curiously, he went on to say: 'I am confident that this approach worked effectively in dispelling the unfounded innuendos and rumours circulating about the task force and Gary Abdallah.'

(In light of the official and legally accepted version of how Abdallah died on April 9, it is hard to say why Noonan was so 'confident' that innuendos and rumours about the task force's supposed intentions had been cleared up. Abdallah, according to all the evidence, hadn't had his fears 'dispelled'.

He was apparently still so nervous of the police intentions that he tried to bail up two detectives with an imitation pistol. (The only other explanation which appears to fit the accepted version of events is that Abdallah was so cocky or so stupid that he thought he could bluff two detectives he must have suspected were armed.)

However, for all the task force's assurances to Abdallah's family and friends, the young criminal still had a problem.

It was this: the police had received information early in the inquiry that another suspect contacted Abdallah the night before the Walsh Street shootings either to 'supply a vehicle as a getaway car' or to join 'the actual offenders' by driving a getaway car.

Noonan qualifies this in his statement, saying the information had 'not been corroborated' and so it was necessary to talk to Abdallah to check if there was any substance to it.

At the same time the task force wanted to talk to Abdallah, he was also wanted for questioning by the arson squad over a fire at a disco in Arthurton Road, Northcote, the previous April, which had caused an estimated $300,000 damage.

Either he was a very active criminal, or people were telling some dreadful lies about him.

When Abdallah finally ended the mystery of his whereabouts by turning up at the St Kilda Road police complex on February 22 with his solicitor, he didn't shed any light on any of his activities. The solicitor, Bruno Kiernan, told Noonan that if his client was formally interviewed over Walsh Street, his answers would be 'no comment' to every question.

Noonan said there would be no formal interview over Walsh Street, only an informal discussion about a car Abdallah had once owned – a 1977 cream Gemini sedan. Abdallah told Noonan the car was registered under a false name and address, and claimed he had sold it to a Barry Ashman about six months before the Walsh Street murders.

He said he would try to find out the date of sale for Noonan. He also claimed he was not close to Jensen and had met him only about three times.

Having exhausted the small talk, Noonan tackled the big question: 'I then told him we had received information that McEvoy and Houghton had spoken to him in the evening of October 11, 1988, and had requested him to get them a car to use. I told him the exact details were not specific, only that he was asked to do something about a motor car.'

Abdallah's answers, at least as reported by Noonan, made it sound as if he had plenty to hide. Abdallah was 'very non-committal on where he was living at that time and on how he learnt of Jensen's death.' He said he did not use telephones 'and in answer to whether he spoke to Houghton and McEvoy that night, made out he did not understand what I was saying; then he said someone was trying to set him up.'

Noonan's recollection was that he had assured Abdallah that 'based on the information we had at that time' there was no evidence connecting him to the Walsh Street killings. But he didn't let him leave without scoring the obvious point: 'I told him that I found it strange that he had been hiding all this time if he wasn't involved in any way.'

Before leaving, Abdallah promised to find the man to whom he had allegedly sold the Gemini, and that he would 'think about' what he had been doing on the night of October 11, 1988, and where he was when he learned of Jensen's death.

He was then interviewed by arson-squad detectives and subsequently charged with criminal damage by fire over the Northcote disco blaze. According to his family, he had taken extra clothes with him expecting to be taken into custody, and was surprised when he got bail and was required to report three times a week to Coburg Police Station on the fire charge.

At least some of what people were saying about Gary Abdallah appeared to be true. He played with matches.

Did he also play with guns?

CLIFTON Robert Lockwood, better known as 'Cliffy' to friends and enemies alike, was no stranger to the Abdallah family and their associates. The big detective had run against Abdallah and his mates while working at Flemington Police Station from 1982 until 1987.

So when Lockwood was handed the investigation into the attempted murder of Darren Hyde after he arrived at work at City West CIB on Saturday March 4, he knew he was looking for the same man the Ty–Eyre task force had failed to find for months.

This didn't stop him trying. Terry Paul Abdallah, three years older than his brother Gary, was living with his mother Beryl Griffiths, brother Kenny and other relatives at their house in Anketell Street, Coburg, when the police came calling on that Saturday morning.

It was around 9am, Terry guessed in a statement some time later. He said he knew the bigger of the two detectives at the door as Cliff Lockwood, but not the other.

Neither side was in the mood for introductions.

Terry Abdallah: 'I got up out of bed and went and opened the front door … the shorter detective, who wasn't Lockwood, said, "Where's the car?" and I replied, "I don't know what you're talking about."'

From that exchange, according to Terry Abdallah, the visit went downhill.

'Both detectives pushed past me … As they walked to the kitchen I kept saying "Get out".' He said that while Lockwood asked another family member questions in the kitchen the other detective took him to his bedroom and asked him again about 'where the car was'.

Lockwood then entered the room, Abdallah said, and asked who was living at the house. 'Lockwood then said, "Who was driving the car?" and I said: "What car?" and he slapped me across the head … As he did this I yelled out "Kenny" and the other detective said to Lockwood, "There's no need for that." Then Kenny came in the room and said, "Yes, I seen that."'

After another exchange Abdallah pretended to call a solicitor on the telephone, and the shorter detective said: 'We had better go.'

'Lockwood walked up to me and said, "That was a mate of mine that got run over this morning," and I said, "I don't know what you're talking about."

'I yelled at him to get out ... Lockwood walked out the front door and down the steps to the gate. I was in the process of closing the wire door and Lockwood turned around towards me and said, "Funny things happen in the dark."'

Kenny Abdallah also testified that he'd heard the parting comment, as well as confirming the detail and the substance of his brother's evidence about what happened that morning.

Question: Was Lockwood running his own race, taking his partner along for the ride, in an independent and quite proper bid to be the tough cop who went into the badlands to track the outlaw everyone in the police brotherhood wanted found?

Or was he, as the barrister for the family, Dyson Hore-Lacy, told the coroner later, an obedient shock trooper in a bigger game controlled by the Ty-Eyre task force? According to Noonan, Lockwood was allowed to run his own investigation from City West CIB 'in the normal manner', on the basis that Abdallah was the prime suspect for the attempted murder of Darren Hyde.

The task force's only contact with Abdallah after the informal interview with him at police headquarters on February 22 had been two telephone calls to Noonan – in which Abdallah failed to clear up the mystery of the 'sale' of his Gemini or his whereabouts on the night he'd heard of Jensen's death. Noonan later insisted that his only instruction to Lockwood was that he should notify him before detaining Abdallah – and not to intercept Abdallah while he was reporting to Coburg Police Station 'as that was the only definite method available to find him when and if the need arose.'

On March 10, Abdallah again went through the motions of 'cooperating' by telephoning Noonan to say the car he had sold was in fact registered in the name of Gavin Barnes at an address in Mulgrave Street, Kensington. And he told Noonan he was 'still thinking about where he was' on the night of Jensen's death.

Meanwhile, the task force was finally managing to get some results behind the scenes. On March 21, detectives traced Abdallah to his correct address: 3/872 Drummond Street, Carlton.

He had been living there more than four months, since November 9. The machinery of the law was slow, but it was sure. The noose was tightening.

On March 23 a 'listening device' was installed in the flat after a warrant was issued by a Supreme Court judge, and the premises monitored 24 hours a day, seven days a week.

Gary Abdallah had thought the task force was very interested in him for some time. He was right.

Late on the afternoon of April 5, Noonan and one of his men, Detective Senior Constable Col Ryan, spoke to Abdallah at his mother's house in Anketell Street, Coburg. 'I told him that daily, we were gaining more and more information about his various criminal activities. I told him to have a good, hard think about his involvement and if he was interested in talking he should contact me personally.'

There was no mention of the small matter of attempted murder in Collins Street. But two days later, evidently resigned to the fact Abdallah wasn't about to take up the invitation to unburden himself about Walsh Street, Noonan gave Lockwood the nod – informing him: 'he could now interview Abdallah so long as he notified my office on his apprehension.'

The checks on the suspect had been thorough – but they weren't reassuring. On April 7, Abdallah hadn't been back to the flat for three days, and the police knew that the rent agreement on the flat (signed by a female friend of Abdallah's) expired that Sunday, April 9.

Once he moved out, he might slip out of reach. The

surveillance had produced no concrete evidence tying him to the Walsh Street murders.

It was time to pick him up on the lesser, but still serious charge, the attempted murder of Darren Hyde.

Enter Lockwood and another City West detective, Dermot Avon, while the task force waited in the wings.

But, just as the action was getting interesting, the microphones were turned off: the 'listening device' was ordered to be removed.

In light of what happened later, much has been made of the possible significance of this. Was it a sinister conspiracy to give police assassins a free hand, or just a coincidence?

Neither, says Noonan, who explains it this way: 'I had decided to discontinue the surveillance and listening device ... as from 7am on April 9, 1989, due to lack of manpower and the fact Abdallah was obviously moving out. [Lockwood and Avon] were informed that the listening device would be removed some time on Sunday and that due to the fact they were not on the listening device warrant they could not utilise it for any reason ... The listening device equipment was to be switched off on their attendance at the observation post.'

Noonan also states that Lockwood and Avon were told to detain Abdallah in the street as he arrived or was leaving the premises – and to notify him so that Ty-Eyre task-force members could 'assist' in the arrest.

'I gave my members an instruction to notify me immediately Abdallah was arrested because I wanted to speak to him at some stage after apprehension.'

It seemed clear the task force still had high hopes of connecting Abdallah to Walsh Street, and regarded the (totally justified) arrest on the attempted murder charge as a convenient opportunity to get him into custody.

The plan was to increase the pressure. Task-force members wanted to strike a deal. 'Tell us what you know and maybe something can be done over the Collins Street incident.' That is why Ty-Eyre detectives wanted Abdallah alive.

But no one had a chance to strike a deal. Lockwood and Avon met a Ty-Eyre task-force detective, Mark Caulfield, at Russell Street just before noon on Saturday April 8, to take over the Abdallah investigation.

Caulfield showed the pair the block of flats at 872 Drummond Street, and said Abdallah had been living in the third flat from the street. He then showed them the school on the opposite side of the road where the task force had its vantage post set up. Lockwood and Avon later stated they stayed until 4pm, then called it a day because Abdallah had not been sighted. They were back at 7am Sunday, driving an unmarked blue Toyota Corona, wearing casual clothes, and each carrying a police-issue .38 calibre Smith & Wesson revolver.

It was a long day. Just when the two detectives might have been intending giving up their vigil is not recorded, but they were still there at 4.26pm – almost half an hour later than they'd worked the previous day – when Avon noticed a cream Sigma parked near Abdallah's flat.

Given that the detectives had been on duty nine and a half hours already, it's tempting to think that if the cream Sigma had not appeared until a little later Avon and Lockwood would have been gone.

And the Sigma's driver might have lived a little longer.

The detectives watched a man they recognised as Gary Abdallah and two others moving furniture and other gear from flat three to a vehicle and trailer parked near the Sigma.

Lockwood: 'As it appeared that these men were about to leave the flats Avon and I agreed to attempt to arrest Abdallah with his car at the flats.

'We then left the school and hid behind a tree at the front of the school.'

The vehicle towing the trailer reversed and left the flats. Abdallah followed in the Sigma. The detectives ran to their Toyota. Avon drove.

He cut across to Lygon Street, then headed north, towards Brunswick.

At first they couldn't see the Sigma; then they spied it turning into Lygon Street from Park Street, ahead of them. Had Abdallah taken a slightly different route they might have missed him.

While following the Sigma, Lockwood contacted D24 and asked the operator to call the task force to advise 'the target was travelling north in Lygon Street.' Lockwood was to say a month later that it had been his idea to arrest Abdallah in the Sigma if possible, to connect him with the car because it had been used in the Collins Street incident.

Avon pulled alongside the Sigma near Albion Street, Brunswick. Lockwood flashed his police badge through the window.

Abdallah drove on for another block before pulling over. He got out of the Sigma quickly, before Lockwood and Avon could.

Lockwood: 'I had my police revolver in my right hand and down by my side.'

Avon: 'I said, "We're from City West CIB. You're Gary Abdallah?"

'He said, "Yeah." I said, "Put your hands on your head."'

While Lockwood checked the Sigma, Avon searched Abdallah, patting down his body and clothing. According to their statements, he found a locking-blade knife hidden inside Abdallah's pants. It was enough to arrest him for carrying an offensive weapon.

Lockwood put Abdallah in the rear seat of the police Toyota, while Avon locked the Sigma. Lockwood told Abdallah they were going to 'have a look at his flat'. They parked in Drummond Street and walked to the front door of the flat.

Lockwood: 'The area that we entered was the lounge room-kitchen area and it was obvious that the flat was being vacated. We did not search this area as the cupboards were already opened.

'I then said to Abdallah, "Let's look upstairs." He then proceeded up the stairs and went into the room on the northern side of the flat.

'This room was in a similar condition to the lounge room in that there was no furniture and just rubbish on the floor ... He then walked out of this room and down a short corridor ... and went into a room at the southern end of the flat.

'Abdallah walked into the room and went and stood in the south-eastern corner of the room. I went into the doorway and looked in and observed that this room was again in a similar condition to the lounge room and the other room.

'After taking this in I moved a short distance into the corridor and turned to Avon, who was behind me [to say] that there was nothing for us here, and we would leave. I then turned back towards the room and would have been in a similar position to that which I had been in before and was intending to tell Abdallah that we were leaving.

'I immediately saw that Abdallah had moved about a metre north along the eastern wall. He was pretty close to the wall and may have been against it. I saw that he was holding what I believed to be a .357 Magnum revolver ... I think he was holding it in his right hand and was using his left hand to support it ... He was bringing the revolver up to the firing position when I first saw it and observed him to continue to raise it to the firing position and aim it in my direction.'

THE tenants in flat two, sisters Tania and Michelle Henderson, had gone out that morning, Tania returning about 3pm and Michelle about half an hour later.

Tania, a 20-year-old solicitor's secretary, read and dozed off in her bedroom. She was woken by noise next door. 'I heard some footsteps on the stairway. And then I heard a fair bit of yelling and then I heard a lot of banging and then a really big bang. I didn't know what the noise was.'

Michelle, 17, had been cleaning the bathroom when she heard the commotion next door. In the statement she made to a Ty-Eyre task-force member a few hours later, she said she had heard a male voice yelling out loudly: 'saying things similar to "Put it down".' Michelle said she thought at the time it sounded as if someone was moving something and another man was yelling at him 'to put it down' before he dropped it.

'Then I heard a number of loud bangs. That's when I thought that they must have dropped whatever they were moving. All the time I heard the bangs the male voice was continually yelling out . . . the only thing I positively heard was when he yelled, "Put the fucking thing down."

'My sister came out of her bedroom and ... asked me whether I heard the noises. I said they were probably trying to move something ... I didn't really think much more of it. Then a short time later I heard an ambulance siren.'

SENIOR Constable Joseph Noonan was at the Ty-Eyre task-force office when a phone call came from Lockwood, who was at the Drummond Street flats.

It was about 4.35pm.

Noonan heard Detective Sergeant Jeffrey Calderbank talking to Lockwood about arresting Abdallah. After Calderbank hung up he, Noonan and another detective, William Panagiotaros, went downstairs and drove to Carlton.

They reached the flats at 4.55pm. Lockwood met them outside the building. He looked shaken. He told them Abdallah had been shot.

When they reached the room Avon was bent over Abdallah's body, giving him mouth-to-mouth resuscitation.

He was later to be charged with the murder of the man whose life he was trying to save.

Noonan stated later he saw 'a large chrome pistol lying on the floor near the eastern wall of the bedroom'. He asked Avon to move aside and checked Abdallah for a pulse. There wasn't any. He gave Abdallah heart massage, stopping at intervals to check the pulse.

'I asked Avon to wait out the front of the flat, as he appeared distressed. I continued to apply heart massage for some two minutes when I stopped and could feel a pulse on Abdallah's neck. I could also see his chest moving and could hear gargled breathing ...'

Noonan went down to the police car to see if an ambulance was on its way. When the first arrived he took the officers upstairs.

JOHN Flanagan had started work early. He was rostered to start his 14-hour night shift with Mobile Intensive Care unit number one at Latrobe Street at 5pm, but when the call to Drummond Street came at 4.58 Flanagan and his partner, Col Evans, were ready. They reached the flat eight minutes later. A second ambulance followed them.

A detective escorted Flanagan and Evans upstairs and into a room. There was a body on the floor. It was young, male and very close to being dead.

The patient wasn't breathing, and had wounds to the forehead, right upper arms, right shoulder and fingers of the right hand. As he and Evans began working to resuscitate the wounded man, Flanagan noticed something else – a revolver lying about 45cm from the patient's right hand.

Ten years earlier Flanagan had been a member of the Oakleigh Pistol Club. Some time before that he had worked as an alarm technician for Wormald Security and had been required to carry a .32 pistol.

He was, therefore, one of few ambulance officers in Melbourne who had handled and fired handguns. When he saw the revolver on the floor of the flat next to Gary Abdallah's body it didn't enter his head that it wasn't genuine. It looked real, although it turned out to be a replica.

Several weeks later, when he made a statement, a couple of things stuck in Flanagan's mind.

When he had noticed the revolver on the floor, he said: 'I asked the policeman, the one who has escorted us up, if it was loaded. He replied that he hoped it was, and he then bent over and had a closer look at it and then replied that he thought it was.

'This same policeman also indicated to me, I can't remember if by word or action, that the conversation in the room was being tape recorded.' In fact, the bugging device had been turned off earlier that day – but the policemen didn't know that.

ABDALLAH arrived at St Vincent's Hospital emergency department at 5.35pm. He already had an airway tube inserted to help him breathe.

His pulse was regular. After an exhaustive round of X-rays, scans and other investigative procedures Dr Peter Smith, the senior surgical resident medical officer, examined the gunshot wounds. By 7pm Abdallah was in intensive care.

Meanwhile, Lockwood and Avon were in a different sort of intensive care. As senior police and the homicide squad swarmed to the scene the pair from City West were the centre of attention. Detective Inspector Lawrie Ratz, who had been on duty as divisional supervisor when he got news of the shooting from D24 at 5.15pm, arrived within ten minutes. He took charge until the homicide squad took over a little later.

As soon as Ratz arrived he was shown to the school building

opposite the flats, where Lockwood was waiting to answer the first of hundreds of questions he would be asked in the following months and years. In later statements, the burly detective had time to compose himself and his story, but the hasty notes Ratz took that night capture the urgency of the story as it tumbled from the shaken policeman.

Everything had gone routinely, he said, until Abdallah had suddenly produced a handgun. 'I screamed at him "Drop the gun, drop the fuckin' gun" a couple of times. He screamed "I'm not doin' nothin," or similar.

'I just kept screaming at him to drop the fucking gun. I must have drawn my gun and his gun was raising and pointing at me. I started shooting at him and he kept raising the gun at me. I must have shot six because I took Dermot's gun and shot one from his, I think. The last shot he dropped to the ground. We rolled him over and pushed the gun away. Avon was giving him mouth-to-mouth and I rang the OP to call an ambulance.'

LEANNE Abdallah was watching Disneyland with her two-year-old daughter when a news flash broke the story that destroyed her peace of mind.

Despite its lack of detail, she later told television reporter Frank McGuire, the message shocked her:'Police have shot a man in the bedroom of a flat in Drummond Street, North Carlton. He is believed to be in a serious condition.'

The fact that normal programming had been interrupted meant it was no 'ordinary' shooting. 'It's Gary', she thought. Everything that her brother and his friends had said in the previous months made her suspect the worst: that her brother was dying or dead, and that he'd been deliberately shot – murdered, in fact.

She was right about the first – and, more than six years on, she was still to believe she was right about the second.

At the Coburg house that police had watched and visited in previous weeks, Abdallah's mother, Beryl Griffiths, who was minding Gary's six-year-old son Michael, also saw the news flash.

Then she got a telephone call from police. She rang Leanne immediately and said: 'It's Gary. Get straight to the hospital.' When Leanne got to St Vincent's, her mother was already at the bedside.

A priest told the family Gary wasn't expected to survive the night.

Leanne Abdallah told reporters later that her brother's left eye was the only sign of life. 'Mum just kept hoping, she believed in miracles, but a doctor told me Gary could last a day, a week or a month, but then he'd die.'

Three days later, on April 12, surgeons at St Vincent's operated on Abdallah's head and neck wounds.

He was returned to the operating theatre three times in the next nine days, but it was a hopeless cause.

The hospital surgical registrar, Dr Michael Murphy, stated later: 'His progress both in intensive care and in the wards was complicated by recurrent chest infections; fluctuating respiratory patterns; loss of body weight despite naso-gastric and intravenous nutrition.'

He was also suffering gastro-intestinal bleeding and septicaemia.

When the end came, no one was surprised. At 5.30am on Friday May 19, Abdallah stopped breathing and couldn't be revived. He was formally pronounced dead at 7.50am.

THE inquest into Abdallah's death opened in July 1989, and finished in October 1994. Evidence taken from scores of witnesses ran to almost 10,000 pages and millions of words, but in some way all related to one brutally simple question: had Abdallah's death been, in police jargon, a 'clean kill', or was he the victim of a police conspiracy?

The second part of the same question was this: was the imitation pistol found with Abdallah's body 'a throwaway' planted to provide Lockwood and Avon with a cover for cold-blooded execution?

These were the big questions that hung over Abdallah's death.

Barrister Dyson Hore-Lacy later put them bluntly at the inquest, accusing Lockwood and Avon of carrying out an execution on the orders of the head of the Tynan-Eyre task force, John Noonan. Tired of waiting for the coroner to come down with his findings, Director of Public Prosecutions, Bernard Bongiorno, charged both police with murder on July 20, 1993.

Avon hadn't fired a shot but he would end up in the Supreme Court criminal dock because of the events surrounding Abdallah's death.

Both men were suspended from duty and stood trial in January the next year.

The prosecutor, John Winneke QC, conceded that Abdallah had the imitation revolver and had threatened police.

He even said that the first six shots fired by Lockwood could have been justifiable self-defence.

But he argued to the jury of seven men and five women that it was the seventh, and fatal, shot which constituted murder.

He said that when the final shot was fired, Abdallah could not possibly have been considered a threat, but was cowering with his back to the policeman yelling: 'I'm not doing anything.'

The case against Avon was thin. So much so that after the prosecution was completed, Justice Vincent gave the jury the opportunity to discharge Avon without even hearing a defence.

Vincent said that if the jury believed the Crown case was 'too tenuous' to justify further argument or consideration they could acquit Avon. 'What I have done is brought to your attention matters which seem to me to raise very, very real problems.'

The jury agreed and Avon was acquitted.

The defence for Lockwood lasted only three days. Essentially its case was that it was impossible to suggest that a policeman's motive changed from legitimate self-defence to murder in the split second between the sixth shot from his own gun and the seventh, after he grabbed Avon's.

After deliberating for five hours on February 22, 1994, the jury found Lockwood not guilty.

He left the court and made a statement through his lawyer: 'I am very bitter that I was charged with murder in the first place and presented for trial by the Director of Public Prosecutions without a committal hearing.'

Later that year Lockwood resigned from the force.

After toiling laboriously through the mountain of material put before him, Coroner Hal Hallenstein produced a 300-page finding, the essence of which is contained in his conclusion in the final few pages.

Despite the apparent complexity of the case and the notoriety and speculation it attracted, his conclusions firmly refuted the conspiracy theory aired by Hore-Lacy, and speculated about by many others.

Hallenstein found that there had been rumours in the underworld that police wanted to kill Abdallah, and these rumours had been fuelled by the aggressive language and behaviour of some police during raids.

But he concluded: 'There is no evidence that police actually intended to kill Abdallah and there is no evidence that Abdallah was killed pursuant to any general police intent that he be killed.'

Hallenstein dismisses allegations that Lockwood had a predetermined intent to harm Abdallah, noting that the claims came from witnesses whose evidence had to be treated 'with caution'.

This was because they were either friends or relatives of

Abdallah's with entrenched anti-police attitudes, and most had convictions for dishonesty.

Specifically, Hallenstein stated there was no evidence to support a claim by Abdallah's friend Wayne Driscoll that Lockwood and other police had assaulted him in Flemington because of his links with Abdallah. Neither was there any evidence that Lockwood or any other police were responsible for shots fired at Abdallah's mother's house in Anketell Street, Coburg, on March 6, 1989.

'Lockwood was ... an energetic policeman on the streets, well spoken of by his superiors in the police force and not liked by some civilian witnesses who in general terms were not particularly supportive of the police,' Hallenstein wrote. 'There is no evidence on which the inquest could conclude that Lockwood was doing anything other than vigorously performing his duty as a member of the police force.'

Hallenstein probed allegations that the imitation pistol had been planted at the scene – specifically the suggestion the weapon might have been handed in to the Flemington police station during a firearms amnesty in 1988 and subsequently taken by Lockwood or other police.

He established that the Flemington property book covering the period from November 1987 to January 1988 had gone missing some time in 1989: that this book recorded any weapons handed in during that time, and that Lockwood had access to the book and the property store while stationed at Flemington from November 1987 to October 1988.

The coroner was also told that Lockwood often returned to Flemington from his new posting at City West in late 1988 and early 1989, to deal with property he was responsible for.

He also heard evidence of an unrecorded imitation pistol being seen at City West, but was satisfied with evidence by a Chief Inspector John Ashby of the police Internal Investigations Department that in June 1989 (two months after the Abdallah shooting), he followed up the sighting and found the unrecorded imitation pistol in question, thereby proving that it was unconnected with the shooting.

Hallenstein dismissed the fact that Lockwood was associated with both police stations at the relevant time: '... there is no evidence that he was involved in the disappearance of the property book from Flemington Police Station or with the unrecorded imitation firearm at City West Police Station. There is no evidence at all that Lockwood had been involved at all with the imitation firearm found at the scene where Abdallah had been shot.'

Hallenstein cited the most compelling evidence in Lockwood and Avon's favour – the independent and specific corroboration by people in neighbouring flats that Lockwood shouted at Abdallah several times to drop the gun.

He concluded: 'The only evidence in inquest and the only sequence of events rendering Abdallah's shooting understandable at all is that Abdallah obtained and produced an imitation revolver immediately prior to him being shot.

'On the facts so far as able to be concluded Abdallah has contributed to a sequence of events leading to him being fatally shot by picking up and pointing at Lockwood an imitation revolver reasonably believed to be real. It was or ought to have been reasonably foreseeable that such an action would be likely to result in instinctive use of police firearms with lawful justification. In these circumstances Abdallah has contributed to his own cause of death.'

Translation: Perhaps Abdallah believed the two police in the flat – or members of the Ty-Eyre task force – planned to beat or shoot him, and the imitation pistol was his only chance to escape.

It seems that Gary Abdallah was frightened enough to play a desperate bluff – and he lost.

• *Cliff Lockwood tried to return to policing but he felt that some of his supervisors always feared he would become involved in another controversy. He felt that he would never be fully trusted again and his word would always be doubted. He eventually quit but still the Abdallah incident followed him. Even in Darwin, years later, workmates would ask him about what happened that day in a small Carlton flat. Eventually he moved overseas.*

TWENTY-SEVEN

OUTGUNNED

*The question is: Why did they
wait for the crime to be
committed before stepping in?*

IT was the heist professional armed robbers dream about. The
bandits had inside information about a million-dollar soft target.
The guards would be unarmed and there was an easy escape
route, or so the theory went.

But there were two groups of trained, armed and ruthless men
descending on Melbourne Airport the cold, windy July day
chosen for the robbery of the decade.

Both groups had done their homework. Both had conducted
repeated surveillance operations and dry runs. Both knew that
precision and timing would be the keys.

But there was one big difference: one group was made up of
three career armed robbers, while the second was the police's
potent strike force, the Special Operations Group. And only the
police group knew that the others would be there.

On the face of it, *Operation Thorn* was right out of a Hollywood script. Armed baddies move in on helpless target, terrorising innocent victims, only to be trapped by the good guys in a shoot-out that leaves one bandit dead, a second permanently disabled and the third lying on his stomach at gunpoint after a high-speed car crash.

But *Operation Thorn* was not a B-grade movie, it was an officially-sanctioned Victoria Police operation, one that raised serious questions about the philosophy of law enforcement in Australia.

Operation Thorn exposed a police win-at-all-costs mentality that placed innocent lives at risk because police deliberately allowed criminals to stage an armed robbery rather than move in to stop the raid. Some of the bandits' victims remain traumatised years later, unable to understand why they were drawn into becoming cannon fodder in a life-and-death drama.

The Coroner, Jacinta Heffey, was left to pull together the pieces of an operation which took months to plan — and only seconds to end in death. The inquest had to look at the death of bandit Norman Lee. Along the way it shed light on the world of hard men playing out a drama in which the safety of innocent people was treated as irrelevant.

Evidence at the inquest showed police being quite prepared to set up an ambush in a public place, where they couldn't be sure that arrests could be made without risks to outsiders.

Police had intelligence, phone taps and physical evidence that a robbery was to be carried out at Melbourne Airport by a group of bandits suspected of being prepared to shoot anyone who got in their way. They suspected the target was the Ansett freight office.

The question is: Why did they wait for the crime to be committed before stepping in?

ON July 28, 1992, the police lay in wait. It was the culmination of a four-month operation involving the armed-robbery squad, the Special Operations Group and the National Crime Authority. On the day of the armed robbery, 52 police were mobilised to catch the robbers at the airport at Tullamarine.

The robbers were no cleanskins. The driver, Stephen John Asling, then 32, had previous convictions for assault and dishonesty offences.

Stephen Michael Barci, then 35, had convictions for armed robbery, selling drugs, assault, aggravated burglary, and intentionally causing serious injury.

Asling and Barci were close mates. So close that, in 1990, Barci was charged with using Asling's passport. The charge was later withdrawn. Police believed they were the core of one of Victoria's more proficient armed-robbery teams, a group that relied on inside information and was prepared to use firearms to succeed.

The two planned and executed the armed robbery of a Brambles armoured van in Port Melbourne in May 1990, in which a shot was fired. They also robbed a Greensborough McDonald's store in 1992.

In the Port Melbourne job, Asling and Barci ambushed two security guards, who were having breakfast, and forced them at gunpoint to lie in the back of their armoured truck. They were taken to a darkened warehouse in nearby Swallow Road where they were bound, hand and feet, before the gang took the payroll of $426,169.81 and the crew's revolvers.

One of the abducted guards was David Lapworth, who later admitted to being the inside man for the robbers. After Lapworth's arrest in April 1992, the armed-robbery squad went after Asling and Barci. They obtained warrants to bug four telephones as part of the operation.

Police said that, while conversations between the men indicated they were planning another robbery, they would never discuss the location over the phone.

It was clear that three men were needed for the job. Police were convinced they knew the name of the third man and even had his phone tapped. He had been in on the Port Melbourne job and was set for the next big robbery. But, with just weeks to go, the third man pulled out. Asling and Barci needed a replacement – and quick. A man who knew the stick-up business and could be trusted.

They turned up a wild card, a small businessman with a minor criminal history, Norman Leung Lee.

Norman 'Chops' Lee was one of the greatest enigmas of the Victorian underworld. He was the only man ever charged over the infamous Great Bookie Robbery, and one of few to survive the carnage that followed it.

Lee was charged by police with the robbery at the Victoria Club on April 21, 1976. The actual amount of money stolen will never be known, with estimates ranging wildly from $1.4million to $12million but likely to be around $3million in untraceable cash.

Lee's best friend was Raymond Patrick 'Chuck' Bennett, the acknowledged mastermind behind the robbery. Bennett was eventually shot dead inside the Melbourne Magistrates' Court, on November 12, 1979.

Lee was alleged to have laundered $110,000 through a solicitor's trust fund, bringing $60,000 into the office in plastic bags.

The allegations were never put before a jury. Lee was released at a Magistrate's Committal over the bookie robbery because of insufficient evidence. The then head of the armed-robbery squad — now retired deputy commissioner, Paul Delianis — said Lee had always appeared quiet and cool.

'The question is whether he was quiet between the bookie robbery and the incident at Tullamarine or whether he was always too clever to come under notice. I think it was probably the latter,' he said. 'He moved in a circle of top crims. It would be a reasonable hypothesis that he was simply not caught.'

Lee was of the old school. Police seized an expensive safe from his business when they were looking for the money from the bookie robbery and took it by truck to the Russell Street police station. Detectives asked Lee what was in the safe. He remained silent. They asked him for the keys. He remained mute. Police phoned a safe expert who drilled out the lock, rendering it useless.

It was empty. But, on principle, Lee refused to assist.

Police used the National Crime Authority surveillance team to follow the key men, Asling and Barci, for three months in 1992. According to evidence from Detective Sergeant Stephen Brown, of the armed-robbery squad, the two men were seen watching cash deliveries from armoured vans at the ANZ bank in Mount Alexander Road, Essendon; at Westfield Shopping Centre, Airport West; the Gladstone Park Shopping Centre; Tip Top Bakeries in Brunswick; and the Ansett freight terminal, Melbourne Airport.

The best bandits use a combination of planning and gut feeling when plotting big jobs. They might check one target for months and then, for no apparent reason, walk away. It is as if living on the edge in a kill-or-be-killed world heightens animal instincts for survival. Police have watched bandits, armed and ready to go, virtually sniff the air and leave a payroll after months of planning. It is always a battle between the two competing elements in a robber's mind, greed and survival. The nerve to walk away from a job separates the elite bandits from the dangerous and desperate who invariably get caught.

Police eventually narrowed the likely armed-robbery targets down to two, Tip Top and Ansett. But what police did not know was that the bandits had the most precious of all contacts, an inside man. They knew an Armaguard security officer.

The guard, Dean Rook, had known Stephen Asling for more than ten years. Weeks earlier, they had run into each other at the Golden Fleece hotel in South Melbourne in the months leading up to the attempt at Melbourne Airport as the gang was looking for its next target. Rook mentioned the type of work he did and what was carried in his Armaguard van.

'I had a couple of beers in me and I was mouthing off,' Rook later told police, admitting he had told Asling details of airport and Tip Top runs. He claimed he was offered a cut of $100,000 from the takings but declined. Crucially, he did not pass any information of this alleged approach to the authorities.

The information provided by Rook must have been enough for Asling. On four occasions in three weeks, the robbers were seen at the bakery, but they were also seen four times at the airport.

Normie Lee used to walk around the airport in a suit, carrying a clipboard like a professional efficiency expert. In a way he was, secretly observing the movements of the armoured van at Ansett's freight depot.

A few weeks earlier Barci and Asling slipped in and robbed the McDonald's store in Greensborough of $3,500 and a security guard's gun. The bandits held guns to two people's heads during the robbery and so terrorised the manager that he could not remember the safe combination.

But it was just pocket money, although they would later use the security guard's gun in the big one they were planning.

Each Tuesday, an Armaguard truck with three guards would arrive at the Ansett freight terminal with huge bags filled with cash. Airport protocol meant the guards would lock their guns in the truck before delivering the bags. As regular as clockwork, the van would arrive between 1.20pm and 1.45pm for the cash to be loaded on to a Kendall's Airline flight to Mildura.

On July 21 the gang was observed parking two getaway cars near the airport, then parking a stolen Ford panel van in the airport. As the armoured truck arrived, around 1.20pm, the driver of the van got out and lifted the bonnet, appearing to check the engine while watching the cash truck. Police suspect a loose engine wire forced the three bandits to abort the mission. The gang could hardly call the RACV to fix the van. It was torched that night. After the false start the gang decided the next cash drop, one week later on July 28, would be the chosen day.

Police found out that the gang had even driven to Bendigo to test fire their weapons in readiness for the job. If the guns were to be used only as a bluff, why did the bandits need a day to make sure each was capable of killing efficiently?

Later, at the inquest, Barci and Asling said the plan to carry extra weapons and ammunition was Lee's. 'If this is true then it supports an image of Norman Lee as a person more likely to try and shoot his way out of a confrontation than to surrender when commanded to,' the Coroner found.

On the day, Asling parked a gold BMW in the car park at the Gladstone Park Shopping Centre and Barci parked a Toyota Corolla in Derby Street, Tullamarine. Both were clearly planted as getaway cars for a job.

The three bandits arrived at the airport in a panel van armed with three pistols and two rifles. The bandits had a .38 revolver, a .357 Magnum, a .380 pistol, a .223 self-loading rifle with 26 cartridges, and a .308 rifle. They also had three rubber masks — two Michael Jacksons and a Madonna — for disguises. It was a toss-up which was more frightening. Barci and Lee also carried spare ammunition. Lee had 12 rounds of .357 cartridges in his pocket. It would do him no good.

The SOG arrest team also brought along a small arsenal, including a 12-gauge pump-action Remington shotgun with pistol grip, semi-automatic pistols, knives and gas masks. No one could accuse the 'Sons Of God' of being under-prepared.

On the day of the robbery, the bandits drove their stolen van to a parking spot about 80 metres from the Ansett depot. The SOG arrest van was parked about 100 metres away in Depot Drive.

Police believed that because of a twist in the law, it would have been fruitless to arrest the men as they were just seated in the stolen van, even though the bandits were armed and clearly about to commit a robbery.

Police were not prepared to charge the men with lesser offences; they wanted them on charges that would result in long jail terms.

They believed a High Court ruling in 1983 precluded police from charging people with conspiracy to commit an armed robbery, without establishing the actual target. But while evidence at the inquest disputed the police impression of the law, it was clear the detectives wanted no chance of any loopholes in their case.

Thorn investigators decided they needed an 'overt act' before they moved. They wanted the bandits to put on their masks, or grab their guns, to make a move that couldn't be disputed in court.

Much play was made at the inquest that police should have moved days or weeks earlier. They could have chosen the least risky time and place to arrest the three.

But the armed-robbery squad, perhaps tired of seeing some of the dangerous men in the country walk free or be sentenced to only a few years, were going for broke. They wanted their case airtight; to do that they wanted to catch the offenders in the act. This would guarantee that the robbers would be put away for 10 to 15 years.

Police often criticise lenient sentencing because they have a vested interest in keeping criminals behind bars. And, for the armed-robbery squad, who hunt the hardest crooks, the stakes are always high. At Tullamarine they couldn't have been higher.

The police plan was to grab the three gunmen before the robbery, but the position of the SOG van left them too little time to intercept the bandits.

They would not move in during the robbery because of the fear the gunmen might take hostages.

This meant they were forced to let the raid take its course, despite a risk the bandits could shoot Ansett staff while it was happening.

The bandits arrived around 1.16pm and parked near the Ansett depot. The armoured van was late. It arrived about 1.45pm.

Asling reversed the stolen van within 30 metres of the Armaguard vehicle. Barci and Lee jumped from the back of the van and ran into the office and grabbed three big red bags containing $1,020,000.

The five-man SOG team was parked in a disguised police van at least 100 metres from the Ansett depot. The police had no chance of stopping the job: the bandits had committed the robbery and were back at the van by the time they arrived. Lee threw two bags in the back of the van and Barci dragged his along the ground.

'As I dragged the bag down the steps I noticed a man in a van to my right. I fanned the gun past him and I was surprised that he grinned at me,' Barci later told police.

'When I got to the van Norm was inside the van on the rear passenger side, squatting. I then picked up the bag I was dragging with both hands and put it in the back of the van. I was pushing the bag in and Norm was pulling it. I then spun around and sat on the rear of the van on the driver's side with my legs hanging down. At the same time Norm grabbed me by the collar of my jacket to help push me in.'

The SOG arrived as the two men were settling in the back of the getaway van. A witness heard the bandits scream 'go, go, go', but the catch on the back door was not in place. 'It was then that Steve hit the accelerator and Norm and I were thrown out the back of the van,' Barci said.

'We were screaming 'stop, stop, stop!',' Barci said, as Asling tried to outrun the police. Not only had the two bandits been thrown out, but one of the three cash bags had fallen, too. Suddenly, it was every man for himself.

Barci and Lee chased the van as the SOG arrest team jumped from its vehicle. According to police, Lee, armed with a .357 Magnum, lowered his gun and appeared to be about to give up. He then raised the gun. 'His actions left me no choice but to fire my weapon to protect myself,' one SOG member said later.

Two SOG police fired, hitting him in the back of the head and to the left side of the chest and left wrist. He was dead by the time he hit the ground.

Another SOG member fired five shots at Barci, hitting him at least three times — twice across the back and once in the left shoulder. He has been left permanently disabled.

It was later found that Barci's gun had fired one shot, probably discharging when he fell to the ground. Asling sped off, reaching a speed of up to 80 kmh. An SOG marksman fired one shot at the tyres, blowing out the rear passenger wheel. The bandit's car was then rammed by an SOG four-wheel drive. Police had left nothing to chance. If the bandits had escaped the inner net, there were road graders on standby to block the only road out.

It was said that one of the SOG members later sang the old song 'We're In The Money' to one of the prisoners. It was the song the bandits would sing to each other during the planning stages for the airport robbery. It was the policeman's way of saying they had been bugged from the start and always doomed to fail.

Barci later pleaded guilty to three counts of armed robbery and was sentenced to fifteen years' jail, with a minimum of ten. Asling was also sentenced to a minimum of ten years for the three armed robberies.

ONE of the main concerns arising from *Operation Thorn* is that police, armed with the element of surprise and outnumbering their quarry 17–1, chose to let the robbery go ahead before moving to arrest the criminals.

Up to 80 staff were counselled after the incident. Ansett and airport staff had been left dangerously exposed during the shoot–out.

Some say *Operation Thorn* was fatally flawed because it involved an armed confrontation in a crowded area. The operation was not as controlled as police would suggest: a shot from the SOG went through the window above a meal area of a nearby office, the bullet lodging in a noticeboard.

Barci made it clear to the coroner what he thought of the operation.

'I believe that the police knew about this robbery well before these events and it could be said that in allowing the robbery to actually take place they participated in a situation that was not only dangerous to the public but which was also a well-planned execution.'

His apparent concern for the public rang a little hollow considering the gang used five high-powered weapons it had test fired a week earlier. The bandits were prepared, at best, to terrorise anyone who got in their way. At worst, they were equipped to murder.

Some Ansett staff were disappointed with police handling of the robbery, but one placed the blame squarely on the bandits. 'They were the ones who put the lives of innocent people in jeopardy. It's a shame they [the police] didn't shoot them all.'

One of the Ansett staff members at the front counter during the robbery, Darren Attard, complained that no one had been warned of the raid.

The chief commissioner, Neil Comrie, disturbed at the number of police shootings, ordered the total retraining of the force under *Operation Beacon*, where safety became the first priority of any police raid.

Under *Beacon* 'the safety of police, the public and offenders or suspects is paramount'. The guidelines also specify: 'The success of an operation will be primarily judged by the extent to which the use of force is avoided or minimised.'

Strict new procedures were put into place stipulating when the SOG could be used. Under the new rules, an operation such as *Thorn* is unlikely to be authorised again.

What the Coroner said:

'The fact that Norman Lee contributed so substantially to his own death by undertaking a violent enterprise would not interfere with the making of an objective judgement as to whether the conduct of the armed-robbery squad did not also contribute to his death. The same consideration and criteria should apply as if the person killed was an innocent member of the public whether by accidental police fire [and we know that three rounds of police fire were unaccounted for on the day and windows in a nearby recreational building were shattered by gunshot fire] or by indiscriminate shooting by robbers. What occurred at Melbourne Airport on July 28 was both foreseeable and avoidable.

'Whether Lee was in fact raising his gun in order to shoot will never be known.

'The three robbers were in possession of far more weaponry than they could need to perform an armed robbery alone. In addition to loaded handguns, they carried extra handgun ammunition; in the rear of the panel van were two Armalite military-style rifles, both loaded. Mr Asling carried a loaded handgun and extra ammunition even though he did not enter the terminal building. Both Barci and Asling agreed in evidence that they had been to Bendigo with Lee to practise using some of the weapons. In evidence they said that being equipped with extra weaponry and ammunition was Lee's idea. If this is true then it supports an image of Norman Lee as a person more likely to try to shoot his way out of a confrontation than surrender when commanded to.

'That a death could result in the course of an apprehension of violent armed offenders in the course of committing an armed robbery on an unknown target in a busy public place in circumstances in which it was known that the robbers had rehearsed by test-firing weapons was not in my view a remote possibility. It was highly foreseeable.

'The possibility of the unexpected occurring, the previously observed unpredictable behaviour of the offenders, the large area to be secured and contained, the possibility of some member of the public behaving heroically and complicating the apprehension – should have all served to demand greater reflection and more objective decision making.

'In their single-minded focusing on catching these "career criminals" the members of the armed–robbery squad overlooked their overriding responsibility to ensure the safety of the public. They are given substantial powers including in this case the power to direct the highly trained members of the Special Operations Group to apprehend their suspects at gunpoint at a time of their choosing. There had been available to them from June 22 onwards an option to arrest their suspects quite legitimately and in circumstances that posed no risk to the public and little or no risk to the offenders. Their failure to do this prior to July 28 coupled with the forseeability of death or serious injury in the course of the arrest on that day in my view amounts to contribution to the death of Norman Lee.'

Postscript: Norman Lee was a fit-looking 44-year-old man of 73kg and 171cm. During the autopsy it was discovered he had a serious heart problem, including a 70 per cent blockage in his left coronary artery. If he hadn't been shot, chasing the getaway van and the shock of confronting armed police at the scene could have killed him.

3 May 1990: Brambles armed hold-up in Port Melbourne: $426,000 stolen. Armed–robbery squad commences *Operation Thorn.*

25 March 1992: As a result of Crime-Stoppers publicity, police get information that a Brambles employee called Lapworth was involved in the Port Melbourne job.

10 April 1992: Lapworth arrested and confesses his involvement. Names Barci, Asling and a man named Kendrick as robbers.

21 April 1992: National Crime Authority commences periodic surveillance on behalf of armed-robbery squad of addresses, vehicles and movements of Barci and Asling. The investigators decide that Asling is their main target.

28 May 1992: Lawful telephone intercepts placed on Barci's home.

2 June 1992: Lawful telephone intercepts placed on Asling's home.

20 June 1992: Armed hold-up at McDonald's at Greensborough (for which Barci and Asling are later sentenced after pleading guilty).

9 July 1992: Special Operations Group becomes involved to conduct reconnaissance with the view to arrest at the appropriate time.

17 July 1992: Lawful telephone taps placed on the robbers' safe house at 10 Dumas Street, Avondale Heights.

21 July 1992: The 'dry run' at Melbourne Airport.

28 July 1992: Norman Lee shot and killed at Melbourne Airport.

TWENTY-EIGHT

JOCKEY HITS A HURDLE

He had a reputation as a tightwad.

HE was a notorious bank robber and escapee but James Edward Smith will always be remembered by the nickname he grew to hate ... Jockey.

Born in 1942 in the middle of the war, Smith was the second of eight children of a battling bush couple. He was raised in Victoria's Colac district and, as a teenager, became an apprentice jockey.

It was a lot of hard work and, like a lot of apprentices, he got too heavy to get many race rides.

His supporters say he turned to crime after an unscrupulous owner cheated him out of promised payment for exercising his horses.

His critics say that even as a teenager he had more larceny in him than Long Bay jail. But it could not be disputed that Smith always loved horses and racing. By the age of 19 he was serving his first stint inside for breaking into shops. It was the start of a long criminal career.

He was soon to team up with a petty criminal who would learn the hard way that crime doesn't pay. His name was Ronald Ryan – the man who later became famous as the last man hanged in Australia after a notorious escape from Pentridge Prison in which a prison warder was shot dead.

Smith and Ryan tried to burgle a shop and it was Smith who tried to shoot his way to freedom but, according to police, his old pistol jammed and he was caught.

In 1973, another faulty firearm stopped Smith from becoming a killer.

This time St Kilda policeman Russell Cook was searching a car when Smith came from behind and tried to shoot him. Again, his gun failed to discharge.

Smith moved to Sydney for a change of luck but was soon charged with armed-robbery offences. In what was to become part of a pattern for almost 20 years, when he was in trouble he ran.

This time he skipped bail but was re-arrested almost two months later, sunbaking on a Melbourne beach.

Taken to Pentridge, he was there less than 48 hours before he used a visitor's pass to walk out of Victoria's then maximum-security prison. Most escapees take a low profile, but Smith found that living a semi-normal life gave him the ideal camouflage. He wanted to be a racehorse trainer so he borrowed a couple of handy names from the top men in the field – Tommy Smith and Bart Cummings.

It wasn't original, but it worked. Somehow he forged a new identity and became a country horse trainer, 'Tom Cummings'.

For three years he lived near Nowra, racing his horses at country meetings and occasionally venturing to Sydney. He should have stuck to the bush.

In 1976, he shot Constable Jerry Ambrose in Sy_ arrest. In 1977, police alleged he broke into bookr_ Tidmarsh's home and, during the robbery, shot him d_

He was later arrested in a phone box in Nowra. Agair_ ____- ing to police, he tried to shoot the arresting officer, Detective Bob Godden. Smith stuck the revolver in the policeman's belly, but the quick-thinking detective managed to stick his thumb between the breech and the hammer.

Smith was originally sentenced to life for Tidmarsh's murder and shooting at Constable Ambrose, but the convictions were thrown out on appeal when it was alleged police fabricated his confessions.

He was sentenced to fourteen years for trying to kill Godden. He was better off in jail. Someone knew his movements and was waiting when he got out.

The day after he was released in February 1992, he was walking with his wife at Bondi when he was hit in the chest, stomach and leg with shotgun blasts. He was close to death but, after a month in hospital, Jockey was back in the race.

According to Mark Brandon Read, Smith was one of the best bank robbers in the country and should have been wealthy. But 'he had a reputation as a tightwad … a man who could have a hundred grand under the bed and go out and pinch a rubbish bin rather than pay for it. He would bite the head off a shilling.'

Which is perhaps why, at a time when he was making good money from selling cannabis and amphetamines, Smith courted trouble by shoplifting a steam iron, kitchen knives and a plastic tray from a Grace Brothers shop in November 1992.

He was caught. To escape he first threatened the store detective with a gun, then forced a terrified couple to drive him away from the Erina shopping centre. Police lost track of him for a few days.

Meanwhile, members of the Melbourne armed robbery squad

...ad their own problems. Career armed-robber Christopher Dean Binse was running red hot.

He had escaped from the Parramatta jail on October 24 and, a month later, had robbed the Commonwealth Bank in the Melbourne suburb of Doncaster of $160,000. Detective Sergeant Steve (Larry) Curnow learned that Binse and two others, including a big name from Sydney, planned to rob an Armaguard truck in Melbourne.

The squad launched a top priority operation, code named *Farnsy*. They found Binse was hiding on a farm near Daylesford. Listening devices picked up that one of the men at the farm was known as Tom.

They didn't know at the time that Tom was Tom Cummings, alias Jockey Smith. Just after 8pm on December 5, 1992, Tom drove from the farm in a white Ford panel van. Police decided to let him go. They knew he would be back and their main target, Binse, was still inside.

Local policeman Senior Constable Ian Harris was on a routine afternoon shift and was unaware of the armed-robbery squad operation in his area when he spotted the van on the Midlands Highway.

He saw the driver was travelling at 80kmh, 20 below the speed limit. He checked on the radio for the 'usuals.' He was told the car had been reported stolen.

He followed the van until it turned into the driveway of the Farmers Arms Hotel in Creswick. Drinkers in the bar stood to watch the show.

Jockey got out of the van and approached the policeman, still sitting in the marked car. After a brief discussion, Harris asked the driver for proof of ownership. Smith went back, grabbed the car manual and used it to conceal a five-shot handgun. In the left pocket of his jeans was a can of mace.

Harris got out of his car and Smith shoved the revolver in the policeman's stomach. He ordered the policeman to hand over his gun but the policeman kept it just out of the reach of the smaller man.

Smith fired a shot into the ground and said: 'I'll give you ten seconds to get your gun out of your pocket and get on the bonnet or I'll blow you away.'

Harris called on the drinkers to ring the police. He knew back-up was only minutes away. But would it be too late? He was not to know that just up the road half the armed-robbery squad and Special Operations Group were watching a quiet farmhouse while he was fighting for his life.

A local called Darren Neil had spent a thirsty day exploring mineshafts and, after a few drinks at a mate's place, decided to get some stubbies at the Farmers Arms. When he saw the police car he decided to keep driving. No need to risk his licence for a couple of beers.

Then he looked in his rear-view mirror and saw a man pointing a gun at the policeman, who was trying to back away.

Later, Neil could not explain his reaction. He told his two young sons, who were in the front seat with him: 'We better go back.'

He got out of his car, walked over to the gunman and pushed him in the chest. Smith responded by firing a warning shot into the ground. Neil then knew this was no game.

He ran back to his car, drove to the entrance of the pub, pushed his kids to safety and then drove back at the gunman.

Smith fired another shot and then pointed his gun at Neil.

It was the split second Harris needed. He grabbed his service revolver and fired three times, hitting Smith in the chest and stomach.

The shots were fatal. Jockey fell at the last.

TWENTY-NINE

GRASPING
AT STRAWS

*He believed Rosenes was
self-interested and manipulative.*

YEARS after the Graeme Jensen case seemed as dead and buried
as Jensen was himself, there was another twist in the tale.

One of the police on the periphery of the case, Malcolm
Rosenes, came forward to say that detectives had planted the gun
found in the front seat of Jensen's car.

But Rosenes wasn't prompted to speak by his conscience ...
he was desperately trying to save himself after being found drug
trafficking. He was trying to strike a deal to minimise his jail
time.

Back in 1988 Rosenes was a surveillance policeman and on the
day Jensen was shot he was on afternoon shift, rostered to be in
charge of a five-member team to assist the armed–robbery squad
and observe Jensen.

He was warned the target was dangerous and 'would more

than likely be armed and had a previous criminal history involving violence'.

Rosenes knew the target well, although they had never met. He had transferred to the surveillance squad in May that year for his third stint. He had previously worked there as a detective and senior detective.

In the month he returned, the surveillance squad was given the job of following a gang of suspected armed robbers, including Jensen, Jedd Houghton and Victor George Peirce.

Rosenes had watched Jensen case a National Bank in Boronia and hold meetings with other members of the gang in the car park of a nearby shopping centre.

On October 11, 1988, Rosenes was sitting in a silver Nissan sedan reading his newspaper when Jensen finally surfaced at 3.20pm and headed to Mower City at the corner of Webb Street and Princes Highway.

Rosenes followed about 15 car lengths behind and pulled into the shopping strip, cruising past the blue Commodore, parking out of sight. Two surveillance detectives wandered into the shop to confirm the suspect was Jensen.

In his police statement Rosenes said one of his team slipped in the car and said: 'It's definitely Jensen, he's about to move off.'

Jensen hopped back into his blue Commodore station wagon as the three unmarked police cars containing the eight armed-robbery detectives barrelled in.

Rosenes would later admit that when he heard shots: 'I froze in my position instead of hightailing it quickly and seeing if Jensen was making a getaway.'

But he soon gathered his composure and drove past Jensen's crashed car before parking and walking back. He spoke to an armed robbery squad detective who told him the suspect was dead.

Rosenes called the four members of his surveillance team and ordered them to meet him at the Berwick Shire Offices. He instructed them to write notes on what they had seen so they would have records for the subsequent investigation.

But, later, those vital notes went missing and were never found.

When Rosenes gave evidence in the Coroner's Court in March 1990, he was unable to explain what happened to the missing notes. 'I believe every possible step humanly possible has been taken. Searches have been undertaken at our office.'

At no stage, either in his original statement or in evidence at the inquest, did Rosenes indicate he had seen anything questionable on the day Jensen was shot. And, strangely for a trained investigator, he didn't seem curious.

'There were ample detectives in the vicinity. I observed it for a short while, again, it could have been five or ten seconds.'

He then walked back past the car. 'At that stage there was quite a gathering.'

It was put to him at the inquest: 'None of your team saw anything at all that the armed-robbery squad did either in the car park or at the time of the shooting or immediately after the shooting until such time as the car actually crashed into the post?' He responded. 'That's my understanding.'

Later he said: 'I saw members of the armed-robbery squad running towards the car and that was it.'

Rosenes was referred to by one of the lawyers at the inquest as one of the three wise monkeys because seemingly he didn't hear, see, or speak.

Rosenes left the court and returned to his solid, but unspectacular career. He became purchasing officer at the surveillance squad because of his uncanny ability to nail a good deal. He then moved to the drug squad where he began to work for himself, not the force. He became a drug dealer and was arrested in a park by Ethical Standards Department police.

As always, the deal-maker tried to cut a deal. He became a Crown witness and in one of his many statements he said the gun in Jensen's car had been put there by police after the suspect was shot dead.

His claim that the Jensen gun was planted was referred to the Ombudsman's office by Chief Commissioner, Christine Nixon. Acting Ombudsman Bob Seamer closed the case after he found the allegation could not be substantiated.

In October 2003 Rosenes was sentenced to a minimum of three years and six months for trafficking ecstasy, hashish and cocaine.

He resigned and was still able to receive $600,000 in police superannuation.

The judge who sentenced Rosenes, Judge Michael McInerney, made it clear that he believed Rosenes was self-interested and manipulative.

He said that he would have to be satisfied on the balance of probabilities that Rosenes was telling the truth before he could give him a discount on his jail sentence.

'Given my already expressed opinions on the reliability of Mr Rosenes, I could not be so satisfied.'